The Sailor's Handbook

The Sailor's Handbook

The Essential Sailing Manual

Pan Books Ltd London and Sydney

First published in Great Britain 1983 by Pan Books, Cavaye Place, London SW10 9PG

ISBN 0 330 26921 6

Conceived, edited and designed by Marshall Editions Ltd., 71 Eccleston Square, London SW1V 1PJ

Editor: Rosanne Hooper

Art Director: Paul Wilkinson

Assistant Editor: Gwen Rigby

Picture Research: Zilda Tandy

Production: Barry Baker

© 1983 Marshall Editions Ltd. London

Artwork by Haywood and Martin
Reproduced by Bridge Graphics, Hull
Typeset by Servis Filmsetting, Manchester
Printed and bound in Belgium by Brepols SA

The Contributors

The Sailor's Handbook was compiled with the help of experts from all the world's major sailing centres. That international input leads to some variations in spelling and terminology which are clarified in the Glossary (page 214). The major contributors are the following:

Colin Mudie is a naval architect with an impressive variety of both power and sail designs to his credit. The most famous include the transatlantic leather boat, *Brendan*, and *Rehu Moana*, the first multihull to sail round the world.

John Oakeley, Britain's top helmsman, has won over 20 major championships, represented Britain in two Olympic Games and in the America's Cup, where he developed the new 12-metre rig. He has won Yachting One of a Kind in USA, Yachtsman of the Year in France and many other awards. He also markets the successful 'Freedom' yachts.

Geoff Hales MBE (Technical Editor) is Technical Editor of Yachting World, and writes on practical matters for the general sailor, particularly about new gear. As a sailor he made his name in 1976 as the handicap winner of OSTAR in *Wild Rival*.

Robin Knox-Johnston CBE the first man to sail single-handed round the world, completed his 313-day trip in 1969. In 1970 he won the Round Britain and Ireland Race and again in 1974 when he set a new record. In 1980 he was Britain's challenger for the America's Cup. He runs a marine consultancy business and has written illuminating books about his experiences.

Michael Richey is Director of London's Royal Institute of Navigation and received, in 1979, its gold medal for outstanding services to the science of navigation. He is also President of the International Association of Institutes of Navigation. Over the last 30 years he has navigated in the major offshore races and crossed the Atlantic alone several times in his junk-rigged *Jester*.

Bob Bond is training manager to the Royal Yachting Association and organizer of the British Olympic team. He was elected Britain's first national coach in 1969 and has since acted as sailing correspondent for BBC TV and written extensively on dinghy sailing, cruising and board sailing.

Halsey Herreshoff (US Editor) is one of the world's foremost naval architects. President of the Herreshoff naval museum and of his own company, he has also advised on several piloting and navigation books, drawn from his wide experience of cruising and racing. He navigated *Courageous* to victory in the 1974 America's Cup.

Ann Welch first made her name as a pioneering flier and glider. That and her round-the-world sailing experience are the background for her knowledge of weather patterns.

Contents

**Introduction to sailing/
Bob Bond**
8 The pioneers of cruising
10 From workboats to
   playboats

**Know your boat/
Halsey C. Herreshoff**
12 Anatomy of a boat
14 Fibreglass construction
16 Wooden construction
18 Metal construction
20 Standing rigging
22 Running rigging

**Wind and sail/
John Oakeley**
24 Choosing sails
26 Sailing dynamics
28 Setting the sails
30 Close-hauled
32 Reaching
34 Before the wind
36 Handling spinnakers
38 Light-weather sailing
40 Reefing for heavy
   weather
42 Riding out a storm
44 Leisurely cruising

Cruising/Geoff Hales
46 Choosing a cruiser
48 Layouts below decks
50 The galley
52 Personal security
54 Staying warm and dry
56 Planning a passage

The cruising grounds
58 Northern Europe/1
60 Northern Europe/2
62 The Mediterranean/1

64 The Mediterranean/2
66 The Caribbean
68 USA: The East Coast
70 USA: The West Coast
72 The Great Lakes
74 Australasia

**Arrivals and departures/
Bob Bond**
76 Successful mooring
78 The different moorings
80 A choice of anchor
82 Foredeck fittings
84 How to anchor
86 Two anchors for security
88 Anchoring emergencies

**Ropes and knots/
Bob Bond**
90 The range of ropes
92 The important knots
94 How to handle rope
96 Splices and eyes
98 Whipping and seizing
   techniques

**Auxiliary power/
Colin Mudie**
100 Choosing an engine
102 How much power?
104 Engine installations
106 Handling under power

**Navigation/
Michael Richey**
108 Reading the compass
110 Confirming where you are
112 Plotting a chart
114 The language of charts
116 Sounding the depths
118 Timing the tides
120 Logging your speed

122 The reason for Radar
124 Radio direction-finding
126 Buoyage systems
128 Navigating by the stars
130 Collision regulations
132 Electronic and satellite
     navigation

**Reading the weather/
Ann Welch**
134 Weather patterns
136 Interpreting the
     forecast
138 The visual clues

Safety at sea/Bob Bond
140 Equipping for safety
142 Signalling for help
144 Recovering a man
     overboard
146 Steering failures
148 Rigging failures
150 Fire hazards
152 Abandoning ship
154 Survival in the water
156 Medical emergencies/1
158 Medical emergencies/2

**The great races/
Robin Knox-Johnston**
160 Rules of the sport
162 The America's Cup

164 SORC, The Onion
     Patch and Bermuda
166 The Southern Cross Series
168 The Admiral's Cup Series
170 The Single-handed
     Transatlantic
172 Round Britain and Ireland
174 Round the World

Care and repair/Geoff Hales
176 Hulls/1
178 Hulls/2
180 Seacocks and skin
     fittings
182 Decks/1
184 Decks/2
186 Standing rigging
188 Running rigging
190 Sails
192 Engines
194 Electrics
196 Tools
198 Paint
200 Below decks

**Boats and the law/
David Johnston**
202 Boats and the law

Facts and figures
204-213

Glossary
214-219

Index
220-222

Acknowledgements
224

The pioneers of cruising

The chronicling of the development of yachting is as incomplete as the history of the evolution of man. It was only when a few amateur sailors began to publish books for the entertainment and education of others that more people became aware that cruising, as opposed to racing, could be enjoyed by ordinary 'landsmen'. Perhaps the most influential volume was Claude Worth's 1910 classic, *Yacht Cruising*.

The craft most readily available to the 'landsmen' were invariably commercial boats nearing the end of their useful working days, but which, with the addition of simple sleeping accommodation, often ex-navy hammocks, and the conversion of the fish-hold into a spacious saloon, made excellent cheap cruising boats.

Many longshore fishermen were employed as professional summer crews by the world's élite. When these men returned home to their fishing villages, they passed on equipment details and accommodation plans to local boatbuilders engaged in converting fishing boats to yachts.

The process has continued to the present day: the classic British motorsailers were derived from the Scottish double-ended fishing boats. The broad-beamed, square-sterned American motor yachts were based on the Gulf prawners and Alaskan salmon seiners, and the sleek Scandinavian yachts owe much to the Viking long boats and the sailing lifeboats, *redningskoites*, designed by the legendary Colin Archer.

Just as previous generations produced famous navigators and explorers, so the last century has given yachting its own pioneers: men who in their time were 'oddballs', some celebrated, others known only because of their writings. Those who cruised the oceans single-handed were probably held in the same awe that we reserve for those who have been to the moon.

Richard McMullen (1830–1891) was the thinking man's sailor. He devoted his life to sailing small boats around the British Isles and became, perhaps, the greatest chronicler of the precise skills of professional seamanship. In his first boat *Leo*, a 20-ft (6-m) cutter, he developed the classic cruising concept of staying offshore in a gale instead of risking

In 1876-7, the millionaire Lord Thomas Brassey circumnavigated the world in his

Edward Knight explored South America in a 28-ton yawl before cruising the Baltic in a converted

Joshua Slocum was the first yachtsman to capture the imagination of the world. In 1898 he stunned his contemporaries when he completed a three-year circumnavigation singlehanded, in his 90-year-old converted lobster boat, *Spray*. Others had sailed round the world in large crewed vessels, but no one alone. When he set out on his 46,000-ml (74,000-km)

Claude Worth drew on his experience of buying, converting and sailing both commercial vessels and purpose-built craft to write *Yacht Cruising*. It was the first manual of seamanship for the increasing number of amateurs. The new breed of owners came from the professional rather than titled classes, and women soon became valuable crew members.

John Voss circumnavigated the world in 38-ft (11-m) *Tilikum*, a converted canoe. He set out in 1901 with a sponsoring journalist, but returned 3½ yrs later alone.

Erskine Childers' best-selling novel, *The Riddle of the Sands*, is based on his cruising experiences in the North Sea and the Baltic and on his own converted life boat, *Vixen*.

Thomas Fleming Day a campaigning journalist who advocated the development of small ocean-going craft, organized the first Bermuda race in 1906.

disaster by running for shelter over shallow tidal banks. The carefully logged thoughts and conclusions he published in *Down Channel* inspired many to take up small-boat sailing.

lavish 170-ft (51-m) schooner *Sunbeam*.

lifeboat, *Falcon*, in 1886.

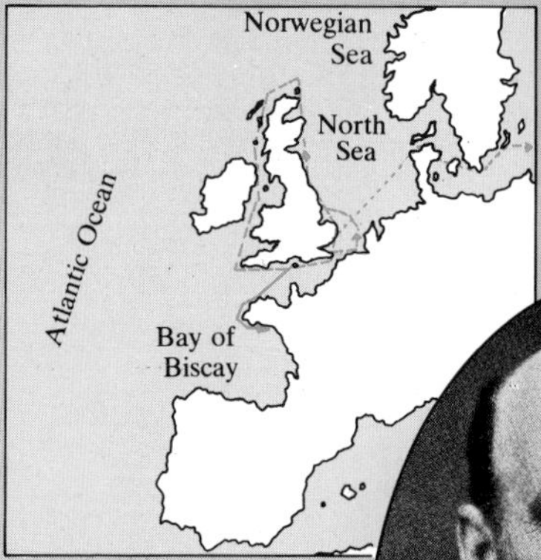

Norwegian Sea

North Sea

Atlantic Ocean

Bay of Biscay

McMullen's cruising routes

Edward Knight

Erskine Childers

Claude Worth's cruising routes

voyage, he was already a celebrated ship's captain. He built his own boat from the wreck of a barque and sailed the 5,000 mls (8,000 km) home to New York from Brazil. His trip illustrates the spirit of adventure exhibited today by men like Bernard Moitessier and Sir Alec Rose.

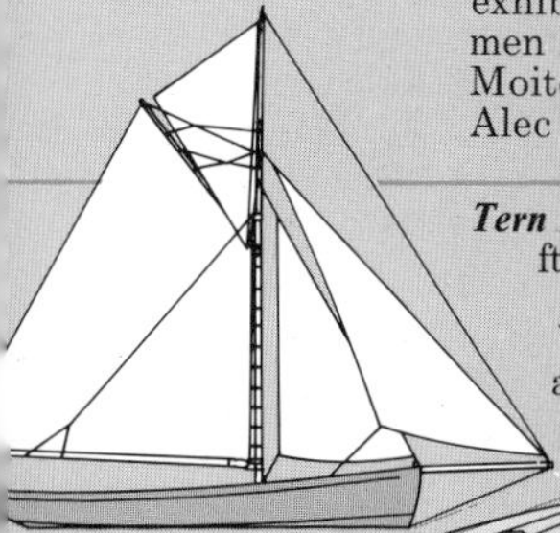

Tern II, *left*, the 30-ft (9-m) yawl in which Claude Worth cruised along the west coast of France in 1912, was one of the most notable of his nine cruisers.

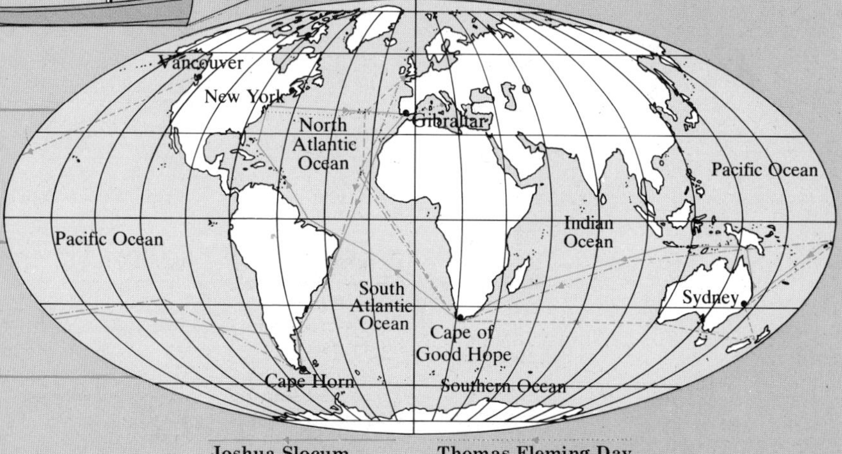

Joshua Slocum

Vancouver

New York

North Atlantic Ocean

Gibraltar

Pacific Ocean

Pacific Ocean

Indian Ocean

South Atlantic Ocean

Cape of Good Hope

Sydney

Cape Horn

Southern Ocean

Joshua Slocum

John Voss

Thomas Fleming Day

Lord Brassey

From workboats to playboats

The first pleasure craft to be described as yachts were, in many ways, similar to the royal yachts of today – lavishly embellished naval vessels, used for cruises and state occasions in peace time and as naval vessels in wartime.

In 1651, Charles II escaped from Cromwell by fleeing to France in the coal brig *Surprise*. On his restoration, the mayor of Amsterdam presented him with the yacht *Mary*. In 1661 Charles's *Katherine* won a wager from the Duke of York, in a race from Greenwich to Gravesend and back.

A few years later, Sir William Perry's twin-hulled craft *Experiment* won the first recorded open-sea race – the Holyhead to Dublin packet – in just 15 hrs.

It was not until the 1720s, however, that clubs were formed to organize sailing in company. The first was the Water Club of the Harbour of Cork, closely followed by others such as the Cumberland Fleet (later to become the Royal Thames Yacht Club) and the Societé des Regattes du Havre, in France. Soon clubs sprang up in the USA, beginning with the Detroit in 1839, the New York in 1844 and the Southern in 1849.

As a result of their close links with the Navy, the early yachts often joined the fleet manoeuvres or sailed in company to France to replenish their owners' cellars.

The Admiralty, recognizing the value of fast ships developed by private individuals, granted the title Royal Yacht Squadron to the Yacht Club at Cowes, which adopted formalized sailing manoeuvres (Admiral Sailing) that were to become a festive feature of the early clubs.

Early races began as friendly wagers between two boats and developed, in the 1870s, into regattas between fleets of boats for specific prizes. As a result, racing rules were drawn up, yachts were classified for racing and a new sport was born.

1660 The Dutch yacht *Mary*, presented to Charles II on his restoration, becomes the first British pleasure cruiser. Based on the fast despatch naval vessels, it is, in turn, used as a model for the first generation of cruising yachts.

1844 The New York Yacht Club is founded aboard J.C. Stevens's schooner *Gimcrack*. In the first race, a time handicap is introduced, allowing the smaller yachts to start first. The winners, however, are the largest entries.

1875 One of the most significant breakthroughs in design is seen in *Jullanar*. Fast enough to beat any other yacht, its great length and small wetted surface will become an inspiration for *Britannia*.

1893 Built for the Prince of Wales, later Edward VII, by G.L. Watson, *Britannia* is one of the first designs to follow the Dixon-Kemp rating rule. *Britannia* sailed for the last time in 1935, having entered 635 races and won 360 prizes.

1720 The Royal Cork is the first club to arrange races for members

1878 Colin Archer builds the first of his legendary Norwegian yachts.

1901 Friendship sloops are built for fishing in Maine and later become pleasure craft.

1749 The first open regatta for commoners is held from Greenwich to the Nore and back. Yachting is no longer confined to royalty.

1775 The Cumberland Fleet, to be renamed The Royal Thames Yacht Club in 1823, is founded. Initially a river sailing club, its best-known yachts are 20–25 ft (6.1–7.6 m) cutters, of broad beam and heavy displacement.

1815 Forty-two gentlemen form the Yacht Club at Cowes, to advise on sailing matters and to sail together in yachts resembling small warships. Renamed the Royal Yacht Squadron in 1833, it organizes racing in the Solent.

1835 America's first recorded yachting race takes place between J.C. Stevens's *Wave* and J. Cushing's *Sylph* off Cape Cod. Stevens, owner of the first US pleasure boat, *Diver*, later takes a part share in the schooner *America*.

1848 *America* wins a race around the Isle of Wight: the first America's Cup challenge.

1855 The Thames Tonnage rule is adopted, to minimize inequality in racing. The effect is at first beneficial, but cunning designers and ruthless owners soon produce narrow and extremely unstable yachts.

1867 Australia adopts competitive sailing when the Royal Prince Albert Yacht Club of Sydney is formed. Within 2 yrs Adelaide has its own club and in 1875 the Royal Perth Yacht Club opens.

1880 The Cruising Club is born – its purpose to produce cruising charts and information.

1881 The Scots cutter *Madge* challenges American centre-board sloops in their own waters and wins all but one race – against *Shadow*. *Madge's* deep-ballasted design influences American yacht architects.

1887 Dixon Kemp attempts to halt the trend towards deep, narrow, 'plank-on edge' style boats, with huge sail areas. His new rating rule, however, eventually leads to wide, shallow 'skimming dishes'.

1891 The famous American designer Nat Herreshoff produces *Gloriana*, a revolutionary cutter with overhanging ends and a cutaway forefoot extending to a very small keel. It outsails every challenging boat.

1901 *Istria*, the first yacht to dispense with a separate top mast, paves the way for the bermudan rig. The topsail is rigged in a track on the upper part of the mast.

1906 Metre classes are introduced to prevent boats becoming unseaworthy. A conference of European yachtsmen approves an international rule which encourages the design of full-bodied yachts with accomodation.

1911 Research in the USA reveals that the bermudan rig is more efficient and lighter than the gaff rig. The triangular sail attached to a single mast is first adopted by small racing classes and later in production cruisers.

1913 The *Jolie Brise* is built in Le Havre as a pilot cutter. Yet, typical of the working boats converted into yachts, it is to have a glamorous racing career and sets the pace for the development of yachts purely for racing.

Anatomy of a boat

Of all the vehicles devised by mankind for transportation, pleasure or business, the boat is perhaps the most intriguing. It's variety is infinite; a penniless youngster on a home-made raft or a millionaire on his gold-plated world cruising yacht both feel a sense of achievement and the satisfying glow that accompanies activity afloat.

Anyone can develop a 'boat sense' through practice or study, and a 1980s 30-ft (9-m) fibreglass cruiser well illustrates the form and parts of a yacht. From bow to stern, such a vessel requires careful design, meticulous attention in construction, and good owner maintenance to make her 'Shipshape and Bristol fashion', fit for the challenge of the sea.

The bow pulpit and lifelines surrounding the working deck contain, forward, an anchor hatch for the ground tackle and, working aft, the raised coach/cabin trunk roof with its portholes, and handrails for the crew to hold on to when going forward in rough weather. The self-draining cockpit is positioned above the water level so that water taken in to it will exit through tubular scuppers or drains. On the coamings round the cockpit are geared winches, driven by hand with a ratcheting winch handle, to promote mechanical advantage when trimming the sheets.

The single mast of a sloop is secured in place by its standing rigging: stiff wire shrouds, the forestay and the backstay. The lower shrouds position the mast at, perhaps, two-thirds of its height, where the upper shrouds bend around spreaders to transfer their tension at a suitably wide angle to prevent the masthead bending to leeward under the pressure of the wind.

Heeling movement, generated by the action of the wind on the sails, is counteracted by the gravity-restoring movement of the keel, – in this instance a short and hydrodynamically efficient lead-filled fin.

Masthead fittings often include a masthead light, wind-direction indicator, an anemometer and possibly a loop antenna for radio direction-finding.

The mast is normally made of a light alloy extrusion and allows internal halyards to be fitted.

The shrouds support the mast laterally.

Spreaders position the upper shrouds for good alignment.

One pair of lower shrouds runs slightly forward of the mast, the other slightly abaft it for maximum support.

The fore- and backstays support the mast upright against halyard tensions.

The halyard winches, used for hoisting sails, often have a brake or ratchet to stop the halyard running back.

The topping lift supports the boom when the mainsail is lowered or reefed.

The mainsheet blocks are attached to the boom and the **traveller**, which slides on a track.

Lifelines, supported by **stanchions,** prevent the crew falling overboard. **The grab rails** provide handholds.

The tiller, the helmsman's steering lever, is attached to the **rudder stock/post**.

The coamings protect the cockpit and main hatchway from spray and form a base for cleats and winches.

Spinnaker sheet winch

The transom, has a pushpit for crew safety, and often a boarding ladder.

STERN AFT

The propeller is a screw, rotated by the engine to propel the boat under power.

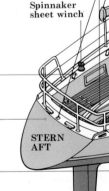

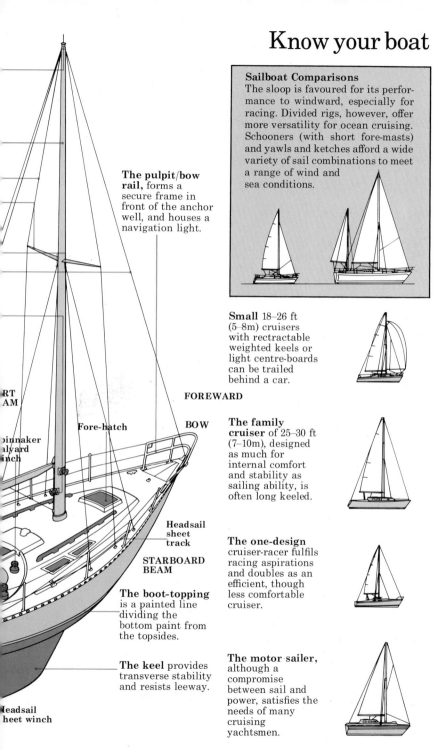

Know your boat

The pulpit/bow rail, forms a secure frame in front of the anchor well, and houses a navigation light.

Sailboat Comparisons
The sloop is favoured for its performance to windward, especially for racing. Divided rigs, however, offer more versatility for ocean cruising. Schooners (with short fore-masts) and yawls and ketches afford a wide variety of sail combinations to meet a range of wind and sea conditions.

Small 18–26 ft (5–8m) cruisers with rectractable weighted keels or light centre-boards can be trailed behind a car.

RT AM

FOREWARD

Fore-hatch

BOW

pinnaker alyard inch

The family cruiser of 25–30 ft (7–10m), designed as much for internal comfort and stability as sailing ability, is often long keeled.

Headsail sheet track

STARBOARD BEAM

The one-design cruiser-racer fulfils racing aspirations and doubles as an efficient, though less comfortable cruiser.

The boot-topping is a painted line dividing the bottom paint from the topsides.

The keel provides transverse stability and resists leeway.

The motor sailer, although a compromise between sail and power, satisfies the needs of many cruising yachtsmen.

Headsail heet winch

13

Fibreglass construction

The majority of yachts and boats today are constructed of fibreglass. This strong and resilient hull material is a combination of a resin (which is made to harden or set chemically) and a strong reinforcement material, usually fibres of glass.

The resin comprises polyester, solvents, catalysts and other additives. The fibreglass is either cloth (a smooth woven fabric), roving (a coarse, basket-like woven fabric), or mat (a random combination of many short-fibre strands of glass).

The post-war explosion in boat production was initiated by the introduction of room-temperature curing resins which revolutionized fibreglass construction.

The process begins with the formation of a smooth female mould (itself usually made of fibreglass laminate) over a precisely constructed wooden plug, which establishes the hull shape. The gloss and colour of a hull are established by gelcoat resin, sprayed against a parting agent, previously applied to the surface of the mould.

Glass and resin are then combined in a hand lay-up process to produce the hull structure. Thickness can be varied by the composition and number of layers and is determined by the correct compromise between the strength and lightness required over different portions of the hull.

A separate deck laminate is produced in the same way; thereafter the real skill lies in the fitting out. This includes the construction of bulkheads (athwartships hull-stiffening panels), joinery of the interior and the proper connection of all elements of fibreglass, wood and metal.

Promoted by developments in the aerospace industry, so-called 'exotic laminates' are entering the boat building trade. Graphite, kevlar, carbon and other new reinforcements promise remarkable strength, stiffness and structural weight-efficiency.

The shape of hull and deck are usually made inside a mould in a hand lay-up laminate process.

Bulkheads and interior units are secured by secondary bond laminates before the deck is fitted.

Stage 3

A fibreglass kit boat can mean a 20 per cent saving in total cost but also a lower resale price. In a Stage 1 kit, the hull, deck and interior framework are supplied. At Stage 2, the interior mouldings are bonded in. Stage 3, complete with engine and deck fittings, leaves only the woodwork to be done. Stage 4 is the finished craft.

The laminate consists of woven rovings, 1, and mat, 2, bonded with polyester resin and sealed with gelcoat, 3.

Through-hull bolts and fittings need to be well supported with a backing plate to spread the load.

The individual components, such as wooden tables, bunks, lockers, deck fittings, metal winches and stanchions are then attached.

Completion of the yacht involves trim, painting, varnishing and check out of all systems. The heads and engine need piping, wiring and controls and deck fittings must be securely fitted.

Checklist
1 Edges and corners on fibreglass hulls should be well rounded for strength, to avoid blow holes and to reduce the chances of chipping.
2 Hull stiffening should be tapered away at the ends or joined to another member to dissipate the stress. Where a stiffener ends abruptly, look for cracks, tears or separations.
3 The hull should be smooth, with no bumps or dimples.
4 A coating of polyurethane paint with added grit will reduce slipperiness on a fibreglass deck.
5 Changes in colour tone, such as yellowing or bleaching indicate ageing and can be painted over.
6 Bubbles, indicating that water is blistering the laminate, must be investigated immediately.

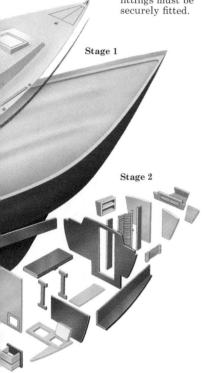

Stage 1

Stage 2

Deck construction normally matches the hull material; however, a traditional wooden deck vastly improves the aesthetic appeal of any hull, particularly of fibreglass. Seams between the planks are caulked in the same way as carvel planks, then 'payed' with gun-applied mastic or hot marine glue. Laid decks are costly, so plywood is sometimes used. Alternatively, a thin layer of teak planks may be laid on top to create the effect of a traditional, laid deck. Since water tends to sit on the deck, a wooden deck needs to be scrubbed regularly. This also produces one of the best non-slip surfaces.

Airex foam in hull cavities improves buoyancy and creates good insulation against temperature, sound and water.

Balsa

Foam

One way of making, a deck-to-hull joint waterproof is by bonding and through-bolting at frequent intervals.

Toe rail

Wooden construction

Since the beginning of time, wood has been the traditional boatbuilding material. Ancient ships, and until the last century, trading and naval vessels were constructed of wood. Interest in yachting and speed under sail led to lighter but strongly built and carefully designed structures. Even yachts of 100 years old, if properly designed, built and cared for, can, and do in some cases, still give service.

Carvel has always been the most common form of wooden construction. Generally, a skeleton of steam-bent oak is formed to support planks from stem to stern. These are made of light wood in small boats and harder woods, such as elm, in larger craft. The seams between planks are fitted with caulking to make the structure watertight.

Clinker/lapstrake construction, common for small boats in the past, is a method where relatively thin, shaped planks overlap each other at the seam. Mechanical fasteners (often copper rivets) join the plank edges, both to seal against leaks and to secure the shell to internal stiffening pieces.

Modern wooden boats are more often built of moulded wood construction, which involves the fabrication of a single glued-ply unit for the entire hull.

Proper design, engineering and construction of hull members is the key to the strength and durability of yachts. Hard-wood keels, bilge stringers, and the clamp, or shelf, at the juncture of the deck with the hull are tied into the hull with bolts, screws or adhesive. The deck, unless of moulded plywood, is strengthened by its athwartships deck beams and is stiffened longitudinally by coamings and cabin sides. Hull form and the stiffness of the entire boat is assured by plywood (or sometimes metal) diagonals or grids.

The choice of good materials is as essential to the durability of yachts as a close fit between members, to keep out water which can promote rot.

The **keel** forms the backbone of the boat and is connected both to a ballast keel and to a lower keel.

The frames, extending athwartships, make up the skeleton, secure the planking and

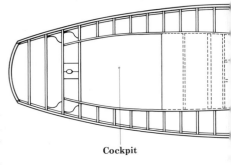

Cockpit

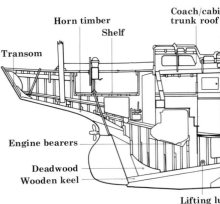

Transom

Horn timber

Shelf

Coach/cabi trunk roof

Engine bearers

Deadwood
Wooden keel

Lifting lu

In clinker/lapstrake boats, planks are both fastened to the frame and joined to adjacent overlapping planks by rivets. The wood swells in the water to form waterproof seams.

Carvel gives a smooth outer surface. Planks are fastened side-by-side on shaped frames. Caulking is forced into the joints to seal them against leaking.

provide hull stiffness. Other stiffening-members include the bilge stringer, the coaming and the house side. The deck beams are joined to the frames by a longitudinal deck shelf.

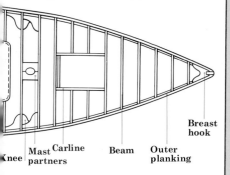

Knee | Mast partners | Carline | Beam | Outer planking | Breast hook

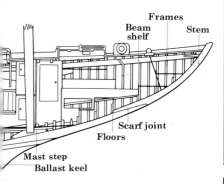

Mast step | Ballast keel | Floors | Scarf joint | Beam shelf | Frames | Stem

Moulded wood construction

A moulded wood hull is made up of three or more layers of wood veneer glued together over a temporary framework, either a hull plug or a firm temporary grid. The grains of successive thin layers of wood are set at different angles for strength and resistance against splitting in all directions. Moulded wood hulls, particularly those with complex, double curvature, can be stiff, durable and weight-efficient. They are smooth both inside and out, and the absence of seams reduces maintenance and the risk of leaks. It was the development of strong, room-temperature curing glues, such as epoxies, that made moulded wood construction possible. Sometimes moulded wood hulls are covered with a layer or two of fibreglass to enhance the strength of the hull structure. Modern hulls of all types are frequently coated with sprayed polyurethane paint, which produces a far more attractive and durable finish than traditional paints. Wood remains the most weight-efficient material for medium-sized yachts.

Strip planking comprises narrow, almost square planking, secured with edge-nailed fastenings. They are glued together, not caulked, which produces a smooth, seamless hull.

Plywood construction involves joining sheets of pre-formed plywood, usually over a skeleton. The topsides and the bottom meet at an angle or chine.

A vacuum bag is used in cold moulded construction to ensure that the veneers adhere to the mould frames. The cover is taped down to the hull surface to form a bag from which air is extracted via a valved airline. Rope net channels allow air to be sucked evenly from the area.

Metal construction

The strength and durability of metal construction are appealing, particularly for larger yachts. Except for small craft, the traditional riveted connections for steel or aluminium have given way to welded hulls.

Two types of hull framing are possible. Transverse framing involves curved, angled or T-section stiffeners inside the hull in the same pattern as the conventional framing of a traditional wooden hull. Longitudinal framing runs fore-and-aft, itself supported by bulkheads.

Welding is used initially to tack shaped and curved hull plates to the framing grid and to position plate edges to each other. Then welding passes are made to fill all butts and seams, for hull strength and water-tightness. Further selective welds are made to ensure satisfactory connection of the hull plating to framing and stiffeners.

During welding, shrinkage of the weld metal as it cools is a critical issue for the ultimate shape. Therefore, a proper welding sequence, from port to starboard and deck to keel, over the plating, must be followed to prevent distortion of the yacht's shape from the desired geometry and to prevent the building up of internal stresses, which may limit the external load-carrying ability of the hull structure.

Skilful lofting – the full-sized drawing-out of hull-shape lines, accurate forming of frames and set-up, plus a proper welding sequence, can achieve an accurate, reasonably smooth hull surface. Nevertheless, for a proper yacht – quality, hull surface, a layer of fairing compound is required over the metal plating. After a priming coat to inhibit corrosion and ensure proper bonding, the filler material is trowelled on, and finally hand-sanded to the desired accuracy and smoothness, using long, flexible sanding planks. Conventional or sprayed polyurethane paint coating finishes the job.

Transverse frames are formed to the desired curved shape from angle- or T-shaped sections. Hand-spiling marks the cut-lines for the accurate trimming of plates. Long plates give a better finish, but are difficult to handle; wide plates make chine construction quicker, but are only suitable for the flatter parts of a round chine hull. A patchwork of different-sized plates speeds up work. Plating is

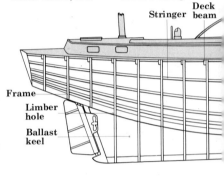

Deck beam, Stringer, Frame, Limber hole, Ballast keel

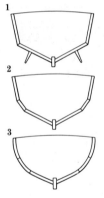

The simple single chine, **1**, allows the use of mainly flat plates. The multi-chine hull, **2**, uses smaller plates, so is stronger and more shapely. Round bar or tube welded into the chine will soften the angle of the rolled chine hull, **3**. Butt welds,

a, are often used in boatbuilding. In thick plate, edges must be chamfered first; on topsides and decks, welds are usually ground flat, **b**. Lap joints are strong, and double bead lap welds, **c**, help to prevent corrosion between mild steel plates. Open corner welds, **d**, produce a smooth curve for coach/cabin trunk roof joins.

curved on rollers or by cramping to frames, or is shaped on hydraulic presses. Plates are joined to each other and to the framing by arc-welding. Deck-edge connections, hatch coamings and bases for

highly stressed fittings are also welded in place. The hull backbone, bilge stiffeners and other main strength members are built up and made secure by successive welding passes.

thole (rounded corner)
Rubbing strake/rubrail
Deck

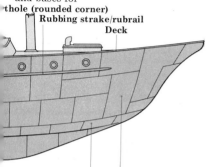

Rolled chine plate   Skin plate

The main advantage of aluminium construction is its light weight. When it was first applied to boat-building it was extremely expensive and vulnerable to electrolytic corrosion. However, the introduction of aluminium-magnesium alloy in the 1930s reduced the problem of electrolysis, and today small, mass-produced aluminium boats are often comparable in price to fibreglass. It is an ideal material for fast racing boats which have claimed many of the top racing trophies.

Choosing a Construction Material

1 Fibreglass is resilient, demanding less maintenance than wood in the first few years, although it needs annual cleaning, waxing and anti-fouling. The smooth, seamless hull is waterproof, although the deck to hull joints can be trouble spots. Fibreglass construction often requires fewer man-hours and, therefore, cuts the purchase price. The high initial cost of the mould, however, means that long production runs are imperative to keep the price down.

2 Wood is the most aesthetically pleasing and the only natural hull material. It is, however, vulnerable to rot and organic growth. Although they have a long working life, traditional wooden boats require a lot of maintenance. Since the cost of seasoned timber and labour is high, marine plywood became the most popular material. More recently, modern epoxy construction has produced low-maintenance boats at economical prices.

3 Steel is stronger for its weight than any other material, although denting causes problems and repairs can be difficult. Steel will not split like wood, nor is it subject to wear and tear like fibreglass. It is economical for boats from 40–70 ft (12–21 m) and good for one-offs. Steel boats also tend to be heavy and noisy and limited in hull shape, unless machinery is available to roll the steel plate. Corrosion is the greatest hazard for both steel and aluminium and all fittings of different metal must be bedded on plastic washers.

4 Ferroconcrete is the cheapest material and favoured by amateur boat-builders. It is strong and continues strengthening for 10 yrs after construction. Durable and virtually maintenance-free, it is also heavy, so best suited to boats over 30 ft (9 m) long. It is time consuming and difficult to achieve accurate dimensions and a good smooth finish.

Standing rigging

A close look at the thickness of a mast and the complexity of its supporting wires will quickly reveal the designed purpose of a boat.

If the mast is thick, the rigging mounted at the masthead over a single set of spreaders, and if the backstay is without a proper adjuster, you have the nautical equivalent of an 'automatic'. You can hoist the sails and relax.

In the 'grand prix' version, however, the mast is patently thin, with a multitude of wires led over several sets of spreaders. The whole rig is tuned by a bank of hydraulic tensioners, which need to be adjusted continually to get the best out of the boat.

Between these two extremes, various combinations exist which permit different degrees of control and adjustment to suit the intended use of the boat. The single-spreader masthead rig with fore and aft lower shrouds (usually taken to the sides of the boat), forestay and backstay, gives the simplest, most robust rig.

The fractional rig has a higher mast and larger mainsails. Since the smaller headsails make it more manoeuvrable in close-tacking situations, it is a favourite with keel-boat and inshore classes, although the smaller spinnakers can be a drawback in light airs. All masthead rigs are set well aft and support large overlapping headsails.

If you are rigging your own kit boat remember that the simple sections will be cheaper to buy and easier to rig. The more complicated rigs require a greater understanding of the stresses involved and need a large, experienced crew to control them.

When buying a production cruiser new or secondhand, make sure that the backstay is adjustable under way. This provides considerable control over the tension, and thus sag, of the forestay for efficient windward work, and over the forward rake of the mast for downwind sailing.

The high degree of control in a fractional rig is effected by mast bend. The backstay exerts forces on the tapered topmast section, while the shrouds and forestay meet at $\frac{3}{4}$ or $\frac{7}{8}$ the height of the mast.

The shorter spreaders on a double rig allow the headsails to be sheeted in tighter to produce more driving power. The streamlined mast needs support from a number of shrouds and stays.

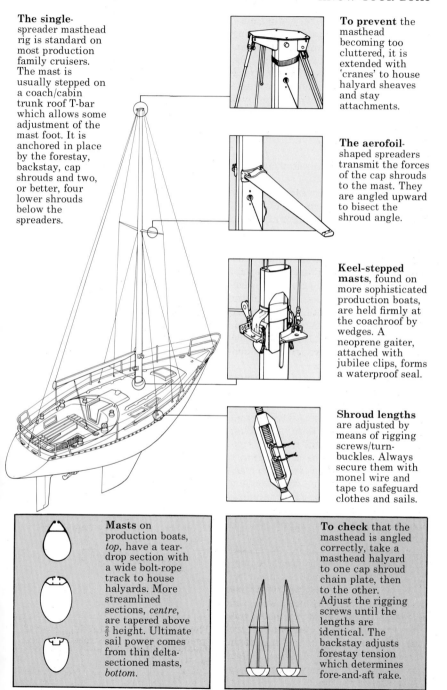

The single- spreader masthead rig is standard on most production family cruisers. The mast is usually stepped on a coach/cabin trunk roof T-bar which allows some adjustment of the mast foot. It is anchored in place by the forestay, backstay, cap shrouds and two, or better, four lower shrouds below the spreaders.

To prevent the masthead becoming too cluttered, it is extended with 'cranes' to house halyard sheaves and stay attachments.

The aerofoil- shaped spreaders transmit the forces of the cap shrouds to the mast. They are angled upward to bisect the shroud angle.

Keel-stepped masts, found on more sophisticated production boats, are held firmly at the coachroof by wedges. A neoprene gaiter, attached with jubilee clips, forms a waterproof seal.

Shroud lengths are adjusted by means of rigging screws/turn-buckles. Always secure them with monel wire and tape to safeguard clothes and sails.

Masts on production boats, *top*, have a tear-drop section with a wide bolt-rope track to house halyards. More streamlined sections, *centre*, are tapered above $\frac{2}{3}$ height. Ultimate sail power comes from thin delta-sectioned masts, *bottom*.

To check that the masthead is angled correctly, take a masthead halyard to one cap shroud chain plate, then to the other. Adjust the rigging screws until the lengths are identical. The backstay adjusts forestay tension which determines fore-and-aft rake.

Running rigging

If you think of the standing rigging as being wire, and the running rigging as rope, one look into the cockpit of a racing yacht will bring home the true meaning of the sailing-ship term 'knowing the ropes'. At least the square riggers coiled and belayed their ropes while sailing to prevent them becoming hopelessly tangled. No such system has yet been devised for modern yachts, which always have a minimum of three sheets occupying the cockpit sole.

The large-crewed racing yacht can cope with this complexity, but the shorthanded cruising-man constantly seeks a simpler rig with fewer controls. One such rig has emerged – the highly successful wishbone rig, found on both sailboards and cruisers.

A ketch or schooner rigged with such sails still needs eight controls to sail and reef it. There is, also, no great financial saving, since the tapered, unstayed masts must be made from expensive carbon fibres or machined from alloys.

An integral part of the running rigging is the rope-handling system of winches, cleats and blocks. It is often more a question of siting winches and controls correctly than installing large numbers of them.

The more expensive are generally worth it because they are better engineered to withstand the massive sheet loadings. Self-tailing winches, which automatically cleat the rope and can be operated by one person, are ideal for cruising boats.

Inspect ropes regularly, especially those subject to constant wear in one small area, and turn them end-for-end at the first sign of wear. As important to long life is the choice of cleats and jamming cleats, since serrated teeth or sharp corners will make the rope wear more quickly. In addition, use fine emery cloth on sheaves, blocks and spars to eliminate sharp metal cutting surfaces.

On a Cat ketch, the unstayed mast with its wrap-around sail is tensioned by the wishbone-shaped boom. The rig is controlled by a halyard, outhaul, sheet and two reefing lines, and is well suited for cruising.

The Junk rig has so far had only limited success on cruising boats. The fully battened sail is easily controlled by a mainsheet and a reefing line, which lowers the foot of the sail into retaining strops.

The large sail areas on the traditional Dutch boat feature a curved gaff and a loose-footed mainsail. In light airs, watersails, attached to spars around the sides of the boat, add to the area.

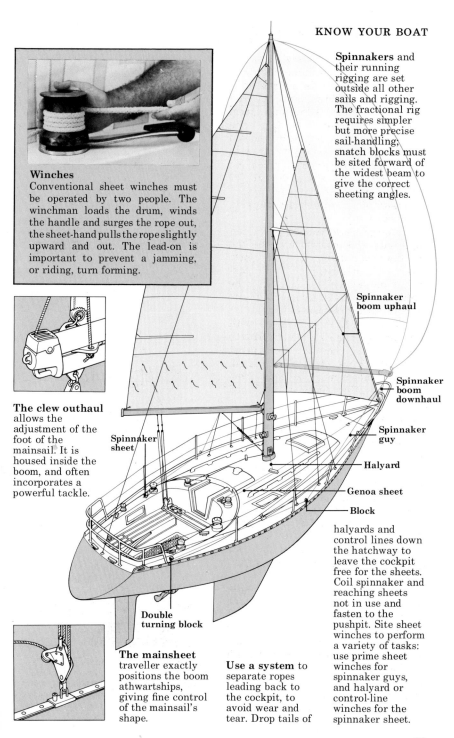

Spinnakers and their running rigging are set outside all other sails and rigging. The fractional rig requires simpler but more precise sail-handling; snatch blocks must be sited forward of the widest beam to give the correct sheeting angles.

Winches
Conventional sheet winches must be operated by two people. The winchman loads the drum, winds the handle and surges the rope out, the sheet-hand pulls the rope slightly upward and out. The lead-on is important to prevent a jamming, or riding, turn forming.

Spinnaker boom uphaul

Spinnaker boom downhaul

The clew outhaul allows the adjustment of the foot of the mainsail. It is housed inside the boom, and often incorporates a powerful tackle.

Spinnaker sheet

Spinnaker guy

Halyard

Genoa sheet

Block

Double turning block

The mainsheet traveller exactly positions the boom athwartships, giving fine control of the mainsail's shape.

Use a system to separate ropes leading back to the cockpit, to avoid wear and tear. Drop tails of

halyards and control lines down the hatchway to leave the cockpit free for the sheets. Coil spinnaker and reaching sheets not in use and fasten to the pushpit. Site sheet winches to perform a variety of tasks: use prime sheet winches for spinnaker guys, and halyard or control-line winches for the spinnaker sheet.

Choosing sails

A conventional bermudan rig for the average cruising boat requires an absolute minimum of a mainsail and one headsail. With a furling headsail, this is probably enough for most of the season. However, it is always worth carrying a small second jib for safety, rather like carrying a second anchor, just in case the furling genoa tears.

Anyone cruising one weekend and racing the next needs more sails. The furling headsail does not lend itself to racing because as it rolls up the sail becomes fuller, which is not ideal to windward. Several sizes of headsail are, therefore, necessary.

The minimum wardrobe for occasional weekend racing is a mainsail, medium-weather genoa, possibly a No 2 genoa which reefs down to No 3, and a radial spinnaker of medium weight. For cruising or racing offshore, a storm jib is essential, both to comply with the rules and for safety.

The movement in sailing today, however, is towards ease of handling. As the conventional bermudan rig involves the expense of a large crew and a full wardrobe of sails to achieve maximum efficiency, over the last five or six years, the Cat ketch (Freedom) rig and Junk rig have been refined.

The Cat ketch has a free-standing mast, usually made of carbon fibre, and has a wraparound sail with only short battens down the leech. The advantage of this 'soft sail' rig is that it can be stowed easily and handled by a single person who hardly needs to leave the cockpit to lower, hoist or even reef the sails.

The Junk rig, also on an unstayed mast, is strengthened and controlled by full-length battens, which makes it a hard sail. Although it appears to be not quite as efficient to windward as the Cat ketch, which, in turn, is less close-winded than the conventional bermudan rig, the Junk sail stows easily and can be handled and reefed from the cockpit.

The Gaff-rig, *above,* the traditional working rig for European trading and fishing boats, now enjoys a revival. Individual sails can be lowered to maintain correct fishing speeds or raised for an efficient downwind rig.

The wraparound 'soft sail' reduces turbulence around the mast, which becomes a blunt but smooth leading edge to the aerofoil section of the sail. More efficient than the conventional rig, this double-sided sail is also easier to handle.

American schooners, now chartered worldwide for long-distance cruising, evolved with such a huge sail area because of the traditional race back to port to sell fish at the best prices.

Wind and sail

When buying sails, beware of black magic circulated by manufacturers and invest in strong, well-constructed sails which may be expensive, but remain in good shape for seven or eight years. For cruising, choose a good-weight cloth in preference to the new plastic laminate which rarely lasts more than a few months.

The mitre, 1, the leechcut, 2, and the crosscut are the most common designs for headsails.

The vertical cut, 3, proved its high performance in the 1981 America's Cup.

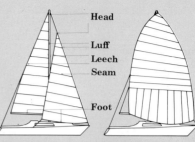

The horizontal cut, 4, is the most popular for mainsails as there is no bias and so no extra stretch on the unsupported leech.

The cruising chute, which is smaller and more easily handled than the spinnaker, has recently improved the downwind and reaching performance of family cruisers.

1 The mainsail takes more wear than any other sail so must be cut for strong winds. Battens wholly support the curved leech (roach).

2 The medium-weather genoa needs a high enough foot to give good visibility ahead and on the leeward side.

3 A No 2 genoa which reefs to a No 3 is useful in strong winds.

4 Alternatively, use a No 3 genoa.

5 The storm jib must be in heavy-weight cloth, preferably fluorescent orange.

6 The cruising radial-head spinnaker is made of light, shock-absorbent cloth. Avoid white to prevent eye strain.

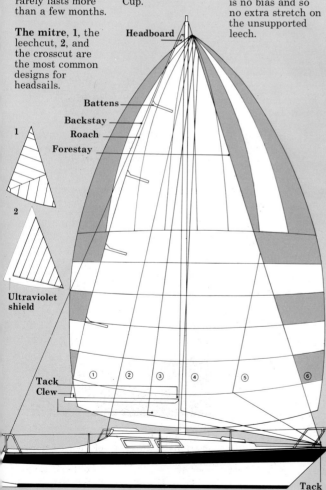

Labels: Head, Luff, Leech, Seam, Foot, Headboard, Battens, Backstay, Roach, Forestay, Ultraviolet shield, Tack, Clew, Tack

25

Sailing dynamics

A boat will not sail straight into the wind, but needs the sails to be full on one side or the other to make it move through the water.

The angle to the wind determines the sheeting position of the sails and which sails to set. The ideal angle for the wind to strike a sail depends on its shape, the type of boat and tautness of rigging. However, in all sailing vessels and on all points of sail, the sails need continual trimming to keep the boat sailing at this optimum angle.

The strength of wind dictates the quantity and sizes of sails to be set. The wind exerts a constant pressure of 1lb/sq ft in a 16-kn (Force 4) moderate breeze. However, if the wind speed increases to 35 kn (gale Force 8) the pressure rises to almost 5 lbs/sq ft.

To keep the same amount of pressure on the boat in Force 8 as in Force 4, and so prevent the boat heeling excessively, the size of sail will have to be considerably reduced.

Sails must be reduced equally to prevent the boat becoming unbalanced. Too much main and not enough jib creates weather helm which pushes the boat up into the wind because the centre of effort is too far back. If there is too much headsail and not enough mainsail, the driving force is too far forward and the boat bears away from the wind.

When the sails are full, the boat would try to move sideways were it not for the keel, which holds the boat upright as well as preventing most sideways slip. Thus, since the boat cannot move sideways through the water, the ultimate forces result in it moving forward.

The angle of heel is important to the speed of the craft. An excessive angle of heel causes the boat to slow down, even though it appears to be going faster. It is, therefore, more efficient and more comfortable to keep the boat on a reasonably even keel.

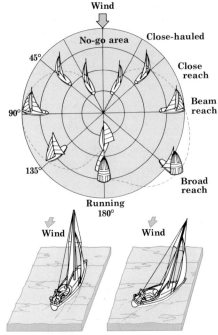

Wind

No-go area | Close-hauled

45°

Close reach

Beam reach

90°

135°

Broad reach

Running 180°

Wind | Wind

Sails, have to be trimmed so that their angle of attack to the wind remains at about 35° *above*. When bearing off the wind, the sheets are adjusted so that the sails maintain their angle but the boat turns.

When beating or reaching, the sails interact to create a slot effect, *below*, and because the compressed wind flows fastest over the curved back of the mainsail, the resulting forces suck the boat forward.

Mainsail

Genoa

The correct centre of effort (COE) is the balancing point of the sail area in relation to the balancing point of the underwater hull shape, or centre of lateral resistance (CLR). It is achieved when a boat needs no rudder correction.

COE

CLR

The boat's speed increases as it moves from close-hauled to reaching. Beyond a broad reach, the apparent wind reduces and the boat slows down unless a spinnaker or cruising chute is set to boost it. A dead run is the slowest point of sailing, unless it is blowing very hard.

The keel stops the boat sliding sideways through the water and keeps it upright. The ballast on the bottom of the keel counteracts the pressure of the wind on the sails, so preventing the boat sailing on its beam ends.

Points of Sailing
The relative speed of any sailing boat is determined by its point of sail or angle to the wind.
1 Too close to the wind, in the 'no-go' area, the sails lift and the boat moves slowly.
2 Close-hauled or beating at 30° off the wind, speed increases as the sails are pinned in tight and at the optimum angle.
3 On a close reach (70°), the sheets are eased out and the boat sails more easily.
4 On a beam reach, at right angles to the wind, speed increases.
5 A broad reach (135°) is the fastest point of sailing, if extra sail is set.
6 Running, or sailing downwind, the sheets are let out to a maximum, and unless more sail is set or the wind kept on the quarter, the boat will slow down.

Heeling force
Leeway
Backward drag on sails
Backward drag on hull
Forward drive
Forward movement
Balance
Keel resistance to side slip

The apparent wind is a combination of the true wind and the wind created by the movement of the boat and feels strongest when the boat is close-hauled. When sailing away from it, the wind feels lighter than it really is. If a 15-kn wind is blowing and the boat is sailing at 5 kn downwind, an apparent wind of 10 kn blows over the deck.

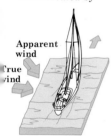

Apparent wind
True wind

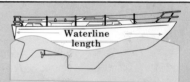

Waterline length

Maximum hull speed. In theory this is 1.5 times the square root of the waterline length and is reached when the waves are the same length as the hull – a wave peak at both bow and stern. Today's lighter boats can exceed this speed by planing on the water surface.

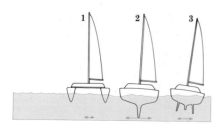

1 A catamaran's width gives it initial stability, but once beyond 90°, it is difficult to right.

2 A cruising boat only heels to a moderate angle because of its hull shape and outside ballast.

3 Alternatively a cruising boat's stability can be achieved by ballast on twin bilge keels and possibly a central stub fin. The same leverage is produced with less draft.

Setting the sails

The starting point of any day's sail is the proper rigging and setting-up of the mainsail and jib on to the spars. Care taken at this stage will prevent snags arising later, such as battens flying out when the sail is flapping.

The first consideration is the weather, especially when you are short-handed. Light winds in the early morning may freshen during the day, requiring a change of headsail, so it is advisable to choose the foresail best suited to the maximum wind speed forecast for the day.

The tack of the jib is fastened to the bow fitting with either a pin, a hook or, for good visibility below the sail, a short tack pennant (length of wire). The luff of the foresail is either hooked to the forestay or, in some boats, fed into a forestay groove, which eliminates the scalloping effect and the turbulence created by hanks.

Once the sails are bent on, the sheets and halyards attached and the boat facing into the wind, the mainsail is generally hoisted first. If, however, the tide is flowing against the wind use the jib to get under way.

Having hoisted the sails, check the tension. On some cruising boats the jib is never adequately tensioned. If it is slack, horizontal creases will run off the luff and a scallop will form between each hank so that the boat sails badly to windward. The luff of the sail should be pre-tensioned to produce a fold in the sail running parallel with the forestay and six inches away from it. When the sail fills, the crease will come out, keeping the flow of the sail well forward. It is always easier to pay out an over-tensioned halyard than to tighten one; the harder the wind, the tighter the halyard should be. If the wind drops, ease off the halyard until the crease just disappears, and if the wind increases progressively tighten the halyard. The luff on the mainsail works in exactly the same way.

Each individual headsail is rigged in exactly the same way. The plungers of the hanks should be on the same side on all the foresails. This avoids confusing the tack with the head, and so hoisting the sail upside down, particularly at night. It also reduces the chances of twisting a hank. Always check that the halyard is not twisted round the forestay before hoisting.

To set the jib, take the bag forward and attach the tack to the bow fitting. Hank the sail on to the forestay, beginning with the bottom hank and taking care not to twist any hanks. Attach the sheets to the clew with a bowline, not a shackle or snapshackle, as these can injure anyone unlucky enough to be hit. Use separate sheets fastened in the middle to the clew, rather than an endless one.

Attach the halyard to the head of the sail, lead the sheets through the fairleads and aft to the cockpit, then secure the end of each sheet with a stopper knot. To hoist, pull hard on the halyard until the head of the sail reaches the top of the forestay, then cleat both halyard and sheets.

The sails act as the engine of a sailing boat. To achieve maximum power, the outhaul tension on the mainsail and the halyard tension on both sails must be sufficient to allow the sails to set wrinkle-free. The sheet must also be tightened until the luff of the sail is just not shaking.

Sail care
Sunlight is a sail's worst enemy, so cover the sails when they are not in use. An ultraviolet guard, fitted down the leech of a roller headsail, will protect the exposed part from the weathering effect of the sun and from dirt and grit. Mildew, which discolours, is prevented by storing sails dry and by hand-washing twice a season.

Check all sails regularly for chafe, particularly where they press on deck fittings or rigging, at reef points, batten sleeves and the foot of the headsail.

To stow the mainsail, start at the leech and flake it on to the boom, left and right, in about 18-in (46-cm) folds, while pulling the leech aft. Secure with a sail tie and continue to the luff. Lash to the boom with sail ties or shock cord.

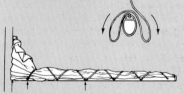

The headsail, neatly rolled and fastened, can be temporarily stowed along the lifelines. To stow below, flake it into a length, **1**, then roll from luff to leech, **2**. Take care not to crease the leech. Pack in a clearly marked bag.

To rig the mainsail, take the bag to the mast and slide the clew of the sail into the boom. Attach the tack to the gooseneck. Fasten the clew to the end of the boom and tension the clew outhaul. Attach the halyard to the head of sail. Fit the slides into the sail track, starting at the head. Fit the stop into the end of the sail track. Fit and secure the battens. When hoisting, check the halyard is running free. Slacken the topping lift so that all the leech tension is taken on the sail itself. When lowering, always tension the topping lift before releasing the halyard. Mark each batten with its pocket number; insert the thin end first and put stiffer battens in lower pockets.

Close-hauled

Close-hauled is the most challenging point of sailing, and the most difficult in which to get the best out of a boat. As it is impossible to make the boat sail directly into the wind, the only way to travel quickly to windward is to climb up into the wind by a series of tacks (zigzags).

The crucial question when sailing to windward is how close to the wind to sail and this is a matter of trial and error. The normal tacking angle – the difference in compass heading between one tack and the other on a cruising boat – in average conditions is about 80–90°.

Some designs, particularly twin-keels, will tack through 90–100°. High-rigged, deep-keeled racing yachts will tack through about 70–80°. Probably the ultimate windward machine, the 12-metre class, will tack through 58° in good conditions. The angle depends not only on the shape of the sails and the boat design but also on the wind strength, the air temperature, the tide and the height of the waves.

The aim when beating is to point as high into the wind as possible, while maintaining the fastest possible speed through the water. If the boat points higher, it approaches its destination more directly, but sails more slowly through the water. If it points farther off, it moves through the water faster, but covers more ground.

Tacking through 90° at a water speed of 5 kn, the boat sails directly to windward at 3.53 kn; pointing higher at a tacking angle of 80°, the water speed may drop to 4 kn and the boat's speed directly to windward falls to 3.06 kn. It often pays to sail farther off the wind and go faster, since it requires a lot of concentration and a well-rigged boat to point high and still maintain speed. When sailing long distances, the wind is likely to change before you arrive, so always choose the tack which is closest to the desired course.

The closest course most boats can sail to the wind is about 35°. The sails are sheeted in as far as they will go without pinching. The apparent wind is strong and the boat tends to heel.

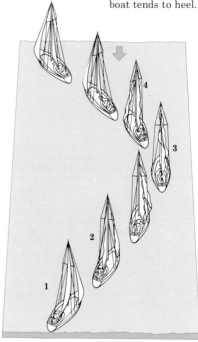

1 Bear away from the wind at least 5–10° to increase speed.
2 Crew 1 uncleats the headsail sheet and holds it on the winch ready to let go. Crew 2 holds the weather sheet with one clockwise turn around the winch ready to pull in. Three more turns will be needed for the final tensioning. Check that the winch handle is in its holder.

3 When all crew are ready, slowly luff the boat up into the wind.
4 As the headsail comes aback, cast off the leeward sheet, push the tiller hard over and as the boat comes through the eye of the wind, haul in the other sheet.

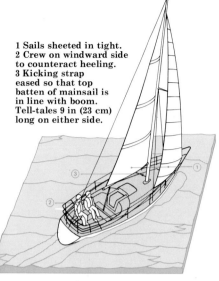

1 Sails sheeted in tight.
2 Crew on windward side to counteract heeling.
3 Kicking strap eased so that top batten of mainsail is in line with boom. Tell-tales 9 in (23 cm) long on either side.

Tell-tales give a visual indication of the trim of the sails and are particularly useful on the headsail. To fit tell-tales, take some threads of wool about 18 in (46 cm) long, make several small holes in the sail with a hot needle (to seal the fabric) and pass the wool through, (9 in – 23 cm – appears each side), tying a knot on each end. Position them 12–18 in (35–46 cm) abaft the luff edge and midway between the seams to avoid the wool catching on the stitching. The tell-tales on each side should stream aft. If the windward one flutters when the boat is close-hauled, it is pointing too high; when reaching, the headsail needs to be sheeted in slightly. If the leeward tell-tale flutters when the boat is close-hauled, it is too far off the wind; when reaching, the sail is too taut.

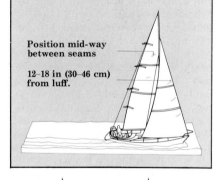

Position mid-way between seams

12–18 in (30–46 cm) from luff.

The optimum speed at which to tack is dictated by the design of the boat and can be established by watching the speed at every turn. The idea is to keep the speed as high as is possible throughout the manoeuvre which means tacking slowly; a fast tack will stop the boat.

Although it can be done in 9 secs, the ideal tacking time on a 12-metre boat is about 23 secs, which allows the boat to maintain her speed during the turn. It is important not to haul in the sheets too violently immediately after a tack, but to wait until the optimum speed is reached.

Wind

Sheet

If the sheets are pinned in too tight and the heeling angle of the boat feels suddenly dangerous, ease the sheets to reduce the sideways pressure on the sails.

Wind   Course

Leeway

Take into account that a boat makes most leeway when close-hauled. A deep-keeled boat may only make 2–5° leeway, a twin-keeled boat may deviate by 15°.

Wind

If the boat stops as it goes about, try reversing the tiller by pushing it towards the intended direction. This pulls the stern over to one side and the sails should fill. Back

the jib by pulling the sheet you have just released and ease the mainsheet. When the bow is 20° off the wind, sheet in the jib.

31

Reaching

Reaching is the fastest point of sailing. In heavy weather it is essential to set the right amount of sail area to prevent excessive heel and to balance the rig to keep weather helm to a minimum. A reefed mainsail and a larger headsail than normal will move the centre of effort of the sail plan forward. This reduces the pull on the helm and also the heeling angle of the boat, and should allow the boat to gain maximum speed very quickly.

In fair weather a spinnaker can be set, although in very light winds a light-weather headsail is preferable since it will not collapse when the boat rolls to leeward: an advantage frequently ignored even by racing crews. If a spinnaker is set the luff tension (the height of the outboard end of the pole) is crucial. The ideal height must be found by trial and error and is reached when the spinnaker will collapse either down its entire leading edge or in the middle.

The spinnaker should not be over-trimmed on a reach; the sheet should be eased until the leading edge just begins to fold, and then sheeted again slightly to keep the sail at its optimum angle. In light weather, the resulting billowing effect increases speed.

In heavy-weather reaching, all the crew should be aft and up on the windward side. This helps to keep the boat upright, the stern down so that the rudder is more effective and the bow out of the water, reducing the boat's weather helm to give the helmsman more control.

In light weather the reverse should happen; the crew should be up forward of the mast and on the leeward side. This keeps the bow down, lifting the flat sections out of the water, so reducing the wetted surface. Increasing the weight to leeward causes the boat to heel slightly, with the result that the sails take up their natural shape through gravity.

On a beam reach the apparent wind attacks the sails at an angle of 90°. On a close reach, this decreases to 70°; on a broad reach, it increases to 135°.

The correct trim of the sails is crucial, so watch the tell-tales and the luff of the sails carefully. As soon as the boat is on course, ease out both the main and jib sheets until the sails begin to flutter, then haul them in just beyond the point where they stop shaking. At this point the sails should be pulling most efficiently. If the mainsheet is eased out too far, causing the wind to strike its lee side, all driving

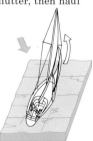

When luffing up into the wind, put the helm down to leeward and sheet in until the tell-tales flutter and luff begins to shake. Then bear off a fraction.

When bearing away, pull the helm to windward and ease the sheets out to increase the flow of wind over the sails and to prevent stalling.

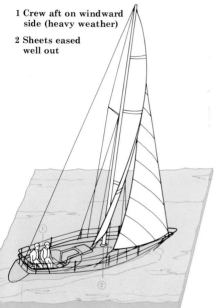

1 Crew aft on windward side (heavy weather)

2 Sheets eased well out

Wind direction
Before setting off, the wind direction can be determined by using any of the following indications.
1 A burgee, a windsock, wind indicator or racing flag, attached to the head of the mast, where the sails and rigging do not distort the wind direction.
2 The position of sails on other boats underway indicates the direction of their apparent wind.
3 Flags, smoke and trees on the coast blow away from the wind.
4 A wind vane or electronic indicator reveals the true wind when stationary and the apparent wind when sailing.
5 Wave direction in the open sea and cloud movement can be misleading.

power will be lost. The solution is to ease the sheets. If both sails are sheeted in too far, the boat will heel sharply and slow down. If the wind draws ahead, tighten the sheets, if it moves farther aft, ease them. On a broad reach, the angle of the boat to the waves may cause it to yaw, so the helmsman should anticipate, rather than fight, the boat's movement.

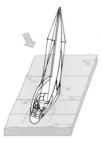

If a squall hits and there is no time to luff up or bear away, let fly the sheets to reduce the angle of heel. The effect will be immediately apparent.

On a reach, the traveller should be as far to leeward as possible and the sails correctly trimmed so that the tell-tales stream aft, flat against the sail.

Weather helm, the tendency of a boat to come naturally head-to-wind when left on its own, is a safety feature which slows and eventually stops the boat if the helmsman has to leave the tiller. Its effect is stronger while reaching than on any other point of sailing and can be reduced by increasing the foresail area. Lee helm, the opposite, occurs when the centre of effort (COE) is too far forward of the centre of lateral resistance (CLR), **1**, and can be cured by lowering the centre-board, **2**, or reducing the foresail area, **3**.

Before the wind

Off-the-wind sailing is a bit like cruising down the Trade winds. Direction is not limited, it is dry and usually much warmer since the apparent wind is less. Steering is not so critical and more sail area can be set (eg the spinnaker or cruising chute).

A course, appropriate to your direction and the tidal stream, will dictate the wind angle to the boat. If it is between 90° and 180° and there is sufficient manpower on board, a spinnaker can be set. This is the ideal wind section to use this sail, and it should be set with just the mainsail, once the genoa has been lowered and secured.

The cruising chute can be used efficiently up to Force 3 with the wind 70–100° off the bow and up to Force 4 or 5 with the wind at 100–135°. If the wind is dead astern, it can be used in a Force 6. It is usually set flying, with no other sails, and is easily handled by a small crew.

If the wind is blowing very hard, a genoa or jib can be set with full mainsail, and with the wind forward of 135°, it can be used on the same side as the main. Once the wind is aft of 160° the headsail can be goosewinged, preferably with a whisker pole if the boat is rolling heavily. This is a good downwind, heavy-weather rig and, as the wind increases, the same format can be maintained by reducing the size of the sails: reefing the mainsail and setting a smaller headsail.

With the wind dead aft, the crew should split into two parties to balance the boat. In light winds they should sit amidships and as far outboard as possible on each side, to act as wing ballast and reduce rolling. When the wind freshens, they should move farther aft to keep the stern down, while maintaining an even distribution of weight.

Running can be the most hazardous point of sailing because of the risk of gybing/jibing and the wind is always stronger than it seems.

Downwind sailing ranges from a broad reach at 135° to a dead run at 180°. With the wind way aft, the sails act like parachutes rather than aerofoils.

Broaching is caused by waves lifting the stern and heeling the boat so that rudder control is lost. The boat then luffs, and heels excessively. To prevent a broach, slow the boat, sail a lower course or let the mainsail twist off at the top by easing the mainsheet.

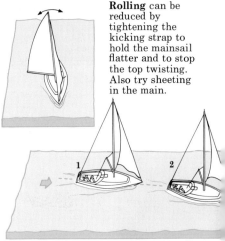

Rolling can be reduced by tightening the kicking strap to hold the mainsail flatter and to stop the top twisting. Also try sheeting in the main.

Gybing/jibing involves swinging the boom over nearly 180° to the other side of the boat. In a controlled gybe, the helmsman bears slightly off the wind, **1**, then orders 'Stand by to gybe/jibe' as he pulls the tiller over, hauls in hard on the mainsheet and cleats it, **2**. The

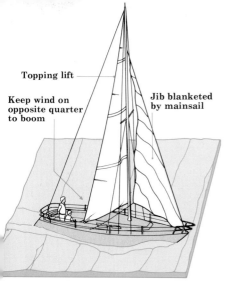

Topping lift

Keep wind on opposite quarter to boom

Jib blanketed by mainsail

Checklist
1 The mainsail, not the boom, should be at right angles to the boat when the wind is dead aft.
2 Keep the wind over on the quarter opposite the mainsail by 5–8° and if necessary tack downwind to stay on course; the increase in speed compensates for the slightly longer distance sailed. This also guards against going into an involuntary gybe/jibe.
3 Move the crew aft to counteract the weight of the wind pushing the bow down.
4 Remember the apparent wind is less than the true wind and reduce sail area before turning into the wind.
5 The topping lift should be attached to give more fullness to the mainsail and to prevent the boom dragging in the water.
6 If the boat has runners, keep the leeward one slack.
7 In a multihull, it is significantly faster to tack downwind than to sail dead before it.

When sailing 'downhill' the helmsman should watch the wind and steer carefully to avoid an accidental gybe/jibe. In a fluky wind, or if the boat is rolling heavily, the wind may catch the front of the mainsail, forcing the whole sail to slam across. This can damage both boat and crew. A boom preventer leading to the foredeck can forestall this. If the jib is not boomed out, it will warn of an imminent gybe by filling on the opposite side to the mainsail. To derive some driving force from the jib, it should be boomed out, so that the boat sails goosewinged, *left*.

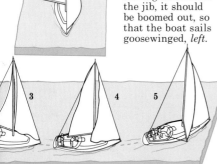

3　　4　　5

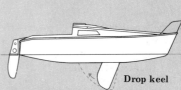

Drop keel

Drop-keel boats are ideal for cruising and are becoming increasingly popular, particularly as trailer sailers. With the centre-board up, they fit into shallow anchorages and sit firmly in a dry berth or on a trailer. When the centre-board is lowered, the keel is deep enough to make the boat very efficient to windward. In many boats, the keel can also be angled aft, which, when reaching, puts the centre of lateral resistance farther aft, so reducing the amount of weather helm and the chances of broaching, When running, if the centre-board is raised, some boats will plane over the water.

crew release the jib sheet and haul it in on the other side, 3. As the boom swings over, held firm by the mainsheet, 4, the crew move to the other side. The mainsheet can now be payed out and the sails trimmed on the new tack, as the crew check the new course is clear, 5.

Handling spinnakers

The spinnaker, which originated from the parachute, is one of the most efficient methods of increasing speed when sailing downwind. It does, however, require a lot of controlling because it is large, very powerful and only attached at three corners.

Care should be taken in setting and in lowering this sail; it is especially important to lower it before an increase in wind speed makes it dangerous. Many difficulties can be eliminated by using a spinnaker control sock.

The equipment includes the sail itself, the spinnaker pole, track on the mast to alter the height of the pole, the spinnaker boom lift and downhaul, spinnaker halyard, spinnaker guy (attached to the windward clew), spinnaker sheet (attached to the leeward clew), winches to control the sheet and guy, substantial turning blocks fixed strongly to the boat, and a bag or turtle to make setting easy.

When cruising, the spinnaker will normally be set only in light and medium winds, therefore a moderately lightweight sail of about 1.2 oz (40g) is recommended. Heavy material will be strong and durable, but will not set well in light winds. The size of the sail is worked out by manufacturers, based on the height of the mast above the sheer line (known as I) and the distance between the forestay and the front of the mast (J).

To trim the spinnaker, always try to keep it square to the wind. If the wind is coming over the quarter, the spinnaker pole will be forward. As the wind comes aft, the pole will also have to be brought aft and the sheet of the spinnaker eased out. The height of the pole is critical to the heeling angle of the boat and varies according to the strength of the wind. As a general rule, try to keep the outboard end of the pole the same height as the clew of the spinnaker. Adjust the pole height on the mast to keep it horizontal.

A spinnaker can be hoisted from a close reach to a dead run to boost the boat's speed downwind.

To set the spinnaker, fasten the bag to the pulpit or on the lee side of the foredeck and pull the three corners of the sail out, **1**. Clip the spinnaker pole to the mast and hoist it to about 6 ft (2 m) above the deck on a 30-ft (9-m) boat, **2**. Lead the guy outboard of the rigging, through the end of the spinnaker pole and, bringing it forward, attach it to one of the clews on the sail, **3**. Bring the sheet forward outside the rigging, fasten it to the other spinnaker clew, **4**, and attach the halyard to the head of the sail, **5**. Hoist the spinnaker pole with the uphaul, **6**, until it is horizontal and secure the foreguy (downhaul), with some slack to the pole, so that, once hoisted, the spinnaker cannot sky, **7**. To hoist the sail when short-handed, tighten the guy until the clew of the spinnaker reaches the end of the spinnaker boom (feed a little out of the bag). Pull the boom back about

3 ft (1 m) from the forestay and securely cleat the guy. Hoist the sail to the top, **8**. Make sure that the halyard is securely cleated, then pull in on the spinnaker sheet, **9**. Lower the genoa and the spinnaker will fill, **10**.

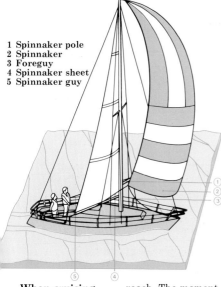

1 Spinnaker pole
2 Spinnaker
3 Foreguy
4 Spinnaker sheet
5 Spinnaker guy

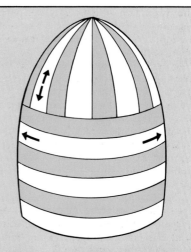

When cruising, the safest way to lower the spinnaker is to bring the boat round to a dead run and let the spinnaker guy go so that the pole goes up against the forestay. Ease the spinnaker boom lift to bring the pole within arm's reach. The moment the crew forward unclips the spinnaker from the guy at the end of the pole, haul in the spinnaker sheet behind the mainsail, on the lee deck. Pay out the halyard at the same rate as the crew can gather in the sail.

The ideal spinnaker design for cruising is a radial head with crosscut base, which produces the most efficient shape in winds from dead abeam to dead aft, and is the least expensive. The panels allow for the direction of stress (*see arrows*). The tri-radial, although expensive, is strongly made and suitable for heavy use; crosscut, starcut and jumbo-foot spinnakers are designed for racing.

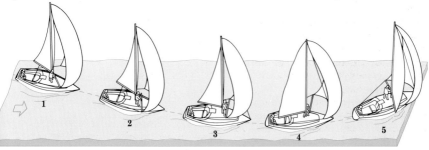

Gybing/jibing the spinnaker should be undertaken only with sufficient crew on board. When it is blowing hard and there are few hands on deck, it is worth considering lowering the spinnaker, gybing and resetting it. End-for-end gybing is the best method for boats up to about 30 ft (9 m). Run off the wind until it is virtually dead aft and square the pole so that the sheet is let out as far as possible, **1**. Unclip the inboard end of the pole, take it across and attach it to the sheet on the other side, **2**. Unhook the outboard end from the original guy and push it across to attach it to the mast, **3**. Gybe/jibe over the mainsail and, at the same time, pull in the old sheet (now the new guy) to draw the pole square across the boat, **4**. Ease out the old guy (now the new sheet), **5**.

Light-weather sailing

Light-weather sailing can give some of the most enjoyable sailing there is. However, to make a boat move at a reasonable speed, the maximum sail area must be set and the weight of the sails kept down to a minimum.

Few yachts are fitted with a full wardrobe and, as a precaution, most tend to have more sails which are suitable for heavy weather. So when the wind is light, set the largest and lightest sail on the boat, such as a cruising chute, large genoa or booster.

It is not advisable to use the spinnaker in very light winds, especially downwind or if the boat is rolling, unless the spinnaker boom can be kept well forward by bringing the wind round on the quarter or beam, to prevent the sail collapsing.

A common mistake in light winds is to pull the sheets in too hard, particularly when going to windward. Instead they should be eased out until the boat points a further 10° off the wind to get the boat moving. Both the mainsail and headsail halyards need to be slackened to produce more fullness in the sails. The mainsail will also fill and generate more power if the outhaul is eased off, the traveller brought to windward and the boom pushed out at least 2½–3 ft (75–90 cm) away from the centre-line. Sailing downwind in light airs, the kicking strap can be tensioned to produce a twist in the mainsail, and the backstay eased to increase speed.

The most effective way to get the boat moving is to sail free for a few minutes, then gradually head up so that the apparent wind increases, which will allow the boat to make way on its own created wind. Some momentum can be maintained if the crew sit on the leeward side. This encourages the boat to heel, and the sails to fill.

Light airs call for patience, a keen eye for signs of gathering clouds or increased wind on the water, and a gentle hand on the tiller.

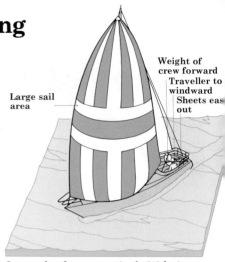

Large sail area

Weight of crew forward
Traveller to windward
Sheets eased out

On a calm day, there is likely to be more wind along the coast: the sea breeze starts to blow on to the land at about 11 a.m. If the early morning wind is off the land, the sea breeze will come in around noon. It blows hardest close to the land and tails off about 10 mls (16 km) out to sea, so it is worth hugging the coast to be sure of wind. At night, the sea breeze dies off and an hour or so later, the land breeze starts blowing off the land. Again it is strongest close to the shore and does not reach out quite as far as the sea breeze.

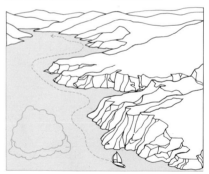

When coastal cruising, take advantage of the old saying, 'the wind will always follow the sun'. In the northern hemisphere, the sea breeze will veer during the day, so that on a south-facing coast, it will go round to a south-westerly or even a westerly direction before dying away. In the southern hemisphere, it will back eastwards.

**The recently
designed** pivoting
spinnaker acts like
a square sail. The
sheets are
controlled like
reins from the
cockpit to swing
the sail. It is
hoisted from its
chute with a tug
on the halyard and
lowered by pulling
a reefing line.

To create a large
and firm sail area,
pole out the No 1
genoa on the
opposite side to
the mainsail. A
boom preventer,
running from the
end of the boom to
the foredeck, holds
the mainsail to
one side and
prevents a gybe.

Motor sailers
If the sails will not fill, the only way
to make any headway in still
weather may be to use auxiliary
power. With the sails up and the
wind forward of the beam, speed can
increase usefully with low engine
revs. Using motor and sail simultaneously can also result in a saving of
as much as 20 per cent on fuel.

Motor sailers are designed specifi-
cally for this combined propulsion,
although their performance in
either mode is inferior to that of a
yacht or a power boat. A modern
trend towards converting yacht
hulls to motor cruisers has produced
designs which give more miles to the
gallon. The advantages of the
modern motor sailer for cruising are
additional comfort and leisure, particularly for the less active, speedier
passages and easy manoeuvrability.

**A versatile
alternative** is the
booster, *above*, a
'double' sail which
opens out into two
large, lightweight
foresails, that can
be set with or
without the
mainsail.

When reaching,
the booster can be
set doubled over
on one side of the
boat. This gives it
twice the strength,
allowing it to be
used in heavier
weather with a
reefed mainsail.

Reefing for heavy weather

Heavy weather is hard, frightening and dangerous and, as most people do not seek it out, it is vital to ensure that every precaution is taken in advance and that the necessary safety equipment is always on board in case the unforeseen should happen.

First, it is essential to reduce sail sufficiently and in good time to control the boat reasonably well. This can be effected by reefing the mainsail and changing the headsail down to a sufficiently small size to withstand the wind strength.

A boat is safer in deep water with plenty of sea-room, so it is wiser to ride out a storm at sea than to risk trying to enter a harbour where the waves will be more treacherous, particularly if there are rocks, a bar or an ebbing tide. Navigation may also be difficult if visibility is affected by the weather.

Severe gales are rare in the temperate latitudes but storm-force winds and hurricanes must be guarded against in the tropics. The dangerous sector of a hurricane lies in the semicircle away from the Equator. To avoid danger, listen to radio weather reports for information about the hurricane's movement.

The biggest problem with heavy weather, however, is that the crew normally give up before the boat. Nevertheless, if all human contingencies are catered for, there is little danger, since the boat will sink only very reluctantly.

This was illustrated in the 1979 Fastnet disaster when, out of all the boats abandoned in the race, only three sank. The 21 others, abandoned by the crew because they thought they were on the verge of sinking, were towed back to port and are now sailing again. The rule should be, only use your liferaft as the boat is about to disappear under the waves, not before. The liferaft is the last resort for it is not nearly as safe as your own boat, although it may appear to be.

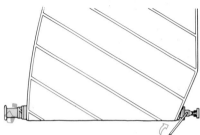

Roller reefing, *above,* seems quick, neat and easy, but it requires skill to get a well-set sail. To reef, release the halyard, and remove the kicking strap from the boom.

Pull the leech aft to keep the foot wrinkle-free. A claw ring fitted over the reefed sail provides an attachment point for the kicking strap.

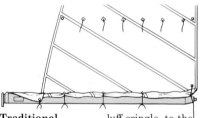

Traditional points reefing allows the reefed sail to set well, but takes time. Tighten the topping lift, and let off the mainsheet and halyard. Pull the

luff cringle, to the boom, and tie. Then pull the leech cringle to the boom, using the reefs pendant. Lash the rest of the reef points under the sail, not the boom.

A modern version of the points system, Jiffy or slab reefing is cheap and easily handled by one person. Tighten the topping lift to

take the weight of the boom. Cast off the mainsheet and slacken the halyard until the luff cringle can be attached to a hook at the gooseneck,

1 Reefed mainsail
2 Reduced headsail
3 Clip harnesses to jackstays
4 Heavy-weather gear
5 Everything stowed

Clothing

The ideal heavy-weather clothing is warm but not bulky: a thermal suit next to the skin; a sweater and quilted jacket and a good set of loose-fitting oilskins with elasticated wrists and waterproof pockets.

Most body-heat is lost from the extremities, so keep them warm and dry with waterproof gloves that allow the fingers to work shackles, knots etc; two pairs of knee-high socks, the inner pair of normal wool, the outer of water-repellant wool, and non-skid rubber boots. Wear a towel around neck and woollen hat: wool takes longer than synthetics to become saturated, but also takes longer to dry.

Woollen hat
Scarf
Sweater
Snug wrists
Gloves
Waterproof jacket
Warm trousers
Oilskins
Woollen socks
Sailing boots

1 Reef early to avoid strain on the gear and crew.
2 Maintain the boat's balance by reefing the mainsail and jib in equal proportions. The feel of the helm will tell you if it is right.
3 Sail close-hauled to bring the boom inboard when reefing.
4 Sail downwind to change the foresail. This keeps the deck drier and steadies the boat.
5 Clip harnesses to toe rails or jackstays to leave both hands free.
6 Stand to windward of the sail when reefing.
7 When points reefing, be sure not to confuse the points on one reef with those on another.
8 Shake out a reef by reversing the reefing procedure. Always untie reef points before the luff and leech.

pull on the reefing pendant, to pull the leech cringle to the boom, and cleat the line. Tighten halyard and release topping lift.

Although expensive, a roller-reefing headsail saves sail changing. It is cut so that the sheets lead aft at a constant angle.

To convert a boat to roller reefing, a headfoil, with attached drum, **1**, and a groove for the headsail luff, **2**, is fitted around the forestay, **3**.

To reef a genoa, attach both sheets to a higher cringle. Fix the parallel luff cringle to the bow fitting, tie the points and re-hoist.

Riding out a storm

How to handle a boat in heavy weather depends on its design. Some will heave-to, others lie better a-hull; some will ride to a sea anchor, and some have to run before the wind. The only way to find out the best method for your boat is to try it out.

The most seaworthy boats ever designed for heavy-weather sailing were the Bristol pilot cutters. They had the ability to heave-to under a staysail only and, as they were very long-keeled, could lie to a sea anchor. A short-keeled boat will sail over the top of the anchor and can cause the anchor warp to foul the propellor or the rudder.

In a modern cruising boat, it may not be possible to lash down the tiller and heave-to under a staysail with much safety, so it is advisable to sail the boat at about 80° off the wind, slowly, with just enough steerage way to luff up or bear away to avoid the worst of the waves.

If the wind becomes uncomfortably strong and you have sufficient sea room, it is often best to run before the wind under bare poles or with a storm jib. Although so small, the storm jib which hanks to the forestay does help to control the boat. It gives a little steerage way, and often reduces the rolling of the boat.

When it is really blowing hard, the circumstances often dictate the best course of action. If the gale is blowing along the course you want to take, it is possible to sail downwind at a reasonable speed under a storm jib.

Although noisy and uncomfortable, lying a-hull is often a safe way to ride out a bad storm. This is simply a question of lowering sails, lashing the boom to the deck so it cannot move, sealing up all the hatches and going below until the storm passes. The tiller must be lashed to leeward so that the boat is always trying to come into the wind. It will make 1–2 kn downwind and probably a little headway.

Breaking waves pose the greatest threat to a boat in heavy weather. A freak wave in a bad ocean storm can cause a boat to pitch-pole, stern over bow. Pooping, when a wave breaks over the stern and fills the cockpit, is a more likely hazard. To prevent this, slow the boat and keep the main hatchway closed.

When running before a storm or approaching a lee shore, the boat's headway can be reduced by streaming warps over the stern.

Five or six 30-fm warps, joined together and towed in a loop in the boat's wake, will slow the boat and may prevent pooping.

Wind

Leeway

To heave-to, ease the mainsail, back the headsail and lash the tiller to leeward. The boat will sail slowly, making a lot of leeway. Yawls and ketches may lie better under mizzen only.

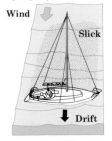

Wind

Slick

Drift

Lying a-hull under bare poles with the helm lashed to leeward, the boat finds its natural angle to the wind. The hull moves to leeward, creating a slick on the weatherside to smooth the sea.

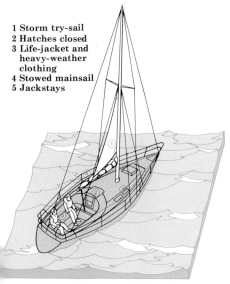

1 Storm try-sail
2 Hatches closed
3 Life-jacket and heavy-weather clothing
4 Stowed mainsail
5 Jackstays

Checklist
At the first sign of heavy weather, or when gale warnings are issued (indicating a Force 8), start preparing for a storm.
1 Double check that everything is well stowed below and lash down anything loose on deck, including the tender. Fasten cockpit lockers.
2 Make sure the boat is watertight. Close and fasten all the hatches. Close the ventilators. Turn off the seacocks to the sink and toilet.
3 Rig the jackstays and issue life-jackets and safety harnesses to each crew-member.
4 Make sure all the crew take a sea-sickness pill or wear an ear plaster, put on extra clothing and have a good meal before the heavy weather arrives, in case the wind takes several hours to subside. Prepare hot drinks or soup in a thermos.
5 Make sail changes in good time. Have stormsails and flares ready.
6 Clear cockpit drains. Ensure bilge pump works. Run the engine from time to time.
7 Listen to the shipping forecasts.
8 Keep an eye on the boat's position and a good look-out on deck.
9 Organize a strict rotation of watches.

The try-sail, when combined with the storm jib, helps to stabilize the boat in even the strongest winds. Often neglected, since the conditions make it difficult to rig any sail, the try-sail nevertheless allows the mainsail to be lowered completely. It is fed into the mast above the furled mainsail, via the sail track gate. It is set loosefooted and sheeted down to either side of the boat, like a jib. To withstand the wind force, the sail is reinforced, particularly at the corners, and triple-stitched along the seams.

A canvas sea anchor is streamed from the boat by a long warp (never chain) and, ideally, a slack tripping line, even though it may tangle with the warp. A Bruce anchor can also prove light enough to make an efficient sea anchor, but only in deep water.

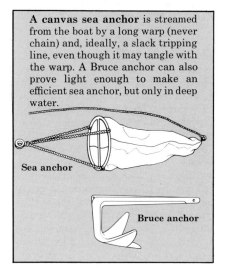

Sea anchor

Bruce anchor

Wind

Drift

With a sea anchor streamed from the bow and a riding sail set on a mizzen mast, a ketch will lie close to the wind and drift to leeward. Sternway, however, may strain the rudder.

Wind

Drift

A sea anchor streamed from the stern allows the boat to follow its inclination to head downwind. It may prevent a broach, but hold the boat too tight and stop it riding the waves smoothly.

Leisurely cruising

Long-distance cruising should be leisurely and enjoyable – so it helps to have a full crew to share the work. But most long-distance trips today are made short-handed, with a maximum of three people on board.

Even so, if thought has been given to the appropriate equipment and supplies, a small crew need not be overstretched. A good self-steering system, the right food and water are a start.

For extensive sailing, the most popular rigs are the ketch, yawl and schooner as a wide range of small sails can be set, which reduces the strains and weight on any individual sail. For example, on a 60-ft (18-m) sloop with a standard masthead rig, the genoa may be around 900–1,000 sq ft (83–93 sq m), whereas a ketch of the same length would probably have a much more manageable maximum sail size of about 500 sq ft (46 sq m).

Roller-reefing gear is a useful addition. A maximum-sized genoa, which can be furled or reefed by one person, eliminates the need both to carry extra sails and to change them each time the wind strength varies.

The same system fitted to the mainsail provides easy reefing and gives a wider choice of mainsail sizes.

On most long-distance trips you will encounter the Trade winds, particularly on the Azores to West Indies route, known as the 'milk run'. As the Trades blow from dead astern at Force 6 to 7, as much sail as possible should be set forward of the mast by booming out the headsails. These can both be set flying or with one hanked to the forestay.

Twin foresails hanked to a twin forestay and boomed out from the mast is another labour-saving and efficient system which works well even in squally weather since the sails balance each other. To counteract the roll of the boat, however, it is best to double-reef the mainsail and lash the boom amidships.

Autohelm
The best electrical self-steering gear on the market is the Autohelm (2000 and 1000 models available), which has sensors to detect any deviation from a pre-set compass course and a control unit to correct the helm. Since it is powered by the boat's electrical system, the batteries need to be recharged every day by running the engine. Small solar panels, designed to recharge the batteries automatically, can now charge up to 4 or 5 amps. They need no upkeep, can be easily mounted on the deck, are flexible and often non-slip.

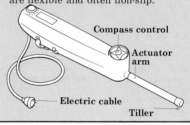

Compass control

Actuator arm

Electric cable

Tiller

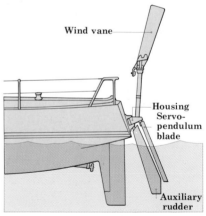

Wind vane

Housing
Servo-pendulum blade

Auxiliary rudder

Mechanical wind vanes, which need no extra source of power, provide the most reliable form of self-steering. Their one drawback is that when the wind direction alters, the boat's heading follows. Sailormat, *above*, overcomes this with a compass which holds the boat on course when the wind shifts. A servo-pendulum magnifies the wind direction data from the vane and turns a large auxiliary rudder.

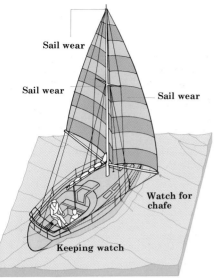

Sail wear

Sail wear

Sail wear

Watch for chafe

Keeping watch

The times of watches depend on the number of crew and length of trip. Ideally, there should be two people on deck, but with only two on board, two hours on, two hours off is the normal maximum by night, with longer watches of 3–4 hrs by day.

In the early days before self-steering gear, many sailors used various improvized systems. When running, the sheets of the boomed-out jibs can be taken back through blocks and lashed to the tiller or wheel, **1**. When the boat turns too far to port, **2**, the leeward or starboard sail flaps and takes the weight off the tiller line, automatically allowing it to swing to port so bringing the boat back on course, **3**. Similar, more old-fashioned systems, which link the sheets of the mainsail and jib to the tiller, can be used.

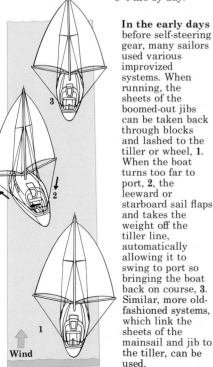

3

2

1

Wind

Checklist
Always choose coloured not white sails to prevent glare hurting the eyes. Watch out for chafe caused by hard wear. Areas to watch on the rigging are the spreader ends, the back edges of the spreaders where the mainsail rubs, and also where the wire stays and shrouds attach to fittings. Baggywrinkles, (plaited rope yarns) wrapped around the shrouds at the end of the spreaders or any area where the sails rub, are a safeguard against chafe. Watch all sheets for fraying and turn end-to-end if the inside strands begin to wear. Ease or tighten the halyards every day to move the point at which they come out of the masthead.

Carry extra maximum-length halyards to replace any which break. Inspect sails regularly for stretch, chafe, mildew, ultraviolet damage or frayed stitching. Check for dried-out sealant around bolts or screws; it can cause leaks. Run the engine periodically to recharge the batteries and to check that it is working. Carry spare parts for the self-steering gear. Check the bilges regularly. To calculate the quantity of food to take, list consumption for an average week and multiply by the estimated number of weeks at sea, adding extra for emergencies.

Choosing a cruiser

Your choice of boat will depend on where you plan to keep it and what you aim to do with it. Deep-water marina berthing, for example, imposes different requirements from shallow or drying moorings, and the boat that needs four experienced people to handle it would not suit a couple with three young children. Since moorings are in high demand in many areas, it is usually better to confirm the availability of a mooring before obtaining a boat – or to buy a suitable second-hand boat, complete with a mooring.

Trailer sailers overcome this problem, but to be big enough for open water cruising (say 25 ft – 7.6 m as an absolute minimum) they are normally so cumbersome and time-consuming to rig that launching and recovery become daunting tasks. Furthermore, a substantial towing vehicle is required. As a result, they have really become boats that can be taken home more easily than most in the winter, or occasionally moved to new cruising grounds.

Long-keeled hulls are often regarded as the traditional choice for a cruising boat, but while they tend to keep the course well, they are also heavy to turn. Modern hulls, with long fore-and-aft fin keels and a separate rudder, can be just as stable as long-keeled hulls, but much lighter to steer and more manoeuvrable.

If you need a boat with good handling astern, a spade-rudder is better than a rudder supported on a skeg. The skeg type, however, is usually stronger and better protected when sailing or motoring ahead, which represents 99 per cent of the boat's cruising time. The remaining one per cent spent reversing can be embarassing, however, if things go wrong.

Cruising catamarans often pay higher rates in marinas, but can moor in shallow waters. They should give quicker and smoother passage times than monohulls of the same length.

The fin keel is the normal design for a modern performance cruiser. The fin must be long enough to support the boat when drying out against a wall in a number of European harbours. The rudder may be of spade type, *above*, or mounted on a skeg.

The twin keel takes $\frac{2}{3}$ to $\frac{3}{4}$ of the water depth needed for a fin keel. But it will stand upright only if the bottom is hard and level. Uncomfortable at times, it is also noisy to windward due to water slamming under the hull.

The lifting-keel boat opens up possibilities for new sheltered cruising grounds and shallow moorings. Drafts can be reduced dramatically when the keel is raised and this also provides an easy way of freeing the boat if grounded.

The long-keeled hull usually has lots of storage space, but heavy displacement tends to make it slower and heavier to manoeuvre than other types, and it demands a more powerful rig to drive it. It has, nevertheless, a comfortable motion.

Trailer tips

Try to avoid putting wheels in the water because if salt water gets into the hubs the bearings will be ruined. Furthermore, by the time the boat can float free, the trailer may be so deep in the water that the towing vehicle must be unhitched and a rope used to join the two together. The best solution is to carry a wheeled cradle on a tipping section of the trailer. The cradle may also fit some standard car-recovery trailers, should you not want to purchase a trailer initially. The boat must be very well secured to the trailer and everything carried aboard must be padded against chafe when on the road. Even a 22-ft boat (6.7-m) will require a powerful car (say $2\frac{1}{2}$ litre engine) to pull it, and remember the clutch has a hard life. You must allow for on-board stores when calculating the weight – and don't go anywhere without a spare wheel.

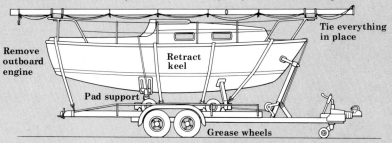

Remove outboard engine

Retract keel

Pad support

Tie everything in place

Grease wheels

Multihulls

The motion is quicker than in a monohull but the boat moves through a smaller angle. A catamaran is usually the cruising man's first choice for it offers more accommodation. However, it is easier to turn a catamaran over than a trimaran when under sail, although in severe conditions, if the boat is just left to drift, the situation may be reversed. Experience will tell how much sail the boat can carry safely.

Multihulls offer fast passages, ample deck space, shallow draft and level drying out – which few monohulls can match. The speed advantage – say 7 kn against 5 may not sound much but in a 60-ml (96-km) passage it could save $3\frac{1}{2}$ hrs and mean an easy daylight arrival. Further, if confronted with a $1\frac{1}{2}$ kn adverse tide, a 20-ml (32-km) passage would take 3 hr 40 mins against 5 hr 40 mins. In very light airs, however, the multihull may well be slower.

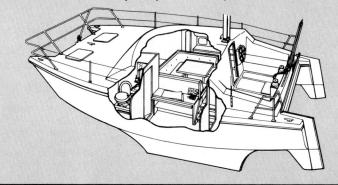

Layouts below decks

Below decks a minimum of sitting headroom is essential though a little more height makes it easier to dress and move around. There should be good hand-holds for safe movement – always two within reach from any point – and lee cloths or lee boards on bunks to allow the crew to sleep comfortably in the windward berths while on passage.

There needs to be room for all except the watchkeepers to rest without using the berths forward of the mast since these normally suffer too much motion at sea. This may limit the size of your crew for a passage, but there is no fun in forcing people to grow cold and tired in the cockpit due to lack of space below.

The more people there are, the more gear and stores must be stowed. Sleeping bags and clothes take up a surprising amount of space, even when packed into soft waterproof holdalls. It is best to allocate each person a locker which can be reached at sea without disturbing a sleeper when more warm clothes are required. All lockers must be dry or clothes must be kept in sealed polythene bags. Oilskins are best hung up inside out to drip without causing annoyance; the heads is often a good place.

The most convenient position for the heads is aft by the hatchway as it saves struggling through the saloon – an advantage for anyone suffering from seasickness. The galley and navigation area also need to be near the hatch so a compromise is needed.

Ideally, lighting should include fluorescents for working areas such as the galley, to allow plenty of light with little battery drain. As they interfere with radio direction-finding, however, they must be turned off when the navigator uses RDF. Bunk lights provide less harsh lighting elsewhere. Galley lights should be coloured red or tucked away so that they do not shine out into the cockpit.

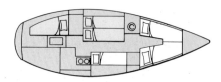

Ideas on the layout for a boat evolve with changes in fashion and the ability of the designers to find new ways of using the space available. A conventional layout for a cruising boat of about 30-ft (9-m),

above, includes more berths than can be used comfortably while under way. These are useful when moored or for a weekend. The boat is wide enough to allow access to the fore-cabin past the heads.

The layout of a racing boat is intended to keep weight out of the ends of the boat, so that it performs well in a seaway, while providing secure sleeping berths for brief

snatches off watch. Total weight and thus comfort are kept to a minimum. Even the navigator is expected to work with primitive facilities.

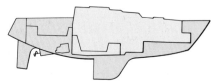

Headroom usually decreases as you move forward, due to hull shape and the angle of the coach/cabin trunk roof and deck. Flatter-bottomed, more performance-orientated boats have less depth below water than

traditional boats, so they must have a high coachroof or sides to provide acceptable standing room. Even more important than headroom is space to lean back comfortably against the saloon back rests.

48

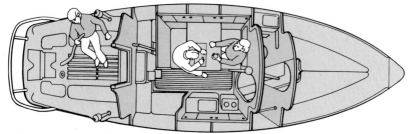

This is a typical cruising layout, as found in the Westerly Centaur. The cockpit is spacious enough for the whole crew although forward visibility is slightly restricted by the high coach/cabin trunk roof. It is roomy below decks, with good headroom and a feeling of space.

The raised dinette table seats four, at a level to give a good view out of the window, though without much elbow room. The table should have good fiddles to stop the plates sliding off, and, ideally, a separate central storage area for various items such as salt, jam, etc. The

dinette arrangement allows for a double berth in the saloon, with the table lowered to seat level with backrest cushions on top. For those who prefer more privacy, the forepeak affords a comfortable double berth, when moored, but would not be used under

way. A fifth person can fit comfortably in the quarter-berth which extends below the cockpit. Stowage is mainly under the bunks in dry, well-lined lockers. The fore-cabin provides access to the anchor chain in its locker, if it should tangle.

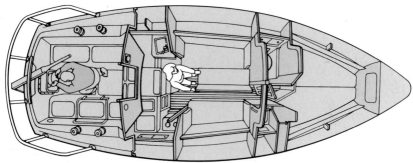

An alternative layout, as found in the Westerly Konsort, makes different use of the space, with an extra 3 ft (90 cm) in length. The roomy cockpit is designed so that when seated, it is comfortable to brace yourself against the opposite seat when the boat heels.

This internal layout is well suited to family cruising, with its capacious saloon and uncluttered arrangement, and there are sufficient hand-holds. It sleeps six comfortably, particularly if there are children. In the saloon the port settee opens out into a double,

still leaving a single settee and a large quarter-berth which doubles as a navigator's seat. The fore-cabin provides an ideal berth for two children. The galley, although a little cramped compared with the rest of the cabin, is well situated by the main hatchway to allow good

ventilation. Konsort proves that a roomy modern layout can be designed into a hull that sails well – a few years ago this would have been considered impossible. Her bigger sister the Fulmar offers even better performance.

The galley

Galley lighting needs to be bright, obscured from the cockpit, and well placed to provide good illumination over the cooker, worktop and sink. The cooker requires a heat shield above it and must be gimballed or have high fiddles for use at sea. Two belts are also useful to keep the cook secure in front and behind, while leaving both hands free for work.

Sink drains need to be large, but it is best to wash up in a bowl because the sink plug is constantly pushed out by the pressure as the boat negotiates large waves, allowing your hot, soapy water to vanish. Water consumption is always a problem in boats and pressure systems positively encourage over-use. A seawater hand pump in the galley helps to preserve precious fresh water, since much food preparation can be done in salt water. It is also a good plan to involve the cook when water containers have to be carried in harbour.

Most boats have ice boxes although ice is not often easy to obtain, while fridges tend to be electrically driven and a drain on the battery. Space below the galley floor provides good cold stowage for vegetables and drinks.

When buying food for an organized menu, remember to include stocks of dry food – biscuits, nuts, fruit, chocolate, cheese, cake – for convenient sustenance in bad weather. Simple hot drinks are always welcome; soups are more nutritious and keep hot longer than coffee in cold weather. A pressure cooker, ideally an automatic one, saves gas, time and a lot of dishwashing. Contrary to popular belief, eggs last for weeks, and tinned butter will keep indefinitely until opened. If tinned food is to be stored in a potentially wet area, write an abbreviated or coded description on the tin top and remove the label. Otherwise it will float off later, may choke the bilge pump and will give rise to countless mystery meals.

The heads need good handholds and permanent ventilation. Easily accessible inlet and outlet valves are also important as water tends to siphon back when the boat heels, if the valves are not closed. Always ensure that instructions for use are clearly displayed and that everyone on board, including visitors, knows how the system works.

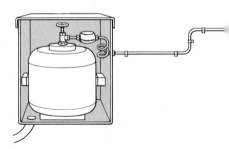

Meticulous care must be taken when installing a gas system to avoid explosions. Flexible pipes should be kept very short and replaced at the first sign of deterioration. If at all possible the rigid pipe should be kept in one length, but if a branch pipe must be taken to a heater or fridge, check the joints periodically. As gas is heavier than air, a drain must run from the bottom of the locker. There must be easy access for disconnecting and changing the bottle, and a valve shut-off near the stove and at the bottle.

Most cooks like plenty of light and fresh air and to be in contact with what is happening on deck. As a result, most galleys are L- or U-shaped and tucked just inside the main hatchway. If the worktop area extends across below the hatchway, ensure that a reliable and positive separation exists between food and feet.

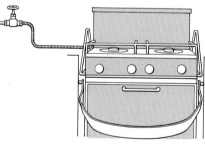

Safety and economy are the watchwords when cooking with gas. Always turn off the tap at the galley end of the supply pipe after use and have a clear 'open/closed' indicator. Beware of drafts from the hatchway which can easily extinguish a simmering flame.

A pressure cooker and thermos flask both save gas. A folding oven is available for stoves without one, and if there is no grill, a toasting rack can be fitted over the burner. Useful additions are a bolt to lock the cooker upright in harbour and another to keep the oven door shut.

Water

1 Conserve fresh water by using seawater for washing up – then rinsing in fresh. Dish-washing liquid works well in salt water.

2 If cook insists on more capacity, it is possible to add extra freshwater tanks. Flexible plastic ones that adopt the shape of the hull are easiest to install, but must be initially cleaned as recommended by the manufacturers. Provided a vent pipe is fitted, they can be linked to the existing water-filling and supply lines. It is tempting to position them in otherwise inaccessible corners, but remember to keep the weight out of the ends of the boat and balance the load each side of the centre-line.

3 If you use the pressure water system at sea, have a back-up pump in case the electrical system fails.

Stores

1 Tinned food is a convenient way of buying in bulk. Foil/packet meals are considerably lighter, and although more expensive, have delicious flavours without the effort of 'dressing-up' bland tinned food – a great advantage when rough seas make cooking a chore.

2 When provisioning for a trip, work out one person's average consumption for a day, multiply by the number of crew and number of days, changing the basic ingredient type for variety. Fresh food, salads, fruit, bread, milk and cheese can be bought at ports of call. In spite of ravenous appetites induced by the sea air, you will almost certainly have too much. Remember to take plenty of fruit juice to supplement water intake and avoid dehydration.

Children

At sea children's food needs to be fun and more of a treat than onshore, to distract and entertain them. Between meals nibbling helps to keep morale and energy high. Allow a good mixture of sweet and savoury, since sailors of all ages often find their tastes change at sea.

Personal security

Everyone on board must have a safety harness that has been adjusted to fit. It should be labelled with the wearer's initials or name, and stowed somewhere easily accessible, complete with a life-jacket. There should also be spares on board. A life-jacket is better than a buoyancy aid because it will turn an unconscious wearer face up, an important point since anyone knocked overboard is likely to be unconscious or at least too stunned to do much towards immediate self-survival.

A safety harness is no good unless hooked to a strong point, the best anchorage being a jackstay between pulpit and cockpit along which the harness hook travels. This avoids the risk and inconvenience of moving the harness hook from point to point.

There should also be strong handholds along the coach/cabin trunk roof, guard rails and stanchions for safe movement on deck. Guard rails are best secured with rope lanyard rather than bottlescrews/turnbuckles so as to avoid a 'closed loop' effect ruining reception on direction-finding equipment. This also means that the lower guard rail can be quickly dropped (by cutting the lanyard) if necessary, to assist recovering a man overboard.

Other deck fittings, hatches, vents, etc., should be well faired so that lines cannot get caught on them.

Every crew member should carry a pack of personal flares in an oilskin pocket, plus a torch and a knife on a lanyard, hung round the neck or waist. The knife's fittings should include a shackle key for tightening shackle pins as well as a hinged marlin spike and blade. It is sensible to adopt a policy for wearing safety gear such as: always wear harnesses when the boat is reefed or at night; always wear life-jackets at night or in fog.

As storage space on board is limited, other personal gear should be kept to a minimum, and well stowed below.

Safety harnesses are no good unless they are worn. There is a normal reluctance to put one on, partly because of the effort, partly bravado and partly because of the implied risk. So built-in harnesses have the attraction that if the weather is cold or wet enough to wear heavy-weather gear the harness is included automatically. The only further effort required is to attach the safety line.

Experienced and inexperienced alike fall into the trap of thinking that an apparently simple little deck job will be just that. When a sail or piece of gear you are holding gives a sudden hard tug, the confidence inspired by a clipped-on harness is immense. The harness safety line should not be long enough to allow you to go overboard to leeward when clipped on to the weather side and there must be eye plates by the hatchway so harnesses can be secured before going on deck.

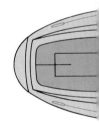

Try not to put heavy sideways loads on stanchions or guard rails, however well fitted. They are vulnerable to determined levering.

Latchway Safety System

The Latchway system is brilliant. An ordinary jackstay lies on the deck, rolls under your feet and tends to get foul of sheet leads. The Latchway system enables the jackstay to be pulled out taut to one side and to be supported at intervals because the special transfastener roller can negotiate these tethers. It is particularly useful when small children are playing on the deck, even in harbour.

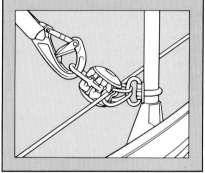

One of the many separate harnesses which can be worn with or without oilskins is the Britax. The colour coding of the straps indicates at a glance which way it should be worn. It also comes in a pouch and each member of the crew should try one, adjust it to fit, and label his pouch. Lirakis is another excellent harness. All safety gear should be kept in a locker near the hatchway.

Safety on deck

1 Casualness on deck at sea can lead to injury or even a fall overboard. Always hold on with at least one hand. Do not leave anything loose on deck which may be tripped over and avoid leaning nonchalantly against the backstay.

2 Conventional spring carbine hooks which used to be standard on safety lines can be disengaged from an eye plate if they are twisted sideways. A much-improved model, the Gibb, used in the Latchway system, requires a positive action to release the safety bar before the spring catch can be opened. It cannot, however, fit round such large diameter fastenings. An even better model, which has a rotating positive latch on the spring catch, will soon be available from XM Yachting. This has the further advantage that single-handed operation is easier than with the Gibb.

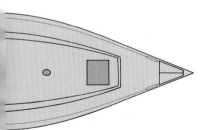

Hook your harness safety line to a windward jackstay, which runs from right forward to right aft on each side of the boat.

Non-slip material is available in various grades and types of grip and in different colours. Stick it in strips on hatches and smooth areas.

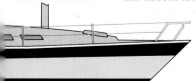

Staying warm and dry

Many people make the mistake of going to sea before preparing for the cold and wet. It is no fun being cold on a boat, so start the warm way. Depending on the weather, clothing can consist of a thermal undersuit, probably of polypropylene, then a quilted Land's end or Javlin-type pile middle layer, with oilskins on top.

The aim of all this gear is to 'wick' moisture – perspiration or condensation – away from the skin and on to the inner surface of the oilskin. These inner layers are infinitely warmer, lighter and less restricting to wear than a pair of jeans and two sweaters – the apparently obvious solution.

The best oilskins have a lining or quilted buoyant layer and a built-in harness. Henri-Lloyd are arguably the best and wear so long that they justify the cost. For inner layers, man-made fibres are easier to wash and quicker to dry than wool, but also smell more quickly. Some theoreticians claim that wool is more efficient, but in practice the convenience of man-made fibre gear is an overriding advantage.

On most non-slip decks almost any type of training or sports shoe should give a good grip, although leather moccasin types are the fashion; these are a little more expensive, but are salt-resistant and very comfortable. Boots must have a good grip to resist lurch on the foredeck in bad weather, and the Geartest trials of a few years ago showed the Javlin/Topsider boot tread to be the most effective.

Some people like to pack their boots full of socks – others like an air gap for warmth; each system works for different people. Similar gear is available for children, who must be kept warm and comfortable, because if they are miserable no one is going to enjoy the trip.

Always take at least one change of clothing and keep shore-going clothes to a minimum. Pack everything in easily stowed soft bags, not a suitcase.

Oilskin checklist
If you plan to spend only daytime at sea, coastal suits will do well. Some people prefer all-in-one outfits, but they are inconvenient if you want to shed layers, so two pieces are usually a better bet for cruising. At night, the benefit of heavy-duty oilskins soon makes itself felt. As well as obvious items, such as attached hoods with adjustable fastenings, good oilies have no seams where they will be under tension and exposed to heavy spray and have doubling patches on seats and knees which provide discardable protection against chafe on deck. There should also be fastenings at wrist and ankle to stop water getting in. A fly makes life easier provided it is watertight.

1

1 Polypropylene long johns and long-sleeved T-shirts make good undergarments, with thermal socks and balaclava.
2 If the weather demands it, the next layer is Hollowfill or Thermalon or Javlin pile – all wash easily and dry quickly, though the Javlin is the least unpleasant to put on damp. The sallopette-type unit is very comfortable and convenient.
3 The next stage is oilskin trousers, to give warmth and protection from damp below.
4 On goes the jacket, ideally complete with a harness. Fasten wrist and ankle straps.

Children and Safety

Children and adults who cannot swim should put on buoyancy aids before going down the marina pontoon (so should all the crew if embarking by dinghy). At sea, well-secured safety harness must be worn on deck and a responsible adult should ensure that they are fastened to a strong point – not just a guard rail – since the jerk of even a child falling can be very severe. A Latchway system allows children to run unrestricted up and down the deck – freedom not permitted by an ordinary jackstay. Explain to children in advance which ropes are likely to run out suddenly, when tacking for example. Keep a calm atmosphere and children won't worry.

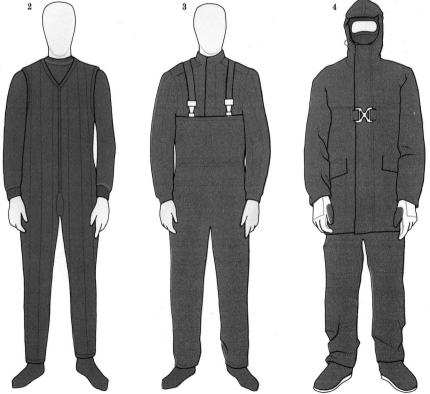

2   3   4

Planning a passage

Half the joy of a passage is the pre-planning, and anticipation. Much of the organization depends upon inter-related factors.

Watches

The experience and number of crew, for example, will determine the length of the trip and the watch-keeping arrangements. On a 30-ft (9-m) boat with two experienced sailors, two with limited experience and two inexperienced, it would be possible to work two watches with an experienced and limited-experienced sailor or, if the weather is kind, one experienced and one inexperienced. One of the two limited-experienced crew would make the third person on each watch. The skipper, however, should expect to be called at any time. Watches of 5–6 hrs can be tolerated by day, with 2-hr watches best at night.

Distance

During 24 hrs you can expect to sail 100 mls, or 60 mls made good, if sailing upwind. When planning the route, check that there are safe and convenient stop-off ports along the way, since a cruise is meant to be a pleasure, not a chore. Boredom can produce sea sickness, and while pills taken in advance help some, others lose their green-tinged complexion when given the helm. A large part of safe navigation is to keep an accurate log of courses steered and distances run between course alterations, to arrive at estimated positions.

Before you leave be sure to acquaint yourself with the laws of the countries you intend to visit. Check that you have all the necessary documents:

1 *Notice of intended departure* must be given to customs, and clearance papers obtained showing that all harbour dues have been paid and giving ports of destination.

2 *Ship's papers* must also be in order. If your vessel is registered in its country of origin, foreign authorities will accept the papers. Some countries will accept the 'International Certificate of Pleasure Navigation', which may save you from officially registering your boat or obtaining a carnet, which gives proof of ownership. British owners, however, are well advised to register their boats officially ('British Registered Ship') if planning a foreign cruise. In the USA any boat with an engine over 10 hp must be registered. If chartering carry the Charter Party document with you.

3 Everyone on board must carry an up-to-date *passport* and a *visa* for the countries that require it.

4 *Health regulations and vaccinations* vary from country to country, so ensure everyone has the correct certificates.

5 The skipper may be asked to produce a *Certificate of Competence* in some countries, especially when navigating inland waterways.

6 Most countries require a complete *crew list*, giving names, addresses, ratings and passport numbers of each crew member. It is advisable to list everybody on board as 'crew', not 'passengers' since some countries may charge for passenger carrying.

7 Check that your *insurance* is up to date. It should cover the area you intend to cruise in, damage received and caused by your boat, personal cover, and contents. If entering by road, check that the insurance covers the boat when trailed, and on the water.

8 Carry the correct *currency* and check on *import/export* restrictions.

9 Obtain all the information possible about the area before setting off. Cruise accounts and large-scale harbour maps are often helpful. Be sure to have the relevant official charts and cruising guides.

10 Remember to take *tide tables, tidal stream atlas* and a *list of lights, radio* and *meteorological services*.

Weather

Plan your passage to avoid the dangerously bad weather, hurricanes, cyclones, typhoons and seasonal winds that occur at certain times of the year, and make the best use of fair winds. *Ocean Passages of the World*, published by the British Hydrographic Department, gives a clear description of winds, currents and weather for all the oceans. You may reach your destination faster by covering more miles with good winds than taking the more direct route, involving storms and doldrums.

The cruising grounds

Azores
Bermuda
Virgin Islands
Canary Islands
Suez Canal
Trinidad
Cape Verde Islands
Galapagos Islands
Panama Canal
Seychelles
Port Moresby
Marquesas
Fiji
Tahiti
St. Helena
Mauritius
Rio de Janeiro
Tristan da Cunha
Cape of Good Hope
Sydney
Cape Horn

Primary routes
Secondary routes

The best time of year to embark on a voyage round the world depends on your point of departure and your route. Essential information about hurricanes, weather patterns, winds, air and sea temperatures and currents are given in both British and US Pilot Charts. A favourite route is to reach the West Indies for Christmas, move on to Panama in January, follow the Pacific Trades and reach the Indian Ocean in August so as to avoid hurricanes. It is best to round the Cape in the southern summer.

Flags
When entering foreign waters, hoist the International Code Flag 'Q' from the starboard crosstrees for customs clearance. Always fly the national ensign of the country you are visiting. This is not just a courtesy; failure to do so is a punishable offence in some countries. Fly your own national flag from the stern of your boat.

Stopping off
The first port of call in any country must be a customs port. Wait to be boarded by a port official or report to the harbour master's office with all the necessary documents. Short spells in port waste time. A 6-hr anchorage in a sheltered bay to save a tide may be worth another 4 hrs lost in port. Many yacht clubs invite visiting yachtsmen to become honorary members during their stay and some, but not all, offer excellent mooring and docking facilities. For long trips, select several well-spaced strategic ports to collect mail. Arrange well in advance for a bank, consulate, yacht club, post office or business to keep it for you.

Inland Waterways
Apply to the country's National Tourist Board for pamphlets giving details of entry permits, regulations, times of opening, information regarding minimum water depths, height of masts and so on.

Courtesies
One of the most important courtesies when sailing in any water is to guard against pollution. All waste should be stored and sealed in plastic sacks until they can be disposed of ashore. Bottles and cans can be sunk in deep water off-shore. Discharge of oil is prohibited and absorbent materials are available to mop up oil spillages. Try to keep noise levels low, and secure your halyard to prevent it flapping noisily against the mast. Keep speed low in congested waters and harbours. When anchoring, keep clear of boats already there. Ask permission before coming alongside and before crossing another boat to reach the shore, and always move quietly across the foredeck. When visiting a yacht club, call on the Secretary before using the facilities. Carry a stern gangway if cruising in the Mediterranean, and plenty of large fenders for inland waterways.

Northern Europe/1

Tranquil cruising in Scandinavia

Cruising Grounds
The tideless waters of the Kiel Canal lead east to the peaceful seclusion of Denmark's 500 islands. Farther north, the Lim Fjord cuts the Danish archipelago, with its 600 harbours, to the rugged west coast of Sweden, warmed by the Gulf Stream. From Göteborg, the Göte Canal traces 250 scenic miles to the east coast where the 24,000 'Skårgard' islands offer some of the best sailing in the world. Alternatively, continue north from Göteborg to Oslo and explore the picturesque south-east coast of Norway with its sheltered anchorages, before continuing up to the dramatic cruising grounds between Stavanger and Sognefjord. From here the wild fjords penetrate the mountains. Anchorages are scarce and a long cable is essential. If venturing on from the Swedish east coast to Finland, the Åland (Alvehanman) islands and the south coast provide sheltered waters, well-buoyed fairways and good fishing. In Finnish waters, check the charts for prohibited zones, and be careful not to trespass. Holland offers varied and challenging sailing, with its large expanses of reclaimed water, the shallow Friesian lakes and the network of inland waterways. Yachts with fixed masts must keep to canals without bridges.

Marina Facilities
Harbours and marinas abound in this area and facilities are generally good. Fuel and water are easy to obtain, direct from hoses in marinas, or from filling stations along the quay/dockside. But carry sufficient gas cylinders on board since they cannot be exchanged. It is forbidden to discharge waste from a boat in the Baltic Sea, so use the reception facilities in the ports. The harbour dues are usually low, but the cost of living is high. Norway has fewer facilities for yachts, so stock up whenever possible. Scandinavian harbours become crowded in high summer, so radio to check in advance if there is space.

Weather

The cruising season runs from mid-May to mid-September. The wind direction is mainly westerly in the summer, although an east wind may blow for several weeks. Variable winds, changing skies, rain and stiff breezes can be expected, but sheltered cruising areas are always available. Visit the Norwegian fjords in settled weather to avoid flat calms, violent squalls and the *fallvaer* wind. Although the Baltic is tideless, unpredictable strong currents sweep round the Sound between Denmark and Sweden. Weather forecasts can be obtained from national broadcasts and coastal radio stations.

The map

The best cruising grounds appear as shaded blue areas and ports of entry as blue dots. In the wind symbol, arrows fly with the wind and the number shows the percentage frequency of light, variable wind.

Buoyage

Belgium, Denmark and Holland use the International Buoyage System at sea, with the Lateral System on inland waters. Finland has the simplest and best system in the world. It includes pairs of red and white or black and white wooden transits which give a lead through channels. In Sweden, keep north and west of black or black and white buoys; south and east of red ones. White stone cairns mark the inner leads and direction of the fairway in Norway, Sweden and Finland.

Charts and Addresses

The 1:500,000 charts cover most of the Scandinavian coastline, and British Admiralty pilot charts are comprehensive. Charts for individual areas are available from bookshops and chandlers in ports and from National Tourist Boards. Scandinavian charts can be obtained from Nautiska Magasinet Skeppsbrön 10, Stockholm; Belgian charts from Ministère des Travaux Public, Brussels; Dutch charts from the Royal Netherlands Touring Club (ANWB), Wassenaarseweg 220, Den Haag. Contact National Tourist Boards for names and addresses of chartering companies, and book early. Other useful addresses include: the Swedish Cruising Club (Svenska Kryssarklubben), Karlavägen 67, 11449 Stockholm. Norwegian Yachting Association, Gronnegate 1, Oslo 3.

Northern Europe/2

Cruising grounds

The west coast of Scotland, with its rugged scenery, sea lochs and outlying islands, remains for the experienced sailor one of the most unspoilt cruising grounds in western Europe. The main centre is in the River Clyde and there are good mainland and island anchorages, but the shore is steep-to and rocky and the wind tends to be gusty. The west coast can be reached from the east coast via the Caledonian Canal from Inverness.

The most appealing area of Ireland for cruising lies off the south and west coasts. Friendly harbours abound between Cork and Bantry Bay. The west coast, although exposed to Atlantic weather, is less prone to fog than the Irish Sea and between May and September the chances of settled weather reduce the need for shelter. The safest ports to aim for in bad conditions are Shannon, Galway Bay, Clew Bay and Donegal Bay.

Farther south, the deep-water estuaries of the English West Country are equally uncrowded, with plenty of sheltered harbours against a cliff and river setting in both Devon and Cornwall. The east coast has a completely different flavour. The shore is flat, full of beautiful rivers, sand banks and mud flats, yet is relatively safe and offers many quiet anchorages. The main yachting centres are found at Burnham-on-Crouch, Maldon, West Mersea, Pin Mill and Brightlingsea.

The traditional home of British yachting is between Chichester and Poole on the south coast. Tiny creeks, fishing harbours and large yachting centres, such as Chichester, Cowes, Hamble, Lymington and Yarmouth, all offer good anchorages. Although it is crowded, facilities in the area are excellent and the Cherbourg peninsula lies a mere 60 mls to the south across the Channel.

In France, Brittany's north and west coasts are spectacular, particularly the stretch between St Malo and La Rochelle – sandy beaches interspersed with rocky outcrops – and such attractive ports as Lezardrieux, Treguier and Morlaix. Strong tides and off-lying dangers, however, call for caution especially when anchoring. The Biscay coast is well provided with marinas, although many of the best anchorages are without facilities.

Canals

The Inland Waterways open up several routes to the Mediterranean. The main access to Paris is from Le Havre, then three canals open up. Another network, joining St Malo with Lorient and Angers, offers an attractive cruising ground and a convenient short route to the Biscay coast, for boats with a draft of less than 3 ft (1 m). The Channel Islands offer numerous anchorages, although deep-water harbours are scarce.

Weather

Although notoriously unpredictable, the weather in this area does follow broad patterns. Britain and northern France are generally subject to prevailing westerly and south-westerly winds. In June, light winds usually accompany fine settled weather, while early August brings stronger, more variable winds, and thunderstorms are common in July. Recently, however, the trend has been towards lighter winds, drier weather and more frequent easterly winds. Tides are strong, particularly in estuaries, and the tidal range is high in north Brittany. The Channel Islands enjoy the most sun. The BBC issues regular shipping forecasts. Phone Jersey Central (0534-23660) for 24-hour Channel Islands forecasts.

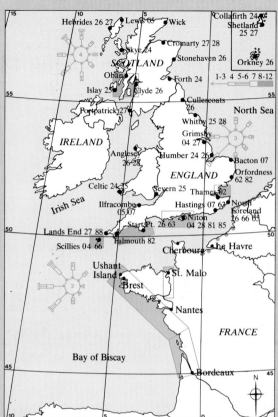

Black dots identify VHF coastguard radio stations (Channel 16), while blue dots mark ports of entry.

Regulations
Until January 1984, any unregistered craft must obtain Customs form C1328 before entering France. Thereafter, visiting yachts will have to be registered. It is no longer necessary to obtain a *permis de circulation* for navigating French waterways. Before entering Britain, unregistered vessels may need the International Certificate for Pleasure Navigation. A registration plate is imperative for all boats visiting Belgium for a period of more than two months.

Charts and Publications
British Admiralty, Imray and Stanford Charts give excellent coverage of the area. French charts and documents are available from: Etablissement Principal du Service Hydrographique et Océanique de la Marne, 13 rue du Chatellier, BP 426, 29275 Brest Cedex. The Royal Yachting Association and French Government Tourist Office issue numerous booklets free, including a list of charter companies and a useful leaflet: *Yachting and Boating in French Waters*.

Useful Addresses
Royal Yachting Association, Victoria Way, Woking, Surrey. Cruising Association, Ivory House, St Katherine's Dock, London E1. Yacht Charter Association, Lymington Yacht Haven, King's Saltern Road, Lymington, Hants. Touring Club de France Service Nautique, 65 Avenue de la Grande Armée; 75782 Paris Cedex 16. Féderation Française du Yachting à Voile, 55 rue Kléber, Paris 16. Jersey Tourist Information Bureau, 118 Grand Buildings, Trafalgar Square, London WC2.

The Mediterranean/1

Riding through the Mediterranean mistral

Cruising grounds

Every boat owner dreams of cruising in the Mediterranean where the sea and sky are blue, the sun warm and the wine and food cheap.

Most boats from northern Europe and N. America come south on the French canals, and emerge into the Mediterranean at either the interesting port of Sète, via the Canal du Midi, the mouth of the Rhône or the St Louis Canal.

The coast west of the Rhône is flat and sandy, but the French government has developed the area as a yachting centre, and giant marinas exist at many places, including La Motte and Leucate-Barcarès. Nearer to Spain, the coast becomes rocky and steep, with some charming old ports such as Canet and Banyuls.

The Spanish coast offers good cruising and the Balearic islands are delightful, but harbours and anchorages are usually crowded.

East of the Rhône delta lies an interesting area of steep-sided, rocky *calanques*, like mini-fjords. There are attractive harbours at Cassis, Bandol and Sanary, and a fine marina at Ile des Embiez.

On the Côte d'Azur, from Toulon to Cannes, the scenery is often spectacular, and the Iles des Hyères, especially Porquerolles, are unusual and worth a visit. Hyères, Ste Maxime and St Raphael are some of the many good harbours.

A succession of lovely creeks and bays then leads rapidly from one charming small harbour to another and so to the legendary Cannes with its millionaires' yachts and glamorous life ashore.

The harbours from here along the Riviera to Menton – Antibes, Nice, Villefranche, Monaco – are among the most fashionable, high-priced and noisy in the world. Nevertheless, they are fascinating, and the sailor can always find peace by cruising south to Corsica and Sardinia.

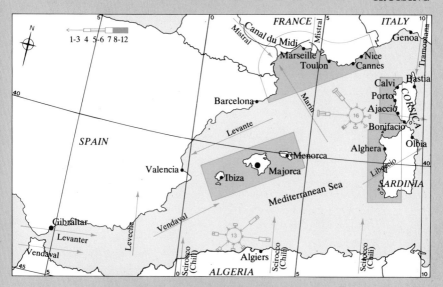

Corsica has magnificent wild and mountainous scenery. The harbour closest to France is Calvi, where Christopher Columbus was born. Going south, steep-sided bays and inlets provide many quite sheltered anchorages, but no harbour or marina before Ajaccio. On the south coast, Bonifacio is a perfect natural harbour.

Less than an hour's sail away, Sardinia's north-east coast offers magnificent anchorages.

Marinas
Almost all the French harbours are marinas, and most can fill every need from water and fuel to camping-gaz. Electricity is often available and is cooler to use on hot summer nights than gas or oil lamps. A stern gang-plank is necessary.

Harbour dues and taxes on foreign yachts can be extremely high, especially on the Côte d'Azur and the Riviera; they are more moderate out of season. The season runs from April to September, with high season in July and August.

In Corsica, most anchorages offer few facilities, so it is wise to stock up whenever possible.

Weather
The ideal time to cruise in this area is May and June. In summer, the intense heat and frequent windless days make an awning essential, but beware the strong winds which can blow up without warning. Weather in the Rhône delta area is generally unpredictable, with strong winds, although the Mistral blows mostly in the winter.

In Corsica the north-west summer winds are usually pleasant and the sea temperature ranges from 16°C in May to a peak of 24°C in August and down to 21°C in October.

Weather forecasts for mariners, broadcast daily, divide the coast into east and west from St Raphael. All French marinas post up weather reports twice daily at the *Capitainerie*.

Chartering Boats
The French government Tourist Office can provide lists of French boat hire companies and names of companies which organize charters and all-inclusive sailing holidays. Foreign boats chartering in France can incur heavy taxes.

Charts and Publications
British Admiralty and French charts cover the whole coast. In addition, Admiralty *Sailing Directions* for the area are essential, and numerous practical and informative books about sailing conditions and harbours have been published.

The Mediterranean/2

Cruising grounds

The Italian coastline is immensely long and anyone cruising there will need to be selective. The Riviera has some attractive harbours, and the Tuscan coast with its outlying islands, among them Elba and Giglio, provide good cruising and shelter. Farther south, the Pontine islands, Ischia, Capri and the Bay of Naples offer beautiful scenery, fine weather and shelter. Northern Sicily provides a chance to see the rarely visited Liparian and Egadian islands.

Rounding the toe and heel of Italy, there are merely adequate ports, and along the Adriatic it is sandy and flat, in marked contrast to the 375-ml (603-km) long, rocky, Yugoslavian coastline, with its myriad islands and inlets.

Generally speaking, as one sails eastward, so the harbours and their facilities become simpler. Italy has many splendid marinas which can provide everything from water to major repairs, but in Yugoslavia there are only a few marinas at the larger cities. The many ports and anchorages range from old walled cities, such as Dubrovnik, to small towns where boats lie alongside the quay. Northern ports are likely to be crowded in July and August.

Greece has everything to appeal to the yachtsman: sunshine, breath-taking scenery and hundreds of harbours and anchorages, usually still simple and uncrowded.

Where there are full marina facilities – mainly near Athens – there, too, will be the tourist crowds.

Coming south from Yugoslavia, Corfu and the other Ionian islands offer delightful cruising and good shelter. On reaching Cephalonia, one can either go eastward through the Gulfs of Patras and Corinth and the Canal to the Aegean, or south along the flatter west coast of the Peleponnesus to Crete.

The Aegean is most attractive, with its islands, mountainous coasts, colourful small ports where you moor stern-to, secluded anchorages and opportunities for all water sports.

Rhodes is the largest of the islands and provides an excellent starting point for a cruise along either the Adriatic or the southern, Anatolian coast of Turkey. This area is little known, but it offers unsurpassed scenery, interesting archeological remains and many sheltered coves and anchorages.

From here you can sail on through the Dardanelles and the Sea of Marmora, through the Bosphorus and into the Black Sea – surely the stuff of which every sailor's dreams are made.

Weather

The cruising season runs from April through October, when the weather is settled, with only local variations.

Comprehensive weather reports are broadcast on 1084 kHz in Italian, at dictation speed. They

follow a pattern and are easy to follow.

In the Adriatic it is easier to use Italian forecasts than to try to pick up the weak-signal Yugoslav reports given in English.

The prevailing day breeze here is the Maestrale, blowing from the north-west, but the south-easterly Scirocco may also blow for days on end.

Greek waters can be divided into four zones, running roughly north and south, each with competely different winds, while by early summer the weather tends to follow a pattern of constant sunshine with occasional thunderstorms until late autumn. Athens radio issues weather forecasts in Greek, with special warnings in English.

The Aegean winds affect Turkish waters also, but along the southern coast there are usually westerly onshore day breezes and in the Dodecanese, strong northerly winds are usual.

Charts and publications

British Admiralty charts and *Sailing Directions* (Mediterranean Pilot Vols 1–5 and Black Sea Pilot) cover the whole area. Charts issued by the Italian Naval Authorities are good and up to date. Yugoslav charts are also useful.

There are many excellent guides to cruising in the area, notably those by H M Denham: *The Tyrrhenian Sea, The Adriatic, The Aegean* and *The Eastern Mediterranean*, all published by John Murray.

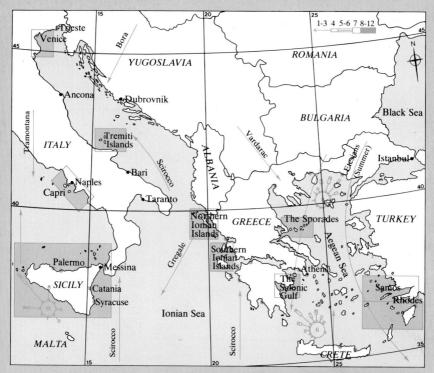

The blue arrows indicate the notorious seasonal winds – often a major hazard when cruising in the tideless Mediterranean.

Regulations

To obtain a permit of navigation in all these countries, it is necessary to fulfil many and varied requirements governing the entry of a boat to their waters, status of the crew, etc; so check beforehand what is needed.

Chartering by foreign yachts is illegal in Italy and Greece, but there are boats for hire locally, and many firms also operate all-in sailing holidays.

Moored in a Greek harbour

The Caribbean

Cat boats in Bermuda

Cruising grounds

The Caribbean draws sailors to its waters like bees to a honeypot. The best islands for cruising are the Bahamas, the Virgin Islands (British, American and French), and the Grenadines, where a wide variety of boats are available for both crewed and independent charters. If bareboating you will need a Certificate of Competence and will have to pay for a cruising permit, fuel and harbour dues. A crewed charter will take care of all the formalities, and will choose your route, but you may need to book up to 6 months in advance. Many charters also include fishing and water sports facilities.

Sixty miles east of Puerto Rico, where the warming Atlantic meets the subtropical Caribbean Sea, lie the incomparable Virgin Islands. Their waters are protected from the Trade winds by scores of islets and cays which offer secluded anchorages. Out of the way harbours, however, are often not clearly marked on the charts, so try to moor in daylight. Many of the islands are uninhabited and the best facilities are found at Road Town, Tortola (BVI); Charlotte Amalie, and Red Hook, St Thomas and Cristiansted, St Croix; (USVI). If you wish to stop every night, and enjoy time ashore, 40 mls a day is a good day's run

To the north, the 700 Bahamian islands offer excellent harbour facilities, particularly at Nassau. Sailing at night, however, is dangerous since there are few lighthouses. For those already familiar with the Bahamas and Virgin Islands, the Anguilla to Antigua stretch, the Grenadines and the north coast of South America are exotic and challenging cruising grounds. The Venezuelan coast is south of the hurricane area and is as yet unspoilt. Living is cheap, but ports with facilities are few and far between. The local people, however, are suspicious of foreign boats, so it is wise to carry a gun.

Weather

Ideal sailing conditions persist for 300 days a year in the Caribbean. Peak time is December to April when the water is beautifully warm almost every day. The islands are warmed by the Gulf Stream and brushed by the Trade Winds which blow at a steady 15–25 kn. The result is an average annual temperature of 25°C. Hurricanes occasionally attack the southern Caribbean between June and November (often in August) but satellite forecasts reduce the danger of being caught unawares. Maritime radio operates on VHF channel 27.

Useful Addresses

For cruising and chartering information contact:
British Virgin Islands Tourist Board, P O Box 134, Road Town, Tortola (809–494–3134). World Yacht Enterprises, 14 W 55th St, NY 10019 (212–246–4811). United States Virgin Islands Tourist Office, 10 Rockefeller Plaza, NY 10020 (212–582–4520).

Chartering Companies

Caribbean Sailing Yachts Ltd, Box 157 (Tel: 4–2741). BVI Bareboats, Box 94 (phone 4–2399). Tortola Yacht Charters, Village Cay Marina (phone 4–2221). Sailors World (phone 775–2080).

Charts

In addition to US and British Hydrographic Charts, excellent chart lists are available from Better Boating Association Inc, Needham, Ma. Imray-Iolaire Caribbean charts are designed for use with Donald Street's Cruising Guides.

Publications

Yachtsman's Guide to the Caribbean, Seaport Publishing Company, 843 Delray Ave, SE Grand Rapids, Mich 49506. *Virgin Islands* Sailing Book Service, 34 Oak Ave, Tuckahoe, NY10707. *Yachtsman's Guide to the Bahamas* Tropic Isle Publishers Inc. P O Box 340866, Florida 33134.

USA: The East coast

Cruising Grounds
The East Coast lends itself to some of the best cruising in the USA. The tree-lined New England coast, with its islands, creeks and rivers, can be divided into four main areas. Beyond the sheltered, land-locked Long Island Sound lies the stretch of island-dotted coast from Buzzards Bay to Cape Cod, with good anchorages at Block Island, Martha's Vineyard and Nantucket Islands, and plenty of natural harbours with good facilities. From Cape Cod to Cape Elizabeth, the more exposed coastline produces some exhilarating sailing, but some of the best sailing is found along the rugged Maine coast between Cape Elizabeth and the Canadian border. South of New York, cruising grounds begin at Delaware Bay, and the Delaware-Chesapeake Canal which opens into Chesapeake Bay, offers thousands of miles of shoreline, particularly good for spring and fall cruising since the summers tend to be hot and still. Inland waterways penetrate 1,000 mls (1,609 km) from the south end of Chesapeake Bay down to Miami, giving access to the winter cruising grounds there. Since temperatures rarely drop balmy days are the general rule even in mid-winter, Florida enjoys year-round cruising. The Florida keys, a chain of tropical islands with a coral reef stretching south from Florida, have become the province of all-in sailing holidays.

Weather conditions
The best cruising months are June to September. The prevailing south-westerly winds bring Force 4–5 winds, and warm, sunny days of 21°C on the water. Occasional easterly winds, however, may bring three-day storms. The tidal range is great in some places, but rarely causes problems, but north of Cape Cod the water is too cold for swimming until late in the summer. The greatest hazard is fog, which settles around Maine, particularly in August. Around Newport, the fog usually burns off when the sun heats the land. There may be fog in Long Island Sound in July and August, and also little wind. Continuous weather forecasts are given on Weather I and Weather II channels and are updated every six hours.

Marinas
The coast is buzzing with natural harbours, and a good port can be found about every 20 mls (32 km). Marina berths tend to be very crowded in summer, so it is worth booking in advance. Most yacht clubs, however, have guest moorings, anchorages or slips for rent, but check in advance.

Buoyage system
Red starboard-hand buoys are left to starboard when entering harbours or sailing clockwise round the coast: north to south down the east coast. This is the opposite to the IALA System A adopted in most other parts of the world.

Charts
The US and British Hydrographic Offices both produce dependable charts for each area. (Soundings are given in feet, not metres.) The Better Boating Association Inc. produces charts in flip-back form, known as *Chartkit*, available from most good chandlers or by post from Box 407, Needham, Ma 02192. The US Coastguards publish charts and booklets for a variety of areas and harbours, including coastal waters, which are available from the National Ocean Survey, Rockville, Md 20852. Boating laws and regulations are given in the Coastguard publication C9290. Several cruising guides condense lists of marinas and services available in each port including: *A Cruising Guide to the New England Coast* by Roger Duncan and John Ware; *A Yachtsman's Guide to Northern Harbours*, Seaport Publishing Co, 843 Delrey Ave, SE Grand Rapids, 6, Mich. Sailing Book Services, 34 Oak Ave, Tuckahee, NY 10707, also publish numerous cruising guides. Some of the large oil companies supply free cruising booklets as well as a cruise service, which will plan out a cruise for you: Esso Touring Service, 15 West 51st St, NY 10019; Gulf Tour Guide Bureau, Box 8056, Philadelphia Pa 19101; Mobil Touring Service, 150 East 42nd St, NY 10017 and Texaco Waterways Service, 135 East 42nd St, NY 10019.

Tranquility and sunshine are part of the Florida scenery. Specially designed cockpit shades, known as 'bimini' tops are essential in this climate and are supplied by the charter sailing boats. Only 100 mls (160 km) off the mainland lie the Florida Keys, the bracelet of islands which boast the only living coral reef in the United States – best explored by skin diving, snorkeling or in a glass-bottomed boat. A popular charter route is between Key West and Marathon, although those with their own boat and the time would find fascinating cruising grounds in the Gulf of Mexico

USA: The West coast

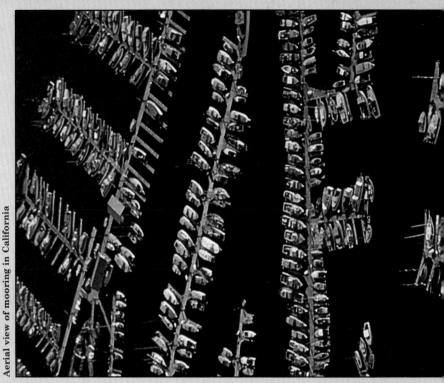

Aerial view of mooring in California

Cruising Grounds

There are two main sailing centres on California's Golden Coast: the Long Beach/Los Angeles area, with its social atmosphere and its off-lying islands which offer some escape from the congested water, and the San Francisco Bay Area. The Bay itself boasts grand-scale scenic cruising. To the north, the coastline grows wild and there are few ports until you reach Puget Sound, which has excellent facilities and beautiful cruising grounds. If you aim to head out to Hawaii, a deep-keeled boat, with stability in the fierce winds and plenty of space for supplies, is most suitable.

Marinas

There are over half a million yachts in California, with the majority in the Los Angeles area. Since natural harbours do not abound here as they do on the East Coast, every vacant stretch of coast has been developed into a marina. The world's largest man-made small-boat harbour is Marina del Ray, which houses 6,000 slips, numerous sailing schools and plenty of rental companies. The Los Angeles area is expensive and approaching saturation. In the San Francisco area, by contrast, the marinas are smaller, well spaced out and so less hampered by congestion.

Weather

The Pacific coast offers year-round sailing, with hot summers, mild winters and fresh breezes. Southern California is blessed with both warmth and strong prevailing north-easterly winds, but every few years hurricanes strike in either August or September. San Francisco Bay, however, benefits from fresh, westerly winds. Rainstorms are rare, but are most likely from December to February. Fog frequently hits the San Francisco area, and sometimes takes days to clear, except inside the bay. Continuous weather forecasts are given on VHF channels which can be fitted into your radio.

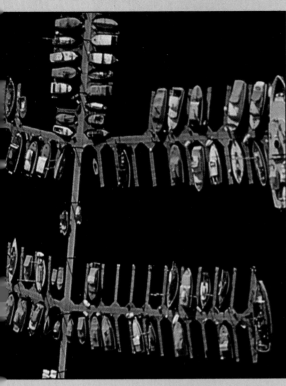

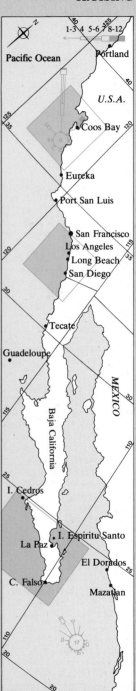

Regulations
Discharge of properly treated waste is allowed in open coastal water, but not in specified areas such as near bathing beaches, shellfish beds and in freshwater lakes. *The Handbook of Boating Laws*, available from Outboard Booking Club, 333 N. Michigan Ave., Chicago, Ill. 60601, lists individual state and federal boating regulations. The Coastguards frequently make official inspections, so be prepared to show documentation, registration, equipment, and to demonstrate navigation lights. Failure to comply can result in a fine of up to $100 (£50).

Charts
Charts for US waters are available from the Coast and Geodetic Survey, Environmental Science Services Administration, Rockville, Md 20852.

Addresses
Chartering companies include: Windships Charters, 54 Jack London Square, Oakland, Ca 94607 and Pacific Marine Charters, 2323 Eastlake Ave, East Seattle, Wa 98102. The *New York Sunday Times* classified section always contains list of boats available for charter. For crewed boats, contact Sparkman & Stephens, 79 Maddison Ave, NY 10016 (Tel: 212-689-9292).

The Great Lakes

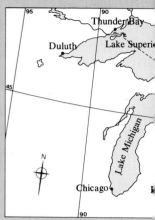

Cruising Grounds

The Great Lakes offer the largest expanse of fresh water in the world – 95,000 sq. mls (247,000 sq km). The St. Lawrence Seaway and other artificial canals have created an inviting opening from the Atlantic into the internal waterways so that the lake ports have become, in effect, Atlantic seaports. The St. Lawrence Seaway, with its 2,000 mls (3,218 km) of canals, rivers, lakes and locks is, however, primarily a trading route and commercial traffic must take priority. For safety reasons boats under 20 ft (6 m) long or one ton may not travel through the seaway.

The waterways are open from mid-May to mid-October for the prime sailing season, before the lakes freeze over for the winter. The Rideau Canal, which also opens out into Lake Ontario, connects Ottawa to Kingston in 125 scenic miles (201 km), punctuated with 48 historic locks and numerous dams. One of Ontario's best cruising areas through the Rideau Lakes, begins 14 locks above Kingston city.

The Thousand Islands, in the St. Lawrence area, is a labyrinth of twisting channels and secluded anchorages. The St. Lawrence Island National Park and Marinas at Kingston and Gananoque provide excellent mooring facilities. The islands lead to the long, narrow Bay of Quinte, near Picton, Ontario – a pretty backwater with plenty of peaceful anchorages – and to Kingston harbour nearby.

The Trent-Seven waterway offers an attractive sheltered passage with excellent mooring and docking facilities, fishing and secluded anchorages. Be prepared for sudden squalls, however, on Lake Simcoe and Chonchiching. Boats with a draft of more than 5 ft 6 in (1.5 m) should contact the waterway office before setting off. The Trent-Seven opens out into the spectacular Georgian Bay, with its 30,000 islands, sandy beaches, and rocky points. It is mainly big-boat water, and smaller craft and trailer sailers will find the best cruising area lies between Port Severn and Perry Sound, through the Thirty Thousand Islands.

In the north lies the world's largest freshwater island, Manitoulin, which has good anchorages and cruising facilities, particularly at Killarney.

The Lake of the Woods, west of Lake Superior, provides 65,000 mls (104,000 km) of beautiful cruising around its shores. Dotted with islands, a maze of channels, and good fishing grounds it forms part of a small-craft route.

There are beautiful and protected inland cruising areas accessible from the Great Lakes by river and canal, and it is possible to cruise to Florida and the Bahamas from 1,000 mls (1,609 km) inland of the Great Lakes. Remember to take plenty of fenders for protection in the locks.

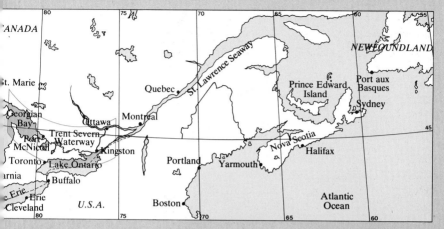

Buoyage

The Great Lakes buoyage system is identical to the coastal lateral system. In this case, the direction from the outlet of the lake is the same as from seaward. So when approaching a lake from its outlet – keep the red mark to starboard, and the black to port. The system is the same on both US and Canadian sides of the border. Although the constructional details of the buoys may vary, colour, number and shape are consistent. Details are given in Canadian Aids to Navigation. Rules of the Road for the Great Lakes are listed in a free Coastguard booklet (CG172).

Weather forecasts

The Coastguard weather forecasts are broadcast continuously on 161.65 MHz. The times of forecasts on other stations for individual areas are detailed in *Radio Aids to Marine Navigation*, available from lock stations and Supply and Services, Canada.

Regulations

Pleasure craft may enter Canada by trailer or under their own power. Customs offices are found at federal harbours, if approaching by sea, and at highway border crossings, if trailer sailing. A permit of entry is issued and must be relinquished on departure. All boats need to display a license on both sides of the bow; these are available from the Registrar of Shipping, Mannlife Centre, 55 Bloor St. W., 9th floor, Box 10, Station A, Toronto, Ontario M5W1A3. Some harbours and canal approaches require permits, available for a nominal sum from most marinas and lock stations. Safety equipment to be carried aboard is stipulated by the Department of Marine Transport and is subject to inspection. Overboard discharge of waste is forbidden and so should be disposed of in port. Check the charts and regulations for boating boundaries and speed limits; always slow down in crowded waters.

Charts and Addresses

Charts of the Lakes and Waterways are available from the Canadian Hydrographic Service, P O Box 8080, 1675 Russell Rd, Ottawa, Ontario K1G 3H6; charts of Lake Michigan, from the National Ocean Survey, Riverdale, Md. 20840. Marina listings appear in *Boating Ontario/Canada* obtainable from the Ministry of Industry and Tourism, Queen's Park, Toronto, Ontario M7A 2E5. *Canadian Aids to Navigation* comes free from Transport Canada, Marine Aids Division, Tower A, Place de Ville, Ottawa, Ontario K1A 0N7. Marine Weather Services can be obtained from Environment Canada, Port Meteorological Office, 25 St Clair Avenue E 3rd floor, Toronto, Ontario M4T 1M2. The Canadian Yachting Association issues cruising information and booklets. *Boat Rentals in Ontario* and other booklets are issued by Ontario Travel, Queen's Park, Toronto, Ontario M7A 2E5.

Australasia

Approaching Sydney Harbour

Cruising Grounds
The Great Barrier reef
offers a lifetime of cruising
in its 2,000 mls (3,218 km)
of exotic coral-strewn
waters along the northern
half of Australia's east
coast. It is besieged by
tidal currents as well as
cyclones in the sailing
season, but the water is
kept warm year round,
with the assistance of the
south equatorial current.
Between the coast and the
reef lie 600 mainly
uninhabited islands. When
approaching an inhabited
island, warn the 'captain'
of the island of your
arrival by radio as a
courtesy; he may allow
you to use the facilities
for a nominal fee.

The Whitsunday Islands
form the bareboat-
chartering centre of
Australia. The 74 thickly-
wooded and sandy-beached
islands, situated 40 mls
(64 km) to leeward of the
reef, offer excellent
facilities at very low cost.
Deserted anchorages
abound, as do sharks,
stonefish and sea wasps, so
beware, particularly if
scuba diving. Local charts
indicate the unusual
currents and conditions.
Farther south, Sydney
harbour and its 16-ml
(26-km) inland coast of
secluded bays and beaches
opens up surprisingly
peaceful cruising grounds,
good anchorages and
facilities.

In New Zealand, trailer
sailers and twin-keelers
which can sit on the
beach, have become the
local style, for mooring
and marina facilities are
scarce. The historic Bay of
Islands, also a renowned
big game fishing area, is a
favoured cruising ground.
The Hauraki Gulf and
Marlborough Sands on the
northern tip of South
Island also offer good
anchorages, attractive
harbours and lovely
scenery – enough for
months of exploration. A
list of radio stations with
call signs, frequencies and
listening times is given in
Sea Spray Annual which
can be found in local
chandlery shops.

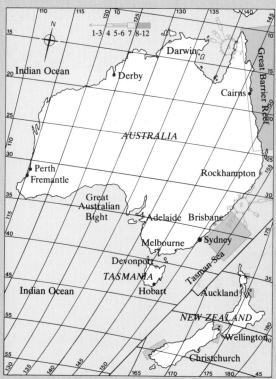

Regulations
Both Australia and New Zealand are largely free from regulations. Cruising boats do not need to be registered, although racing boats do. Visiting yachts are allowed to stay only one year in Australia free of import duty, with a one year extension. Anyone coming from smallpox or yellow fever infected countries must be vaccinated, except for children under a year old.

Charts
British Admiralty charts and Australian Navy Hydrographic charts cover the area. Port Information Manuals are available from port chandlers.

Moorings
Moorings and marina facilities are scarce in many areas and there are usually long waiting lists for marina berths. Moorings are usually controlled by the maritime authority of the particular State government and can be rented for a small annual fee. So if you are planning a short cruise, use the excellent anchorages.

Weather
The best cruising time is April to October, when north-easterly sea breezes blow at a steady 10–12 kn on to the north-east coast. They are, however, interspersed with cyclones.

Useful addresses
Cruising information is available from the appropriate State Tourist Office. Chartering companies include Sail Australia Pty Ltd, 23a King George St, Lavender Bay, North Sydney, NSW 2060; Halvorsen Boats, PO Box 21, Turramurra, NSW 2074; Clippers Anchorage Pty Ltd, Coal and Candle Creek, PO Box 63, Terrey Hills, NSW 2084; Australian Bareboat Charters, Box 115, Airlie Beach, Queensland 4800; Queensland Yacht Charters, PO Box 2821, Sydney, NSW 2001 and Mandalay Sailing, PO Box 218, Airlie Beach, Queensland 4800.

Successful mooring

Too often, skippers find themselves fazed by the crowded conditions (and the omnipresent spectators) when the time comes to exercise their skills at mooring and anchoring. A little practice soon produces an understanding of the factors affecting the handling of the boat at slow speeds.

Manoeuvring under sail is one of the purest forms of sailing, although now, regrettably, it is becoming the province of those who like to frequent uncrowded anchorages, because many harbour authorities now actively discourage sailing in the waters under their jurisdiction. All mooring and anchoring manoeuvres, under sail or power, must be undertaken slowly, accurately and with intelligent use of wind and tide.

Many marinas are located in estuaries where the tidal stream must be taken into account when planning to berth or to leave. Tidal streams are, too frequently, overlooked in the apparent shelter of a marina complex, so when using an unfamiliar berth or boat, check the tidal flow on a mooring buoy or pile to gauge the extent to which turns and approach and exit routes must be modified.

When reversing, always operate the engine gently unless your boat has a folding propeller. Modern designs are not generally very good at going astern because of the usual 'fin and skeg' keel and rudder configuration. Boats with spade-rudders however, are very controllable in reverse.

Before attempting to approach or leave a mooring, weigh up all the observed variables against the known turning characteristics and drifting attitude of your boat. Determine the principal danger areas and make your plan known to everyone involved.

Mooring successfully is to achieve your aim without causing bother or damage to other water users – it does not matter if what you do is unorthodox.

Downwind, jib only

Crosswind, mainsail only

Upwind, both sails

Mooring under sail requires slow speeds. The boat's angle to the wind dictates which sails to use. An upwind approach is best carried out under both sails. On a reach, when the wind acts as a controllable accelerator, use the mainsail only. When approaching downwind, a small, easily lowered headsail provides some control. Whenever possible, however, luff up and moor under mainsail only.

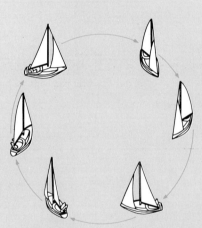

The boat's stern swings out when turning, in the same way as a supermarket cart. When going astern, the bow swings wide. Use

Tiller   Wheel

this 'skidding' effect to slide the bow or stern into or out of a marina berth.

When reversing to starboard, push the tiller to port or turn the wheel to starboard.

Arrivals and departures

Drift

The natural drifting attitude assumed by a boat is determined by its shape and reflects how it will respond when manoeuvring, since it will perpetually strive to take up its natural position. Shallow-draft boats drift more readily and have a larger turning circle than deep-keeled boats which have greater 'bite' in the water. The height of the hull above water (the freeboard) also influences a boat's windage. High bows tend to blow away from the wind, high deckhouses cause sideways drift. Strong winds exaggerate drifting tendencies and may even stop the boat completely.

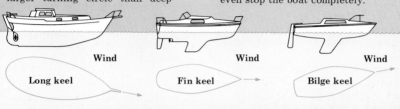

Long keel   Wind

Fin keel   Wind

Bilge keel   Wind

Wind

When
approaching or leaving a mooring, remember that the boat turns in a wider circle towards the wind than away from it.

Modify turns to account for the tidal flow. In still water the boat will make a perfect circle once well started in its motion.

When turning
towards a weak tide, the boat will swing out, etching a figure 9 in the water.

Circling away from a weak current elongates, rather than compresses, the turn into a figure 6.

When turning
towards a strong tidal stream, the boat is forced into a tight turn.

A boat is pushed downstream while it turns when circling away from strong tides.

Checklist

1 Use all the boat's equipment to aid you. Ropes and fenders are your principal allies; your worst enemy is speed.

2 Always have an escape route in case things go wrong. It should take you away from the mooring, allowing time to reappraise the correct approach. It is more seamanlike to abandon a bad approach than to crash.

3 Use a vacant mooring buoy to experiment with approaches and departures. Try to keep the bow or stern within 3 ft (1 m) of the buoy, both uptide and downtide of it. If you overrun the mooring, engage neutral and wait for the buoy to bob up again to avoid fouling the propeller.

4 Sailing boats are notoriously unpredictable when going astern. Use reverse as a brake, or to kick the stern into a berth or away from an obstruction. To steer in reverse, push the tiller away from the direction you wish the stern to go or turn the wheel towards it. Try facing the stern to orientate yourself.

5 Determine the natural drifting tendencies of your boat by experimenting under bare poles.

6 In tidal waters, establish the state of the tide, and check mooring lines frequently.

The different moorings

Most marinas offer alongside berths in finger pontoons/slips. Some, however, have pairs of piles (fixed wooden or metal stakes driven into the sea bed), which provide fore and aft attachment points. In many harbours, tidal estuaries and creeks, traditional mooring buoys are still available.

Before approaching any mooring, ensure that no ropes are hanging over the side. Start the engine, check the water, gears and fuel. Lower and stow the sails.

Prepare two short mooring warps by passing an end outside the lifelines and rigging and back through the fairleads to a cleat or mooring post at the bow and stern. Loosely coil the free ends of the warps and lay them on deck amidships.

Securely fasten the fenders on the side they will be needed, and lay the boathook on the coach/cabin trunk roof. Modify your approach to allow for the wind and tide.

When planning to moor at a marina, remember to book a berth on your VHF radio, unless you need only a temporary fuel or visitor's berth.

Enter cautiously along the row opposite your berth to allow a wide swing in. When the boat's beam passes the end of the pontoon/slip, two of the crew can leap ashore with bow and stern lines, and a short burst astern should stop the boat. Securely cleat the bow and stern lines, rig springs and, if necessary, breast ropes, then adjust fenders for position and height.

Before leaving, ensure dues have been paid, warm the engine and brief the crew. Release bow and stern lines last and reverse slowly out of the berth collecting shore crew on the way. Clear, coil and stow warps and clean and stow fenders.

When moored in a trot, perhaps six deep, obtain the cooperation of boats either side and slip out in the same direction as the strongest element: wind or tide.

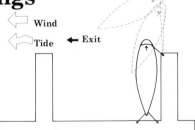

To leave a finger pontoon/slip when wind and tide are both moving across the exit of the berth, rig a doubled line from the stern cleat to the end of the windward pontoon, and reverse. When the bow is almost clear, snub the doubled warp around a sheet winch, and turn the tiller to swing clear. The line will run clear when one end is freed.

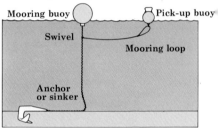

Approach a swinging mooring so that the crew can hook the small buoy aboard and secure the chain to the bow cleat. Point into the strongest element to coincide with the heading of moored boats. If they face in all directions, try a downwind approach.

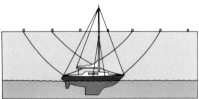

Plan to arrive at a tidal wall near high tide, to get the lines ashore easily. Check the water depth at low tide and the position of ladders. Protect the boat with fenders, fender boards and anti-chafe and, if berthing outside another boat, take your own lines to the jetty.

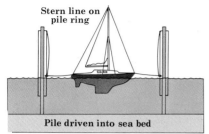

Stern line on pile ring

Pile driven into sea bed

Tools of the trade
The minimum number of mooring ropes required is: two the same length as the boat (breast ropes); two, 1½ times the length – usually the strongest pair – (springs); and two twice the length of the boat (bow and stern ropes). Also known as lines, warps and springs, they should be three-strand and also reasonably stretchy. Floating polypropylene rope is ideal. Use plastic tubes or old sail material to protect the warps from chafe, particularly where they rub against the quay/dockside.

1 Stern line	4 Aft spring
2 Aft breast line	5 Fore breast line
3 Fore spring	6 Bow line

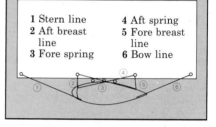

When mooring to piles, approach against the strongest element, usually the tide. Slip a doubled stern line round downtide pile. As the bow reaches the uptide post, slip the bow line through the mooring ring. Haul in on stern line and pass through the ring. The boat lies between the two posts.

Anchor

Fouled anchors

Buoys

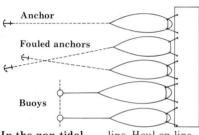

In the non-tidal Mediterranean, boats are usually moored stern-to-quay/dock. Reverse slowly towards line of buoys parallel to quay and attach a bow line. Haul on line running to the quay and secure stern lines to quay. Alternatively, drop a bow anchor well out and swing stern to quay.

Fenders absorb the shock when coming alongside and protect the hull once moored. They should be attached to cleats, toe rails, cabin-top grab rails or stanchion bases, but never directly to the lifelines, because this imposes unfair stress on the guard rail. Each should be fitted with a 5–6 ft (1½–2 m) line. Always keep a minimum of six fenders on board.

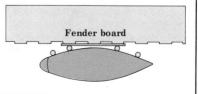

When mooring alongside a quay/dock, particularly one with buttresses, attach a ladder or plank of wood outside the fenders so that the board rests against the quay.

Wind

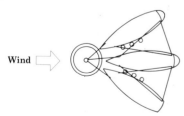

To leave a large mooring buoy when sandwiched between two boats, release your neighbour's stern-line, then your own line from the next boat. Motor slowly ahead to push the windward boat. As a leeward gap forms, release the bow line and reverse out.

Fender board

A choice of anchor

As marinas with their parking facilities have burgeoned, the factory-produced boats have not encouraged anchoring skills; often they are not equipped with even the basics for lying to an anchor.

But as sailors gather experience, they tend to venture away from protected marinas to the independence of anchorages in remote areas – and as a result anchoring assumes greater importance.

As a rough guide, the standard equipment for a cruising boat should be a large main anchor, rigged with a chain, and a smaller kedge anchor, with a short length of chain and a long nylon warp. The strength and high-stretch properties of nylon minimize the snatching loads experienced in rough conditions.

The main anchor should weigh 1 lb (0.5 kg) for every 1 ft (30 cm) of boat length and the kedge about 20 per cent less. There is no substitute for weight, despite marked advances in design.

When cruising, carry two different types of anchor, to suit the conditions of the sea bed. For example, to equip a 30-ft (9-m) boat for cruising in the Caribbean or the English Channel, you would need a 30–35 lb (14–16 kg) CQR main anchor with 30 fm (54 m) of chain, size $\frac{5}{16}$ in (4.5 mm) and an 18–20 lb (8–9 kg) Bruce kedge anchor with 6 m of chain, size $\frac{5}{16}$ in (4.5 mm) and 100 m of braided or cable laid nylon warp, size 18 mm. If you are venturing into rocky or weedy anchorages, take a 25-lb (11-kg) fisherman's anchor. When sailing off the USA, you will need a Danforth, plus a yachtsman's anchor for holding in storms.

Chain is sold in 15 fm lengths, and sized in inches across the metal of the link, while rope is sized in millimetres diameter or inches circumference, so use conversion charts when ordering. Anchor winches are designed to accept a specific size of chain, so order both together.

The traditional fisherman's anchor is useful when cruising in areas with rocky sea beds. As only one fluke digs in to the sea bed, it relies on its own weight and that of the rock it snags for holding power, and it may drag in loose sand.

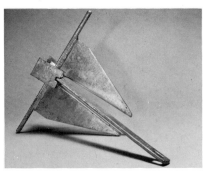

The Danforth, an American design, holds well in mud, sand and river mouth silt, but is unreliable in rock and weed. Its crown design and flat flukes make it easy to stow but often hard to break out from the sea bed.

A bow shackle, 1, passes through the last link in the anchor chain and the pin is secured with non-corrosive wire.

A swivel, 2, inserted at any join in the anchor cable, allows the system to turn freely.

The table headed: Size of chain, 1, weight of CQR type anchor, 2, size of nylon warp, 3, and displacement in tons, 4.

1	2	3						4
7/16"	55lb 25 kg	2¼"						20
		5.6 cms						18
	45lb 20 kg							16
								14
	35lb 15 kg	2"						12
		5 cms						10
3/8"	25lb 11 kg	1½"						8
	15lb 6 kg	3.8 cms						6
5/16"		1"						4
	51lb 2 kg	2.5 cms						2
		(ft): 20	24	28	32	36	40	44
		(metres):	7	8	9	10	11	12

The CQR 'plough' anchor is designed to burrow beneath sand, mud, weed, shell and overlying gravel, as well as into mixed sand and rock. The hinged, angled shank encourages the anchor to bite, although it often takes a while to hold.

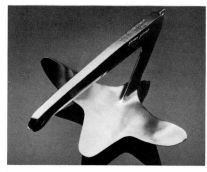

The Bruce anchor, designed to secure the giant North Sea oil rigs, slices deep into sand or mud with its semi-circular flukes. Light to handle and with high holding power to weight, it is efficient on short scope but may drag in rock.

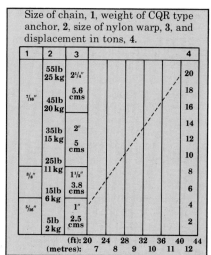

To join rope to chain when the rope is too thick to go through the last link, unravel about six turns. Loop strands 1 and 2 through the last link and unravel 3 six turns more. Lay strand 2 into 3's place. Join 2 and 3 with an overhand knot and tuck in 1.

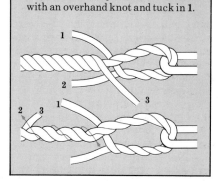

A D-shaped shackle, 3, is used to join each 15-fm (27-m) length of chain. The rounded end faces the anchor to prevent fouling when it is let out.

Mark the anchor rope and chain with, for example, one knotted cord or coloured stripe for each 30 ft (9 m).

Foredeck fittings

In very severe conditions, the loads imposed on deck fittings are enormous, especially if the yacht is pitching into a confused sea. It is essential, therefore, that when your equipment is put to the test, every part of your anchoring system is man enough for the job. Equipment is only as strong as the weakest link, so choose each element carefully.

Few production boats are fitted with adequate bow fittings, capable of receiving the chain or warp from any angle. Even quite substantial fittings are often not adequately secured to the hull with bolts and backing pads. This may not matter in normal situations, but can become critical in extreme conditions, so check and, if necessary, reinforce all the attachment points.

Ideally, a bow fitting should have two large rollers divided by a substantial metal fence. The sides should be high enough to accommodate the largest chain and a large-diameter dropnose pin should be added to prevent the chain jumping out.

When buying a boat, check that the bow fitting is sited so that the chain does not foul the forestay fitting as it is hauled in, particularly if there is an anchor windlass.

Once the anchor has been laid, the rope or chain is wound round a cleat or bollard. Rope can be tied with a bowline. The end of the rope or chain must be secured to a large through-bolted eye by means of a light line which can be easily cut away in an emergency. In theory, you should never let your chain out so far – but it happens!

It is becoming common practice to stow either a Bruce or a CQR anchor in the bow roller, to which it is attached by a steel pin. The chain can be fed down to the locker below through a navel pipe. It may have a watertight cover, or a hinged cover with a slot for a link of chain.

Pulpit stowage in a moulded deck well, *above*, leaves the anchor ready for use, with chain and warp attached. The end of the warp should be secured to a cleat or eye in the well.

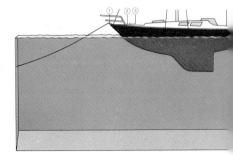

Ideally, a bow fitting should have two large rollers, *left,* with a dividing metal fence. High sides to the fitting and a large diameter pin should prevent even the largest size of chain from jumping out. A windlass, hand operated, *left,* or electric takes away the strain of hauling in an anchor. The CQR anchor, *below,* is conveniently stowed in the bow roller for ease of handling and held by a strong steel drop-nose pin.

The anchor chain is led on board through a bow roller, and is held in place by a large-diameter pin or a chain pawl. After it has been hauled in, by hand or windlass, it is secured to a post or cleat on the foredeck, **2.** In many boats the chain is fed below through a navel pipe, **3.** The last link of the chain is secured to a metal eye bolt, with a light line, which can be cut in an emergency.

Checklist
1 When dropping anchor, do not stand on chain or rope.
2 When paying out or hauling in, never take a turn around your hand.
3 Sit on the foredeck with feet braced against the base of the pulpit. Try to pull by straightening your legs, not bending your back.
4 Never cleat chain or rope with a half hitch; it will often jam.
5 Always buy chain which has been tested for strength and calibrated.
6 Be sure the chain locker is well ventilated, as the anchor will bring plenty of slime aboard.
7 The working anchor is let out over the port bow in the northern hemisphere, since the wind veers as a low front passes. If a second anchor is let out over the starboard bow during the blow, the two cables will then not cross as the boat swings round.
8 Stow anchor warp loosely in a well or rolled up on a reel.

The chain must be secured to the boat so that it will not slip, yet can be easily released, even under load. For this purpose, a post or bollard is preferable to a cleat. Take two turns around the bollard, **1,** then take a loop under the taut chain and slip it over the bollard, **2.** Cleats used for securing chain, **3,** should be large and mounted on a wooden pad to raise them above the deck. Take one turn round the cleat then twist a loop of chain over the front end of the cleat, **4.**

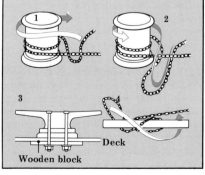
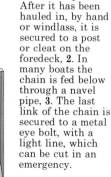

How to anchor

Watch out for local styles of anchoring, when venturing into new cruising areas. You may be accustomed to laying two anchors, up and down, in a strong tide but find when you cruise in foreign waters that it is customary to lay anchors across the tidal stream. If its swinging pattern is different, your boat will cause chaos with neighbouring boats at the change of tide.

Careful preparation is needed before dropping the anchor over the side. First the anchor must be freed from its stowage and positioned, ready for release at the appropriate moment. As you will usually anchor under power, the mainsail should be loose-stowed, all the ropes brought inboard and headsails removed from the foredeck to give ample space.

If the chain has been detached from the anchor, shackle it on and secure the pin with wire or thin line. If you are using a windlass, check that the brake can be released by slacking it right off and moving the gypsy, then tighten it. If paying it out by hand, flake about 5.5 fm (10 m) of chain along the deck ready for anchoring. If using rope, put the drum in its housing or ensure that rope which has been flaked into a locker is free to run out.

Your final approach to your chosen spot should be into the strongest element so that when the anchor is released, the boat drifts away from it. Never drop the anchor at the spot where you wish the boat to end up.

If you are anchoring in a rocky area or one which is known to contain debris, it may be wise to rig a line to the anchor and attach a float which will show at high water – usually a fender with ANCHOR written on it. In crowded anchorages, however, it is almost impossible to use an anchor buoy since an unwary newcomer is likely to moor up to it or catch it in his propeller.

If you still want a line, lash it to the chain and bring it back on board.

A lunch hook – anchoring for a short stay to eat a meal or sit at a favourite anchorage – highlights the value of a second anchor. Its light weight and short length of chain and nylon warp allow younger members of the family to practise the 'black art'. If other boats have used chain instead of rope in a crowded anchorage, do likewise, to follow their swinging patterns.

For a short stay of a few hours, twice anchor cable to water depth (short scope) with a kedge anchor is usually enough. If you extend your stay you will need to lay your main anchor and more chain.

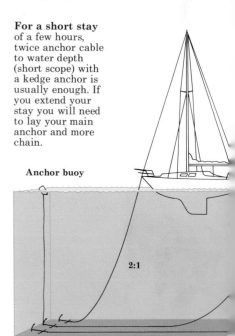

Anchor buoy

2:1

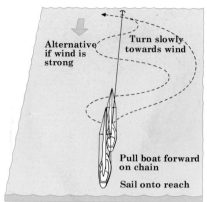

Alternative if wind is strong

Turn slowly towards wind

Pull boat forward on chain

Sail onto reach

Seek an anchorage sheltered from the wind and waves by land and off-shore reefs. Consult the chart for good anchorages (indicated with an anchor symbol), for water depths and tidal information. Use the echo sounder to verify the depths and, since anchors hold best on flat surfaces, to locate areas free from ridges, holes and slopes. Use a lead 'armed' with grease to collect a sample of the sand, shingle, mud, weed or coral on the sea bed. If it picks up nothing look for any marks on the lead that may have been made by rock.

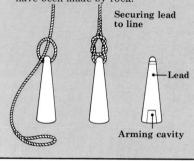

Securing lead to line

Lead

Arming cavity

When it is time to leave, and the boat is pointing towards the wind hoist the mainsail. Haul in enough chain to break out the anchor and cleat it. Sail the boat in a broad arc until the chain begins to slacken, and can be hauled in. Tack and sail slowly towards the anchor until it can be pulled on board. As the boat sails on, stow the anchor gear and set the headsail.

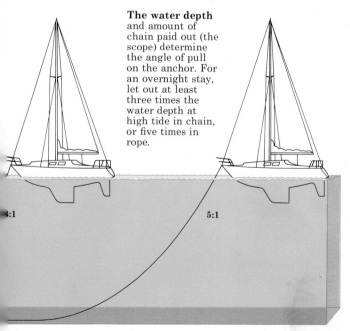

3:1

5:1

The water depth and amount of chain paid out (the scope) determine the angle of pull on the anchor. For an overnight stay, let out at least three times the water depth at high tide in chain, or five times in rope.

If strong winds are expected, or if the tidal current is strong, pay out chain to five times the depth. Choose a well-protected anchorage, check every shackle and pin and set the anchor firmly by going astern. This will also take out slack in the chain on the sea bed. The weight of the chain gives extra stability to the anchor and ensures horizontal pull, free from stretch or tugging. To hold the boat steady in gale conditions, a second anchor is often advisable.

Two anchors for security

Major anchoring problems can arise when strong winds and tides are opposed, causing the boat to swing wildly around its anchor. If more than 1 kn of tide or 15 kn of wind is expected, drop a second anchor, to allow the boat to lie securely between two fixed points.

The use of two anchors requires careful planning and preparation. In case you have to weather out a gale, carry a large mooring swivel to which both anchors can be attached without risk of tangling the chains. This method does, however, mean that the anchors take the strain alternately rather than together.

To take the strain on both anchors simultaneously, lay the ground chain across the wind or tide. The easiest method is to lay the kedge with its long warp, and motor across the wind or tide. When the warp runs out, drop the main anchor and, as the boat swings back toward the kedge, veer the chain and take in the slack of the kedge warp until the boat lies mid-way between both anchors. Then attach the warp to the chain and release the chain until the knot is about 10 ft (3 m) below the surface.

The last anchor down is normally the first to be taken up. If the mooring swivel is used, the smaller anchor may have to be retrieved with the anchor buoy. When it is stowed, haul the swivel aboard, cleat the chain and bring in the buoyed rising chain. Once the swivel from both ground and rising chain is removed, shackle the chains together before stowing. Haul in the rest of the chain and the anchor.

Anchoring offshore is another traditional skill to suffer from the proliferation of marinas. To anchor under sail, first determine the depth and nature of the bottom, drop and stow the headsail. Once abeam of the anchorage, gently turn head to wind, drop anchor as the boat comes to a standstill and lower the mainsail.

Lee shore survival

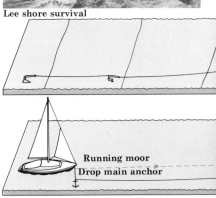

Running moor
Drop main anchor

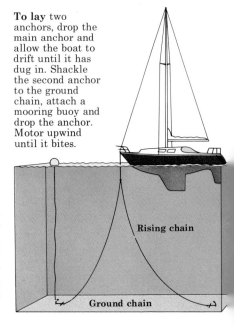

To lay two anchors, drop the main anchor and allow the boat to drift until it has dug in. Shackle the second anchor to the ground chain, attach a mooring buoy and drop the anchor. Motor upwind until it bites.

Rising chain

Ground chain

If gale force winds are blowing you on to a lee shore, it is safer and cheaper to anchor as a last resort than to run the boat on to mud flats or rock. Use the anchors in tandem: drop the kedge, attach its cable to the crown of the main anchor and lower both. Veer most of the chain and cleat. Attach a mooring swivel to the end of the chain, fasten two warps to the inboard eye of the swivel. Take the warps back to the main winches, which are designed for heavy loads, then secure.

Checklist
1 Approach your anchorage against the strongest element – wind or tide. Have anchor and cable ready on deck in good time.
2 Always anchor at least two anchor scopes (lengths of cable lowered) from any other boat, and, if anchoring with chain, allow yachts with nylon rope a wider berth.
3 The boat that anchors first has 'right of way'.
4 To test if the anchor is holding, pull gently on the chain or warp. If a grating, snatching action can be felt, the anchor is skimming over the bottom, probably on its side.
5 Even though the anchor appears to be holding, it may drag when the tide changes.
6 A thick warp is easier to pull on than a thin one.
7 When using nylon warp, guard against chafe.

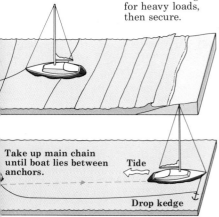

Take up main chain until boat lies between anchors.

Tide

Drop kedge

If your main anchor chain is made up of three standard 15-fm (27-m) lengths, shackle a mooring swivel to the centre of the 30 fm (55 m) which will become ground chain. Remove 15 fm (27 m) at the D–Shackle, and attach to the free end of the swivel, to form the rising chain. The second anchor chain is then shackled to the swivel or the kedge warp attached to the main anchor chain, *below*.

If precision is required, anchor under power rather than sail. Start the engine, lower the sails and motor gently against the wind or tide, to help slow the boat and give greater control when neutral is engaged. When the chosen point is reached, and the boat almost stationary, drop anchor. The wind will push the boat back away from the anchor, pulling it along the sea bed until it digs in. A powerful burst astern will check that the anchor is holding well. When leaving under power, plan your course, brief the crew and motor forward to break out the anchor.

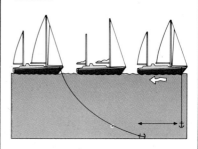

Mooring swivel

ing chain

1 **Three turns round chain**
2 **Back over warp**
3 **Take loop through bottom two loops**
4 **Tighten with care**

Anchoring emergencies

Anchoring skills are often learned the hard way so, whenever possible, anchor a good distance from other boats. This allows more room for manoeuvre, more time to react if you drag, and an easier departure.

A dragging anchor can be the cause of a lot of damage so always check that the anchor is holding. This can be done by feel, with a hand on the chain: if the pull is steady, the anchor has set; if it snatches, the anchor is skimming over the bottom probably on its side. Try letting out more warp or chain; if it still will not set, however, it must be hauled up and dropped elsewhere. Transits (aligned landmarks) or compass bearings can also be used to indicate any movement from the original anchoring position.

In fog, rough weather or potentially dangerous situations, it may be necessary to organize anchor watches. One member of the crew is constantly available to check transits and bearings to ensure that the boat is not drifting.

When the anchor will not leave the sea bed, you have a fouled anchor. Let out some rope or chain and motor in a circle, keeping tension on the warp, and occasionally go astern away from the anchor. If fouled under a rock or in a crevice, it will come free. If this does not work and there is some give in the chain, winch it in and release it suddenly. If the offending obstruction was rope or chain, the anchor may then fall free.

Power cables can be a hazard, so if the chart shows wavy magenta lines or you can see yellow diamond shapes on the shore line, do not anchor. If you do foul a power cable, buoy the last 15 fm (27 m) of chain and report to the local harbour master to find out if the wire is 'live'. With old cables, haul in the cable to get the wire as close to the surface as possible, somehow slip a rope under it to hold it and lower the anchor free.

A visual reference can determine if the anchor is dragging. Once the anchor is set, and the boat settled, line up two stationary objects. Take another transit at right angles to the first. Draw a circle on the chart around your position of a radius equal to the length of cable out. If the transits put you outside the circle, you are dragging, not swinging.

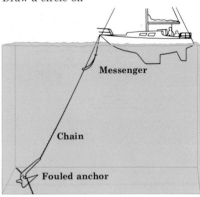

Messenger

Chain

Fouled anchor

If a fouled anchor cannot be freed by motoring round it in a circle, try using a messenger. Lower a loop of chain with a very large shackle on a line down the cable. Shake it about until it reaches the anchor and slips over it. Attach a buoy to the last 15 fm (27 m) of chain and drop it over the side. Motor fast away and try to jerk the anchor out in the opposite direction with the messenger line.

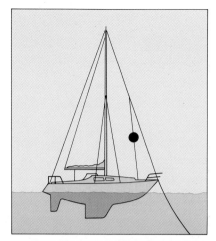

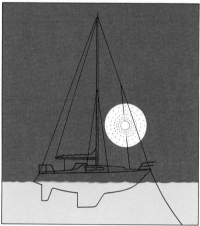

The yacht's tender can be used to lay a second anchor. An inflatable will operate more efficiently astern, particularly when towing a very long rope. Flake the warp into the tender so that it does not increase drag as you row away. When enough cable for the depth is in the tender, make fast the other end to the boat. If the anchor is very heavy hang it under the tender with a rope strop secured with a slip knot. Row or motor upwind or tide as quickly as possible, then across to the anchor point, release the slip knot or lower the anchor to the sea bed.

The tender may also be needed to retrieve a firmly entrenched anchor.

1 **Form bight with one rope**
2 **Thread second rope through bight, and around it**
3 **Then through under itself and tighten Pull to release**

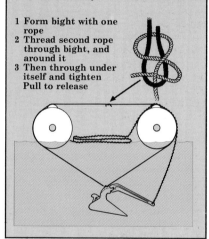

In daylight, you must, by law, display a black spherical ball forward of the mast. At night, carry an all-round white anchor light in the same position.

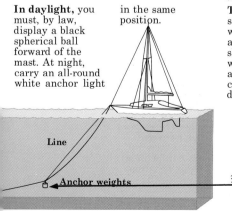

Line

Anchor weights

To dampen the snatching action when a boat is anchored in waves, shackle an anchor weight or another anchor over the chain. Slide it down on a line

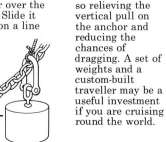

until it lies midway between the sea bed and the surface. This 'angel' makes a curve in the cable, so relieving the vertical pull on the anchor and reducing the chances of dragging. A set of weights and a custom-built traveller may be a useful investment if you are cruising round the world.

The range of ropes

One of the greatest sources of confusion on board a boat is the multiplicity of ropes required to hoist and control the sails, and to moor or anchor. The illusion of chaos is only heightened by modern practice which dictates that most ropes must be led aft to the cockpit.

Rope manufacturers have tried to simplify matters by producing colour-coded ropes as an aid to identification, and designers have incorporated rope-handling systems into some production craft, in an effort to tidy up the cockpit.

Modern synthetic ropes are now so refined that they duplicate the easy handling characteristics of the very best natural fibres, but have the great advantage of being resistant to rot and heavy wear.

The arch-enemies of synthetic rope are grit and sunshine. Grit squeezes between the strands and finds its way to the interior of the rope where it saws away at the inner fibres, and ultraviolet light accelerates the decay of synthetics, so wash them occasionally in fresh water and stow them in a dark locker after use. Abrasion is a frequent problem with halyards and control lines which constantly wear in the same place.

If the halyards run inside the mast, a permanent messenger line will allow a new halyard to be attached and fed through. If the messenger breaks a bicycle chain (or a sink plug chain on smaller masts) will serve as an efficient weight for encouraging the line down the mast, and can be hooked out through the bottom sheave.

Damaged ropes should be replaced immediately, but in emergencies a thinner rope can, if necessary, be interwoven to replace the damaged strands. Old sheets and halyards make excellent mooring lines, especially in commercial harbours where you may want to protect your best warps from oil and grit.

Three-stranded or laid rope makes good mooring warp. The lightest synthetic, polypropylene, is quite suitable, since it floats. It is also the least expensive.

Polyester three-strand rope is pre-stretched during manufacture and is ideal for sheets and halyards, which should not 'give'. It will not shrink but may kink when wet.

Imitation manila is strong, smooth and shares the handling characteristics of natural fibre. Yet it will not rot or swell when wet.

Plaited rope, such as polyester 16-plait, gives the combined strength of 24 components and stretches 3.6 per cent, ideal for control lines and halyards.

Nylon rope stretches, but is twice as strong as manila and easy to handle, wet or dry; 16-plait nylon rope will bear heavy loads and is used for anchor warps.

Braidline consists of a plaited core of extra-strong inner fibres within a friction-resistant flexible plaited sheath which is easy to handle and grip. Strong, high-stretch and shock-absorbent, nylon braidline makes excellent anchor cable or halyards. It is soft, flexible, and does not kink or harden.

Ropes and knots

Bosun's bag

Every cruiser must carry the basic rope-repairing and improving equipment. Plastic tape is useful for sealing the ends of strands, to prevent unravelling and to guard against chafe. A gas lighter or blow torch can be used for heat-sealing. Whipping and seizing tools include some spools of waxed and unwaxed whipping twine, two sailmaker's needles and a well-fitting sailmaker's palm, used as a thimble. The Swedish fid, an alternative version of the marlin spike, is useful for splicing synthetic rope. Sail-repair tape must also be included, and spare pieces of sailcloth for each weight of sail which can double as anti-chafe protection for warps and running rigging. A knife with a wooden handle is useful: heat the blade on the cooker to cut and seal a rope in one move.

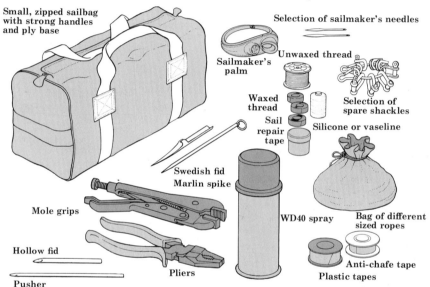

Small, zipped sailbag with strong handles and ply base

Selection of sailmaker's needles

Sailmaker's palm

Unwaxed thread

Waxed thread

Selection of spare shackles

Sail repair tape

Silicone or vaseline

Swedish fid
Marlin spike

Mole grips

WD40 spray

Bag of different sized ropes

Hollow fid

Pliers

Anti-chafe tape

Pusher

Plastic tapes

For easy recognition, many modern boats are equipped with colour-coded ropes. The system below is a good example.

Halyards
1 Genoa/jib (port/starboard) – blue
2 Spinnaker (port/starboard) – orange
3 Mainsail – black
Sheets
4 Genoa/jib (port/starboard) – gold
5 Reaching/change sheet – red
6 Spinnaker sheets (port/starboard) – red
7 Spinnaker guys (port/starboard) – blue
Control lines
8 Spinnaker pole downhaul – red
9 Baby stay tensioner – black
10 Clew outhaul – gold
11 Cunningham – blue
Mainsail
12 1st reef – red   13 2nd reef – blue
Running backstays
14 Port – red   15 Starboard – blue

The important knots

Strictly speaking a knot is found at the end of a rope, but the word has come to include a 'bend', used to tie two ropes together, or a 'hitch', used to secure a rope to another object. The simplest way to learn to tie the appropriate knot for the purpose is to volunteer for the deckhand's job when mooring or rigging the boat.

The best multi-purpose knot, and favourite of scouts and guides the world over, is the bowline. It can be used to secure a line to a bollard, a ring or a crossbeam; to fasten a safety line around your chest, or to haul someone out of the water; to make a bosun's chair or an improvised ladder. It is easily undone and imposes less strain on the rope than other knots: 42 per cent loss of strength, compared to 55 per cent with a reefknot and 50 per cent with a sheetbend.

A bosun's chair can be made from a doubled bowline by spreading the two loops for the bosun to sit in and hoisting him aloft on the halyard. This can, however, be extremely uncomfortable as the lower part of the body is compressed. If possible, make a permanent bosun's chair by incorporating a wooden seat, particularly if the bosun intends to work aloft. Thread the ends of two rope strops through a hole in each corner of the seat and splice them underneath it; then seize the strops together to form an eye.

In no circumstances should a snap shackle be used to attach the chair to the halyard. Instead, use a large D shackle and tighten the pin with pliers. Use two halyards, one for hoisting and one as a safety line, which should be secured round the chest of the person hoisted. Once the halyard is fixed to the seat, lead it back to the largest sheet winch or mast halyard winch and when the bosun is seated, smoothly winch it in, taking care to avoid riding turns. Another crew member maintains a steady hand over hand pull and watches the man aloft.

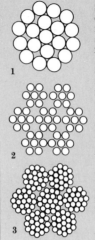

Steel rigging is either rod or wire rope. Shrouds and stays are made from stainless steel 1 × 19 wire rope, **1.** Seven wires twist anticlockwise round the central strand. The other 12 form an outer clockwise-twisting layer. 7 × 7 wire rope, **2,** may be used to splice on end fittings. Halyards should be flexible 7 × 19 galvanized, rather than stainless steel, rope, **3,** which can be spliced into the rope tail.

The simplest knot is the overhand or thumb knot, used to stop the end of a rope running through a block or up the mast.

Also made by the thumb or over the hand, the double overhand knot can be used on the end of genoa sheets, halyards and reefing lines, but not on spinnaker sheets or guys.

The figure-of-eight knot is also used to prevent ropes escaping, but if left can prove difficult to untie. For extra bulk, the end can be passed through a second time.

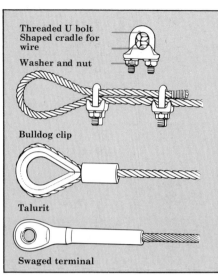

Threaded U bolt
Shaped cradle for
wire

Washer and nut

Bulldog clip

Talurit

Swaged terminal

Wire-to-rope connections
Where wire standing rigging connects to the mast or adjustable rigging screws, it must be bent to form an eye or opened into a self-locking device. In an emergency, such as dismasting, a good temporary eye can be made by bending the end into a loop with a mole wrench and securing it with the correct-sized bulldog clips. A talurit eye, suitable for small craft, consists of a soft nickel sleeve which is crimped over the doubled-over wire and secured under great pressure. The wire is bent round a metal thimble for reinforcement. In the swaged terminal, a hard metal or plastic core is inserted into the end of the splayed wire.

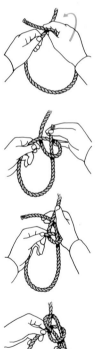

To make a bowline, hold the rope about 6 in (15 cm) from the end with your 'working' hand. Lay the end over the rope, palm down, supporting the rope with the other hand.

Twist the working hand away from you so that the rope end points up towards you through the loop which is produced.

Grasp the crossover between your finger and thumb. Take the end up and behind the rope then feed it down through the loop.

Tighten the knot slowly so that the loop and the turn are in equal tension. The end should be 2–3 in (5–8 cm) long.

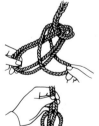

For a doubled bowline (on the bight), start to tie a large loop in the end of a rope with a single bowline.

Make the first stage of the bowline with a loop instead of an end. Pass the loop round and down over the lower part of the main loop, to form a second loop.

Work the single loop slowly up and put it over the doubled rope close to the original single knot.

Spread the two loops to form the seat of a bosun's chair.

How to handle rope

Handling and coiling ropes
Always coil ropes or the ends of ropes not in use, as kinks will reduce their strength and may jam in a block when the coil comes free. Use both hands to coil a rope, supporting it in, say, the left hand and feeding it with the right. Swing the arms apart, gathering a length across the body, then swing together to collect the coil. A coiling rhythm produces even lengths of rope. Coil right-handed rope clockwise and left-handed rope anticlockwise; braided rope should be snaked into a figure-of-eight. Hang up ropes not in use rather than lay them in the bottom of a locker. When breaking open a new coil, lead off an end anti-clockwise, or the rope will kink.

Coil rope clock-wise and twist to flatten.

When only 4 ft (1.22 m) of rope remain, take three turns round coil.

Pass the looped end through top of coil.

Take loop right over top of coil and pull free end to fasten.

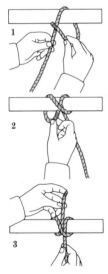

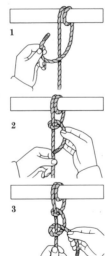

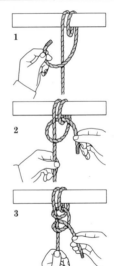

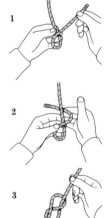

A clove hitch is used to attach a fender to the grab rails. Pass the rope-end forward over the rail, **1**, bring it up to the right, behind the standing part, **2**. Loop over the rail and tuck in to the crossover, **3**.

A more secure variation on the clove hitch is to wrap the rope once round the rail, **1**, and then tie two half hitches on the standing part, **2**. It is used to tie a rope to a spar, rail or shroud.

A fisherman's bend will secure a rope to a ring or an anchor, and thick rope to a thin shroud or lifeline. Pass the rope through the ring twice, **1**; pass the end round, **2**, and back through the turns, **3**.

The figure-of-eight overhand hitch is a secure, and useful stopper knot. Loop the end through the ring, **1**, take it back round the standing part, **2**, then thread it back through the loop, **3**.

94

When heaving a line, always re-coil the rope and check (by eye) that it is long enough to reach the quay or another boat before throwing it. Hold a few coils in one hand and throw the rest of the rope in tighter coils by swinging the arm back and leaning the opposite shoulder towards the target. Aim well above the target and allow the rope to fly free.

A rope may jam or slip if it is incorrectly cleated. Always take the rope to the back of the cleat first and take a round turn around the base, 1. Then take several figure-of-eight turns around both horns, 2. For extra security, take a final full turn round the base of the cleat, 3.

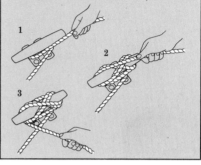

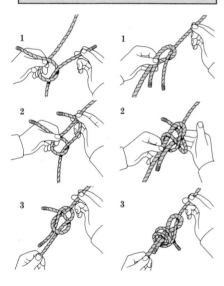

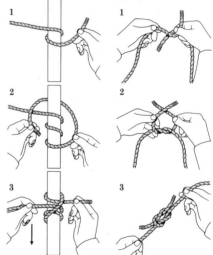

Use a sheet bend to join two ropes. Make a loop with the thicker rope, 1, and pass the other up through it, around the back, 2, then across under itself, 3. Both short ends must lie the same side or it slips.

A double sheet bend is used when one rope is much thinner. Make a loop in the thicker rope, 1, continue as for a single sheet bend, 2, but making two turns or more, 3.

A rolling hitch can be used to free a sheet or halyard from a riding turn on the winch. Wrap the end twice round the sheet, 1, take it back, make a half hitch, 2, and tighten, 3. Wind the end on a free winch.

When tying reefing points, use the reef knot which holds well under pressure, but is easily freed. Tied correctly, 1, and, 2, the reef knot appears as two symmetrically linked loops, 3.

Splices and eyes

Splicing is the joining of two ropes in an attempt to preserve their strength. After a few basic starting sequences, it consists mainly of tucking the strands over and under each other. The simplest and quickest way of forming an eye in a rope or joining two ropes together is the tuck splice. The tucked join, **1**, is made by twisting the ends of two ropes together. The tucked eye, **2**, is formed by laying the end of the rope under a strand in several places. Whip or tape the ends.

1

2

Preparation is essential on all synthetic ropes because they unravel easily. All splices are started by untwisting the rope to the desired length. At the point where the unlaying ends, tape or whip the limit of the strands and the end of each strand, to prevent further unravelling. Join two ropes together with a short splice to get the feel of the sequence of tucking in the ends. Always make the tucks against the lay of the other rope, and at right angles to it.

1

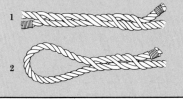

2

3

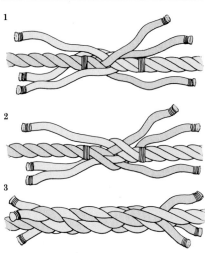

1

2

3

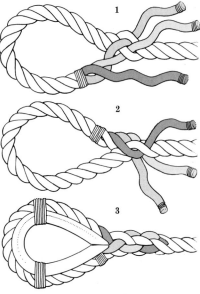

To make a short splice, unlay the ends of both ropes for three turns, **1**. Mesh the strands together so that each passes between two strands of the other rope, **2**. Splice in one end at a time, passing each over its neighbour and under the next strand, against the lay of the rope. Repeat twice. Pull the ends tight, turn the work over and splice in the other three strands, **3**. Tighten and roll between the hands; trim and seal the ends.

To make a permanent eye, unlay four turns, form a loop and tuck the centre, then the left-hand strand against the lay, **1**. Turn the splice over to tuck in third strand, **2**. Take two extra tucks. Cut the ends and heat-seal. To reinforce a 'soft' eye, incorporate a metal thimble, **3**, and secure with whipping.

To splice rope to wire, first unravel 9 in (22 cm) of the wire and whip the junctions; 7 × 7 wire can be divided into 2 × 2 and 1 × 3 to produce three strands. Unravel about 1 in (2.5 cm) of the rope, 1, and, meshing the wire and rope strands as evenly as possible, whip the rope firmly to the wire. Tuck in the wire strands against the lay, taking care not to kink the wire, 2. Tape and tuck the rope and protect the whole length with an overall whipping, 3.

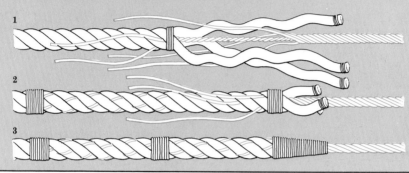

Mooring warps are usually made from eight strands, with two pairs running clockwise and two pairs anticlockwise. When splicing, the clockwise strands must be worked anticlockwise. Tape the ends of each pair of strands a different colour for clockwise and anticlockwise. Unlay three turns and put a whipping round clockwise strands, 1. Tuck uppermost clockwise pair, pointing to the left of the rope, down between clockwise pair, 2. Tuck in left pair and two remaining strands, as shown, 3.

Whipping and seizing techniques

Working with twine is an ideal way of introducing younger crew members to the skills of seamanship and since most heat sealing tends to break down after prolonged use, many owners are now taking up the whipping twine, palm and needle, as their predecessors did. First whippings should be quick and made without using the palm and needle to close up an already fraying rope. Raid the bosun's bag for waxed whipping thread. All whippings should be made against the lay of the rope to stop it twisting open. Take 18 in (46 cm) of thread, and beginning 1 in (2 cm) in, lay a loop of thread along the rope in the direction you are working and cover it with tightly wound thread. Put the end through the loop, pull the protruding thread and cut both ends to form a simple and secure whipping.

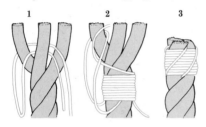

For a sailmaker's whipping, open a 3-strand rope and thread a loop of whipping thread loosely round one strand, **1**. Close the strands and wind the thread tightly round the rope, thread the end between the strands, and bring the loop back over its original strand, **2**. Pull the loop tight with the bottom end of the whipping. Tie the thread tightly to the top end with a reef knot, but make two or three twists to form final part of knot, **3**.

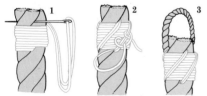

For a palm and needle whipping, push the doubled thread under one strand. Wind thread to top, take in another strand and tighten, **1**. Lead thread down to the base and back until the three grooves are filled. Finish with half hitches, **2**. To make a halyard strop, make a sailmaker's whipping and stitch a loop across the top, **3**.

An alternative way of joining ropes or making eyes, if it is not possible to splice them, is to lash them together with thin twine using a lot of tight turns. Known as seizing, this is particularly useful when joining plaited ropes. Another method is to stitch through both parts.

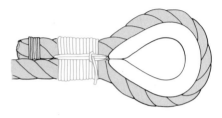

To form an eye with seizing, make a loop in the end of the seizing and attach it securely around the doubled ropes. Wind it round, using a marlin-spike hitch to tighten the turns. Make about eight turns, then loop the seizing around one of the points of the eye or lead it down inside the seizing through the looped end and tie an overhand knot.

A marlin-spike hitch is made by inserting a marlin spike into the loop of a slip knot so that more power can be applied when whipping or seizing the end of a rope, since twine is hard to grip firmly.

To join two ropes together at regular intervals use a crossed seizing. This is made in the same way as seizing an eye, but two or three turns are taken round the centre. Finish with two half hitches or by sewing the seizing into one of the ropes.

Having fun and playing with rope helps you to understand it better. You can often collect offcuts from your local chandler or occasionally your local rope maker. Youngsters lucky enough to go sailing regularly should each have their own bosun's bag containing many different samples of rope.

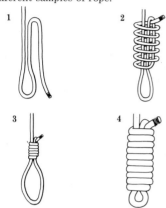

A hangman's knot will keep a young crew occupied for quite a while. Loop the end of the rope and double it back, 1. Make 13 round turns with the rest of the rope's end and pass it through the loop at the top, 2. Tighten up the round turns so that they grip firmly, 3. Now you have a running noose, 4.

A running figure-of-eight knot is useful for scooping up a floating object from shallow water, or even for tying parcels. Loop the end, twist it round in a figure-of-eight and tighten.

To attach a hook or swivel to a fishing line, loop the line through the eye, make four or five round turns. Bring the end down and tuck it back through the eye. Tighten it gently, especially if it is on a hook.

Blocks and tackle

Before the days of winches, blocks and tackles were used to lift heavy loads, to hoist sails and move spars. On modern boats, the best example is the mainsheet system, which has blocks and ropes to reduce the pull transmitted to the helmsman. The power of a purchase is calculated by counting the number of lines coming from the moving block or blocks. The simplest mechanical advantage is gained by using one pulley block on the load to be moved, such as the boom. It halves the effort required to pull the boom in and so has an advantage of 2:1. The bottom block here acts as an anchorage and turning block for the rope. A further advantage is gained by inserting another block at the moving point, to produce a 3:1 purchase. A fourth block with its own anchorage point will double the leverage power to 6:1. Applications on modern yachts include lifting out engines for overhaul and hoisting dinghies aboard.

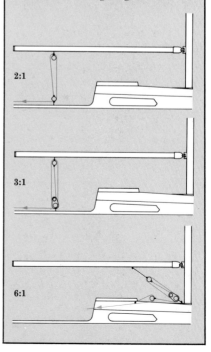

2:1

3:1

6:1

Choosing an engine

The basic decision for most owners is between petrol and diesel. Petrol/gasoline engines are lighter, smoother, less noisy and cheaper than diesel but they use expensive, potentially dangerous fuel, and need reliable electrical ignition systems. Diesel engines use a smelly but cheaper fuel and can remain reliable, despite periods of non-use. Few petrol engines are fitted as standard today.

Both types are available in 2- and 4-stroke form; 2-strokes are lighter and use more fuel, and are generally employed where light weight is important. Thus 2-stroke petrol outboards are often used for small, fast sports boats, and 2-stroke diesels in large, fast motor yachts.

The next consideration is the type of drive. The traditional system uses a propeller installed permanently under the boat and connected more or less directly by a shaft to an engine fitted inside the hull. This has the advantage of simplicity, but the propeller may be vulnerable and hard to get at. If the boat is of a size to take the ground regularly, or to be trailed, it may be much more sensible to fit an inboard/outboard drive. On boats under about 25 ft (7.6 m), it is probably easier to fit an outboard petrol engine, clear of the accommodation.

An increasingly common and inexpensive installation in lightweight sailing boats and small motor boats is the sail drive, where a petrol or diesel inboard engine is mounted through the hull bottom on a fixed outboard-type leg.

Two other factors should influence choice. Remember that the bigger and heavier a boat is, the bigger the propeller needed, regardless of the speed and power of the engine. Secondly, since boat engines are subject to heavy condensation in a salty atmosphere, maintenance is important. If you seldom use your boat choose outboard petrol or inboard diesel.

Outboard engines are convenient and cheap for smaller boats, the lower maintenance costs offsetting the heavier fuel consumption. Bracket mountings usually allow them to be lifted clear when sailing or even stowed below decks.

The sail drive consists basically of an outboard-engine-type propeller leg mounted through the bottom of the boat and driven by an engine mounted inboard. It is most suitable for modern sailing boats since it is convenient and simple, with the engine weight placed to best advantage. A folding propeller is often fitted.

Cavitation is caused by water vapour forming on the propeller but the term is loosely applied to any condition where the propeller races without gripping the water.

The exhaust is often discharged through the centre of the propeller in outboards or inboard/outboards. The straighter waterflow past the blades increases exhaust efficiency.

Cavitation

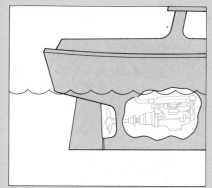

The straight drive is the simplest installation, with minimum loss of power. The engine is connected directly to a shaft and propeller, which can be well protected in an aperture, *above*, or in the open, supported by one or two shaft brackets.

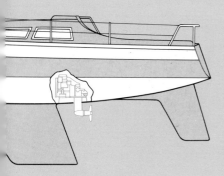

This compromise is generally used for higher-powered installations, where it is an advantage to fold the propeller leg out of the way for sailing or grounding.

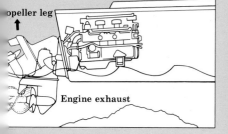

opeller leg ↑

Engine exhaust

Choice of propeller

A marine propeller works by the action of each blade creating lift from its aerofoil-type section along the line of the shaft – in a similar way to an aircraft propeller.

The slim two-bladed propeller is slow-moving, like a glider, and gives highly efficient lift for small power. It is, therefore, used for comparatively large hulls driven by small engines, and usually needs a reduction gear to reduce shaft speed.

With more power, the blade area has to increase, and with faster engine speeds, it is necessary to reduce the overall diameter to prevent too fast a tip speed: the resultant need for blade area has led to the three-bladed propeller, often with quite broad blades.

Three-blade propeller

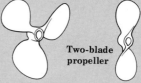

Two-blade propeller

Propellers come in all manner of blade shapes, but two specialized types should be mentioned. The 'weedless' has extended blade tips to prevent weed catching in fouled waters. The other, the 'cleaver', uses a special blunt-tailed form for ultra-high-speed racing power boats.

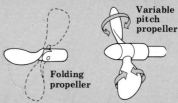

Variable pitch propeller

Folding propeller

The effect of centrifugal action throws the blades of folding propellers out into their working position when the shaft is turned. The blades of variable pitch propellers can be set in a number of positions, usually including reverse and a feathered position to reduce drag.

How much power?

The power required to drive a boat at any given practical speed increases with its weight, and for the same weight, decreases with length. The potential maximum or economical cruising speed varies greatly with the type of hull.

Heavy displacement hulls – some motor launches and most older-style sailing yachts – are limited by the wave-train they set up around themselves, and are at maximum speed when travelling essentially on one wave. Modern light displacement sailing boats and faster launches are shaped so as not to build up stern suction at speed. This means more power can be used to drive the hull up and on top of the single wave, so that it is partially supported by the effect of speed as well as buoyancy. Beyond this semi-planing range, boats shaped and powered for it can climb over the single wave until the bow drops and they plane along, supported more by water pressure than buoyancy.

Whatever the hull, a quite modest increase in speed can require a great deal of extra power and fuel. However, in deciding the engine power needed, some further allowances must be made. First, to meet local conditions, such as tide races, where extra speed may make the difference between getting home or not. Second, windage and rough seas increase hull resistance anything from 10–50 per cent, and extra power may be needed to compensate where these factors are important. Again, if high speed is important, 10 per cent drop-off in output must be allowed for as the engine gets older. High ambient temperatures can cause a drop of up to 15 per cent.

Any increase in engine power must be taken into account in the propeller design, since the extra loading from wind and seas may cause a breakdown of the flow over the blades, and may necessitate an even greater power allowance.

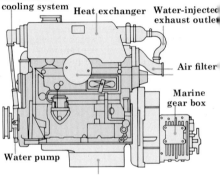

Exhaust 5% · Air filter 3% · Alternator 5–? · Gearbox 1–3% · Pumps 1%

Listed engine output is usually given for a standard engine with essential accessories, in ideal conditions. In practice, the climate is not likely to be ideal and the fuel may have less calorific value. Power will also be taken from the engine by the generator and any pumps, etc. There will be further losses in a reduction gearbox and from bearings and glands. The propeller will have a propulsive efficiency of about 50%.

Freshwater cooling system · Heat exchanger · Water-injected exhaust outlet · Air filter · Marine gear box · Water pump · Engine sump

The true marine engine has a large, heavy cast-iron block with wide galleries to prevent caked salt obstructing the salt-water cooling system. Although reliable, such engines are much less economical than an automotive engine adapted for marine life. Marinizing entails replacing all the aluminium castings by marine-grade aluminium alloy, and arranging a closed-circuit freshwater cooling system, cooled in turn by pumped salt water. Other changes involve redesigning the engine sump, fitting a marine gear box, and adjusting the carburettors or injectors.

Power output

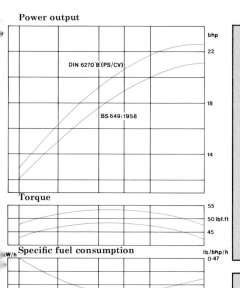

Speed potential
Differing power requirements for different boats can be compared by taking the square root of the water-line length as a proportion of the speed. A displacement hull, for example, will be powered economically at $\sqrt{\frac{V}{L}}$ of about 1.0 (5 kn/25 ft WL) and will have a maximum speed potential of about 1.5 (7.5 kn/25 ft WL). A semi-planing hull will have the same economical speed but a maximum potential up to about 3.5 (17.5 kn). A planing boat will have a speed potential from 20 kn up and, because it will have got over the 'hump' in climbing its wave, will have an economical cruising speed of about 22 kn, possibly more.

Power curves in makers' brochures give maximum output over the range of revolutions. Here, the top curve shows how power is developed as engine revolutions increase. The middle graph shows the range of revolutions over which the engine delivers most torque. The lower graph marries fuel consumption to revolutions. It can be seen that at about 2,000 RPM the engine develops high torque for low fuel consumption.

Electrolysis
Any metal object in salt water or even in a salt atmosphere, takes up a particular value of electrical potential. An electrical current is set up with any other metal object of a different potential though the salt electrolyte and the natural circuits can be greatly increased by electrical currents from the boat's fittings. The flow is from the high potential, or cathodic, item to the low potential, or anodic, fitting which is subject to corrosive attack. The potential of different metals can be listed in a galvanic table, with stainless steel, titanium and nickel near the cathodic end and aluminium alloys and zinc near the anodic end. Any metal will deteriorate in salt water in the presence of one of higher potential. Lumps of low-potential metal, such as zinc, are often fitted to hulls as sacrificial anodes to attract corrosive forces away from more valuable items such as bronze or aluminium propellers.

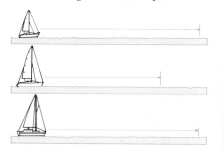

The heavier of two boats of the same size and windage requires more power to reach a specific speed. For craft of the same weight, hull length is the governing factor, the shorter boat needing more.

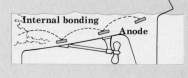
Internal bonding   Anode

Engine installations

Most engines and installations start out as reliable units, but they need protection and maintenance if they are to remain so. Good access to all parts is, therefore, important.

The majority of engines are fitted on flexible mountings, since it is not practicable in light boats to provide the massive bearers necessary to absorb vibration. As the engine itself is vibrating freely, the connections to it must also be free to flex. The propeller shaft too has to absorb the movement, usually by a short intermediate shaft fitted between two flexible couplings. However, if the engine is infrequently used, a flexible stern gland, sometimes with a flexible coupling can be a successful compromise.

Safety in the fuel systems starts with electrical earthing of the filler plate and tank and fuel lines, to eliminate the possibility of sparks from static electricity. The fuel piping should be strong and well protected, and the flexible connection to the engine should have a 5-min fire rating. Cut-off cocks for the tank should be easy to reach from outside the machinery space. Marine fuel is often dirty and contaminated with condensation, so fuel lines must have big filters and tanks must be cleared of water regularly.

Some engines are air cooled, but most use a pumped sea-water supply with an inter-cooler to cool a fresh-water system. Some or all of this water can be injected into the exhaust to cool and silence it.

Exhaust lines must be looped up high or fitted with water traps to ensure that sea water cannot run back into the engine, despite heeling, and cooling-water outlet pipes must have special valves for the same reason.

All engines need plenty of air, both for consumption and for cooling, and a power fan should be installed to increase circulation in the engine compartment, if necessary.

The modern diesel engine is still comparatively large, heavy and slow running. It needs heavy mountings, shaft and propeller, a well-maintained fuel system, and good sound insulation. Care should be taken to prevent the diesel smell from pervading the boat.

Stainless steel or ungalvanized mild steel tanks are usually fitted, as diesel attacks zinc coating. The supply line is taken from a bottom sump to avoid airlocks.

Flexible connection

Fuel system

Drain cock

Earthed filler plate

Siphon break pipe

Outlet seacock

Return line

Supply line

Exhaust system

Drain cock

Exhaust elbow

Exhaust system

Earthed filler plate

Drain Cock

Supply line

Exhaust section

Fuel tank

Siphon break pipe

Outlet seacock

Flexible exhaust section

Inboard petrol/gas engines are used for their initial cheapness, light weight and high performance. They must be carefully installed to be safe, with special care taken to cater for any fuel drips, and vapour alarms fitted. Spark-proof fans should be used to clear the bilges of fumes before starting up.

The ignition system is highly vulnerable to condensation, damp and salt. The engine should be run often to dry out the system.

For minimum drag, propeller shafts are made thin, often of aluminium bronze or stainless steel. Shaft bearings are commonly rubber, and water lubricated.

104

Easily changed
duplex-type filters – more than the engine-maker requires – should be used.

Water separators
help to protect against condensation in both shore supply and the boat's own tanks.

Ideally, fuel lines should be solid, and clipped to sturdy structures, to reduce movement. Ensure that any joins are low and airtight.

High-compression
engines need plenty of air, preferably trunked to the air inlet, with a fan sucking more air into the engine room itself.

Seacock

Flexible connections to engine

Exhaust elbow

The petrol/gas line is usually taken from the top of the tank, and joints made high up so that any leak will not drain it. An easy-to-reach cock is needed to cut off fuel when the engine is not in use, or in case of fire.

Install batteries carefully: they contain sulphuric acid and give off explosive hydrogen when charged. Too much engine heat reduces their life.

Most engines are cooled by filtered salt water. Some use a heat exchanger arrangement to a closed-circuit freshwater system in the engine.

Flexible mountings
Most engines are fitted on flexible mountings to insulate the hull from noise and vibration. The type of mounting, **3**, is chosen to suit the vibration characteristics of the engine and varies from hard to quite soft. Other connections must suit this free movement, e.g., shaft arrangements, **1**, vary from a single flexible coupling, **2**, to twin universal joints with an intermediate cardan shaft. Usually a thrust bearing is needed on the propeller shaft to take the load off the mounts. Pipe connections for fuel and water need a final flexible section; those for the exhaust are usually made with a bellows joint.

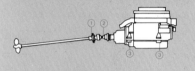

Exhaust systems
Exhaust lines usually inject engine cooling-water into a high elbow close to the manifold by means of a self-draining pipe, sometimes with a silencer, to a transom or shipside outlet. Water injection both silences and cools, so reducing the need for elaborate insulation. Sometimes the exhaust is discharged through the bottom, close to the engine, using a small auxiliary exhaust pipe to prevent back pressure affecting the engine; this can greatly reduce the exhaust smell on deck.

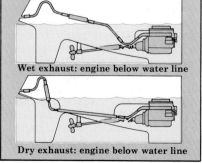

Wet exhaust: engine below water line

Dry exhaust: engine below water line

Handling under power

Boats are generally used under power in crowded anchorages or when sea or weather conditions are difficult, so it is essential to know how your craft will handle.

Any boat hull slides through the water and rarely goes exactly forward or backward; it is also susceptible to the effects of wind, sea and tide. Although the hull is turned slightly by the movement of the rudder, it is the increased water pressure, induced by this movement on one side of the bow or keel, which produces the greatest turning moment. Under power, this effect can be augmented by the strong thrust of the propeller jet stream, deflected to one side by the rudder.

When turning slowly in close quarters, a quick burst of power against the rudder will swing the boat without producing much headway. Also useful at such times is the paddle-wheel effect of the propeller, which makes the turn appreciably tighter in one direction than the other.

The mechanics of steering astern are the same as those for ahead, and a good astern-steering form must have suitable hull surfaces. The modern sailing boat with a fin keel is usually particularly good. The effect of the propeller stream is much reduced but propeller paddling can prove useful. An outboard-powered hull, especially one with two engines, can often be driven stern-first into its berth.

In really bad weather, the boat under power alone is best motoring slowly into the wind and sea. In gale force conditions, when you have to run with the waves, you may have to go astern occasionally to prevent the boat broaching. The boat under sail can improve its state by running the engine, even quite slowly. The extra power helps to stop the jerky motion and improves the stability of the air-flow through the sails. In light airs, too, an extra push from the engine can dramatically improve the airflow.

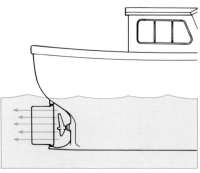

The propeller needs plenty of clear water around it to work efficiently. This means that it should have the minimum of hull obstruction in front of it and that the blade tips should have good clearance from the hull.

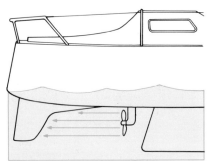

A modern sailing boat is very easily steered. The propeller is only required for propulsion. In a less manoeuvrable vessel, such as a heavy long-keeled boat, the propeller jet stream should pass the rudder to improve steering.

A propeller which rotates clockwise moves the boat to the right.

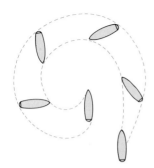

Turning circles vary from boat to boat, and from port to starboard depending on hull steering qualities, propeller rotation and thrust deflection. At full speed, most modern boats will turn in two boat-lengths.

A boat slips sideways as it turns, but it will, typically, behave as shown in the drawing, *above*.

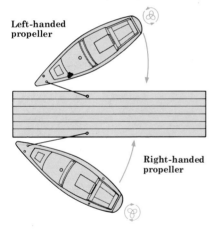

Left-handed propeller

Right-handed propeller

A propeller which turns clockwise when viewed from aft is termed right-handed; one which turns anti-clockwise, left-handed. Most petrol engines have right-handed, and most diesel engines left-handed propellers. A propeller tends to paddle the stern of the boat in the direction in which it turns. In both mooring positions shown, the boat is brought alongside by using propeller thrust deflected by the rudder.

Engine failure

Most engine failures result from fuel contamination, a blockage in the water-cooling system, or the effects of a line caught around the propeller. If unable to carry on under sail, the boat should be anchored for repairs, and the engine switched off. A propeller can sometimes be freed if one person, well aft, pulls hard on the line while another turns the fly-wheel in the right direction by hand. When anchoring is impractical, a motor boat can employ windage and tidal streams to retain some control over the direction of drifting; tide against wind can be used to push the boat far enough sideways to reach shallower water or avoid an obstruction.

In a flat calm and strong tide, the anchor or any weight can be lowered until it just drags along the bottom, slowing the rate of drift. The tidal flow past the hull can then be used to slew it around bows-on to the current, and induce a line of drift with a strong sideways effect.

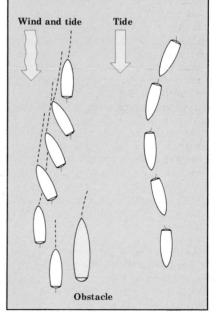

Wind and tide   **Tide**

Obstacle

Reading the compass

Position on the Earth's surface is generally expressed in terms of latitude and longitude. In coastal navigation and a pilotage, however, the position of a vessel is more often identified in relation to the coastline or seamarks, such as buoys and light-vessels, or even the nearest danger point.

There are two basic, fundamentally different ways of determining position at sea: 1 By dead reckoning (DR), which is the application of direction and distance travelled to the boat's last-known position, taking into account the effects of wind and tide. 2 By fixing the position in relation to outside objects such as points of land, the sea bed, radio transmitters or astronomical bodies. Because the knowledge of the course steered and distance run and the effects of wind and tide will necessarily be approximate, the accuracy of the dead reckoning position needs to be up-dated, whenever possible, by fixes.

Direction at sea is measured in relation to north, nowadays clockwise through 360°. Charts are oriented to true north, the direction of the Earth's geographical North Pole. The magnetic compass, however, which is used to steer courses and take bearings, points to magnetic north.

The difference between true and magnetic north at any place is known as the variation. Compass north may vary from magnetic north because magnetic interference within the craft causes deviation. The difference between true (chart) north and compass north, the sum of variation and deviation, is known as compass error and must be allowed for in all chartwork.

Distance (or speed) at sea is measured by some form of log. The unit of distance is the international nautical mile of 1,852 m (6,076 ft); speed is measured in knots, that is, one nautical mile per hour.

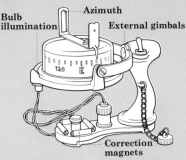

Azimuth

Bulb illumination

External gimbals

Correction magnets

The standard or steering compass is often gimballed so that the card remains horizontal in spite of the boat's movement. Some modern compasses, such as the Sestrel-Moore, *above*, can be read both from the top, looking down, and from eye level. Compass cards generally show the three-figure notation 000°–359° in abbreviated form and mark off every 2 or 5 degrees.

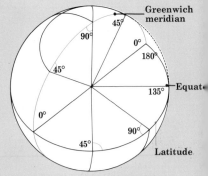

Greenwich meridian

45°

90°

0°

180°

45°

135°

Equat

0°

90°

45°

Latitude

Position of Longitude is measured in degrees, minutes and seconds of arc east and west from the Greenwich meridian, which passes through the site of the original Greenwich observatory. Latitude is measured in arc north and south of the Equator, as viewed from the Earth's centre. Degrees and minutes of longitude represent the angle at the centre of the Earth between any longitude and the Greenwich meridian. Each degree of latitude is divided into 60 mins, each of which equals approximately one nautical mile (1,852 m/6,076 ft).

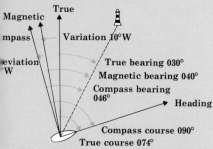

Magnetic | True

mpass | Variation 10°W

eviation
'W

True bearing 030°
Magnetic bearing 040°
Compass bearing 046°
→ Heading

Compass course 090°
True course 074°

To establish

compass error, *above*, observe a known true bearing, such as a transit marked on the chart or a distant lighthouse. Suppose it is 030° true, and the magnetic variation (from the chart) is 10° W, then magnetic north lies 10° west of true north, and the magnetic bearing of the lighthouse will be 040°. The bearing is then taken with the compass, which reads, say, 046°. Deviation is thus 6°W.

Magnetic north

North pole   True north

mb line

Variation,

the difference between true and magnetic north, with its annual rate of change, is given on each compass rose on a chart. Variation is west if magnetic north lies west of true, and vice versa. To convert magnetic bearings to true, add the easterly variation and subtract the westerly.

Projecting the

curved surface of the Earth on a flat map involves some distortion. The Mercator chart is constructed so that a course can be laid off as a straight line which will cut all meridians at the same angle. Drawn on the globe this 'rhumb line' would spiral towards the poles.

Deviation

Compass north may differ from both magnetic and true north because of magnetic interference within the craft itself. The extent of deviation varies with the heading, and is named east or west of magnetic north. When compass north is east of magnetic north, add the deviation to convert from compass to magnetic bearings. Large compass errors are corrected by a qualified adjuster and the residual deviations recorded on a card, *below*.

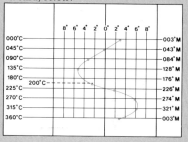

	8°	6°	4°	2°	0°	2°	4°	6°	8°	
000°C										003°M
045°C										043°M
090°C										084°M
135°C										128°M
180°C										176°M
225°C	200°C									226°M
270°C										274°M
315°C										321°M
360°C										003°M

The compass should be sited as far as possible from sources of magnetic interference, such as metal, electronic and electrical equipment. The higher the compass, the further it will be from the influence of the engine and iron ballast keel and, on a steel boat, from the hull. It must be located at least 3 ft (0.9 m) from switches and any instruments containing magnets.

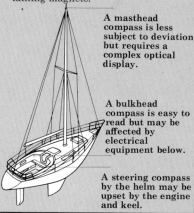

A masthead compass is less subject to deviation but requires a complex optical display.

A bulkhead compass is easy to read but may be affected by electrical equipment below.

A steering compass by the helm may be upset by the engine and keel.

Confirming where you are

A position line is an imaginary line at some point along which the observer's position must lie. The intersection of two position lines fixes the position, although three produce a more reliable fix. All methods of position fixing, whether astronomical, by visual compass bearing, radio direction finding, etc., yield position lines, albeit from widely different sources. Position lines from any source can be combined to produce a fix.

The greater the angle of intersection of two position lines, the less will any error in either of them affect the accuracy of the fix. For two position lines a right-angled cut is ideal, for three, 60°.

Position lines obtained at different times can be advanced (or retarded) to a common time by applying the course-made-good and distance run between observations. This running fix is used in coastal navigation when only a single object is visible, or in astronomical navigation when, say, the altitude of the sun is taken at successive intervals so that its bearing will have changed sufficiently to produce a good cut. A running fix is generally inferior to simultaneous observations because the course and distance are seldom completely accurately known.

Some idea of the accuracy of each of the position lines will enable an estimate to be made of the accuracy of a fix. In general, because none of the position lines will be entirely accurate, the intersection of three position lines will result in a 'cocked hat', the size of which will give an indication of the reliability of the fix. The position will not necessarily lie within the cocked hat and the cautious navigator will assume a position near to it, biased towards the nearest danger.

In coastal navigation, the most frequently used position lines are those obtained from visual compass bearings.

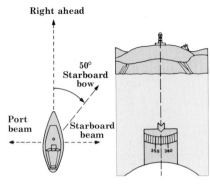

Right ahead

Port beam

50° Starboard bow

Starboard beam

A relative bearing is the angle between the boat's heading and the direction of the object. A beam bearing is 90° from the boat's heading, not 90° from the course-made-good. A bearing 50° to starboard is named 'Green Five Zero'.

To take a compass bearing, identify a landmark on the chart, sight it through the ring or V of the compass and read off the bearing. Correct it from magnetic to true and lay it off on the chart. The closer the object, the more accurate the position.

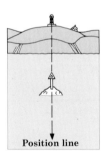

Position line

The transit (in USA **range**) of two well-separated aligned objects gives a position line which can be laid off on the chart without instruments. Beam transits can be used to check the boat's progress against the tide, ahead transits to follow a course.

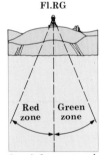

Fl.RG

Red zone | Green zone

At night, sectored lights can help to indicate position. If the boat crosses from, say, the red sector to green, a position line can be drawn along the change-of-colour line. There are many systems of sectored lights, especially in the Baltic.

110

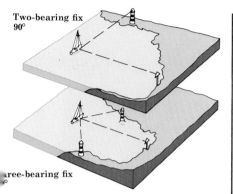

Two-bearing fix 90°

Three-bearing fix

The compass
bearings of two or more landmarks onshore will fix the boat's position. When using only two position lines, they should cross at a broad angle for accurate results.

Three bearings
will give a more reliable fix. Ideally the three marks should be about 60° apart, and never less than 30°. The position lines will rarely intersect at one point but form an error triangle or 'cocked hat'.

Sea horizon distances
Distance measurement of an object gives a circular position line which can often be combined with a bearing to give an instantaneous fix. Thus, a vertical sextant angle of an object of known height combined with a compass bearing of the object provides one of the quickest and most reliable fixes. Given the height of the object and the observer's height of eye, the sextant angle is converted into distance by means of a table or by calculator. The top of the object, or the light in the case of a lighthouse, is brought down to the shoreline immediately below it.

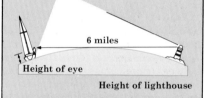

6 miles

Height of eye

Height of lighthouse

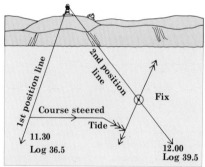

1st position line

2nd position line

Course steered

Tide →

Fix

11.30
Log 36.5

12.00
Log 39.5

A running fix can
be obtained from a single landmark by observing two bearings with, say, half an hour's interval between them. Read the log at the time of the first bearing, steer a steady course for half an hour, take a second bearing and read the log for distance travelled. Plot the two position lines and the course-made-good. Draw a line through the second position line parallel to the first at a distance along the course-made-good corresponding to the distance sailed. The intersection of the position lines will be the fix.

Estimating distances
Distances at sea can be hard to assess, particularly as short distances are often over-estimated and long distances foreshortened. The following clues will give a rough distance guide, as seen from 7 ft (2.1 m) above sea level in good conditions and with a moderate sea.
3 miles (4.5km) – Horizon
2 miles (3.2km) – Large buoy just visible: small buoy lost: windows are dots.
1–1½ miles (1.6–2.5km) – Rigging of a large vessel visible.
1 mile (1.6km) – Colour and shape of large buoys visible: small buoys shapeless: people are dots.
450 yards (410m) – Man seen walking or rower pulling.
250 yards (228m) – Tide ripples round buoys.
100 yards (91m) – Faces visible.
The distance of a boat from a cliff can be determined by the number of seconds it takes for a blast on the fog horn to echo: 1 sec = 200 yds (183 m).

Plotting a chart

A boat's course is the direction in which it is moving, but because of the set (direction) of cross-currents or tidal streams and leeway due to crosswinds, the course will not necessarily be the same as the heading. The course-made-good is the direction followed between fixes; the track, which may involve a number of courses, is the path followed by a vessel over the Earth's surface.

Dead reckoning (DR), which is the determination of position by keeping an account of the courses steered and distance run, is usually worked out on the chart, although the DR position may also be obtained by using tables or a calculator.

The two main problems in chartwork are, 1, when the effect of tidal streams or current and leeway are taken into account, 2, to find the course to steer to make good a certain direction and to find the position known as the estimated position (EP) after steering a certain course for a known distance.

Tidal stream information is obtained from tidal stream atlases which show, in relation to high or low water, the hourly rate/drift and set of the stream; similar information is often tabulated on the chart. Leeway is generally estimated from experience of the boat in different conditions. A rough idea of leeway angle can be obtained by comparing a bearing of the wake with the course steered.

When working from the magnetic rose on the chart or with a special plotter set to the magnetic variation, only deviation of the compass need be taken into account. However, it should be remembered that tidal stream information is given in true not magnetic directions. Whether you choose to work in true or magnetic, be consistent to prevent errors creeping in. Working in magnetic usually saves one calculation, and, in consequence, perhaps one error.

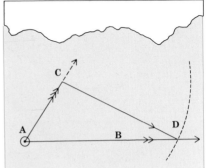

To find the course to steer to make good a certain direction, pencil in the required course on the chart (**AB**). Then plot the rate/drift and set of the tide or current to establish how far it will push the boat in, say, one hour (**AC**). With the dividers set at the distance the boat will travel in one hour, intersect the required course at **D**. The course to steer, allowing for tide, will then be **CD** and the distance made good in one hour/**AD**. Allow for leeway when necessary by steering upwind of the course to steer.

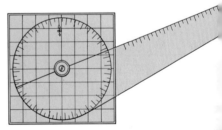

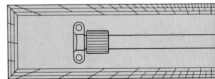

The chart table should measure at least 24 in × 30 in (58 cm × 75 cm). Basic equipment includes up-to-date charts, nautical almanac, tide tables, pilot books, log book and note pad. A practical selection of plotting instruments would consist of: a Hurst plotter which is above all useful for plotting

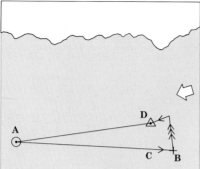

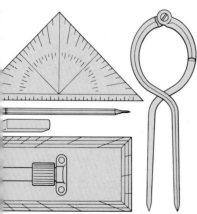

MARK	COURSE & DISTANCE	REMARKS
⚓ 5·5m	↑	SPIRE ⌀ CHIMNEY PIER Lt 065°c
No.4 ◿△◺ 200°c	a/c 125°c 1·5 M	F.S ⌀ TOWER LEADS TO ⚓
No.1 △ R.W 1 mile	a/c 085°c 2·6 M	
FAIRWAY ◫◺ R.W ½ mile	015°c 0·5 M	Tidal stream astern 2·0 kt.

Navigator's notebook
Before entering or leaving a harbour, translate information on the chart into a Navigator's notebook, *above*. The sequence for the safest departure route commences at the bottom. Leave fairway buoy to port, distance ½ ml; steer 015°M for 0.5 mls. No. 1 buoy is now 1 ml abeam to port. Alter course to 085°M for 2.6 mls, until No. 4 beacon is abeam to starboard, bearing 200°M. Alter course to 125°M to bring flag staff and tower in transit which leads to anchorage in 1.5 mls. Anchor in 5.5 m of water when spire and chimney are in transit and pier is bearing 065°M.

To find your estimated position, plot the course steered (**AC**) from the last known position (**A**). Modify the angle to account for leeway and mark the dead reckoned position, **B** to correspond with the logged or estimated distance travelled. Plot the set and rate/drift of the tidal stream **BD** to indicate the effect of the current (for the time it took to sail **AB**). The point **D** is the EP and **AD**, the course- and speed-made-good. The log book must be kept up-to-date with details of distance travelled and course steered. Whenever an accurate fix is obtained, the old EP can be ignored.

magnetic bearings; a roller rule which can be rolled across the chart with one hand to lay off courses and bearings; a pair of dividers for measuring off distances; a navigational set square or Douglas protractor. Soft pencils (2B), a sharpener and a square rubber that will not roll are also indispensable.

The chart symbols, *below*, are a universal form of shorthand when plotting a course. Use the 24-hour clock, e.g. 18.30, not 6.30 pm. Symbols in blue represent those used in USA.

+ ⊙ **Dead Reckoning position**	⇉ **Course-made-good**
△ ▢ **Estimated position**	⇶ **Tidal stream**
⊙ △ **Fix**	⟶ **Position line**
→ **Course steered**	⇐⇛ **Transferred position line**

The language of charts

Visualize a light within a globe throwing the shadows of coastlines on to a cylinder. The cylinder is then rolled to produce a flat surface, and you have the basis of map projections.

The problem of the nautical chart, however, is how to represent the spherical surface of the earth on a flat piece of paper *without* distorting the features used by the navigator. Except in very high latitudes, for specialized purposes or for harbour plans, the Mercator projection is almost universally used at sea. One of its properties is that a straight line will intersect all meridians at the same angle.

The largest-scale chart should always be used. The larger the scale, the more detailed will be the information given. In addition, errors in plotting on a large-scale chart will cause less error in the position than on a small-scale one. Much of the information given on charts is expressed in standardized abbreviations and symbols, listed on Admiralty Chart 5011 and US Chart No. 1. Because buoyage, lights and other features change from time to time, charts have continually to be updated from *Notices to Mariners*, issued weekly. The date of publication of a chart is printed outside the bottom margin in the centre or in the bottom left-hand corner, and new editions are shown to the right of it. Corrections are entered at the bottom left-hand corner.

Charts are published in the US and Great Britain by the national hydrographic authorities with world-wide coverage and the chart catalogue shows what charts are available throughout the world.

Sailing Directions, or pilot books, are published by the same authorities and give information about local conditions such as, conspicuous landmarks, harbour approach courses, port facilities and so on. They are a necessary adjunct to the charts, whose information is necessarily incomplete.

Chart symbols are grouped as follows: coastal and natural features, harbours and buildings, buoys and beacons, radio and radar, fog signals, dangers, depth contours, quality of the bottom, tides and currents, the compass rose.
1 Radio mast exhibiting red lights.
2 Light beacon flashing every 3 secs, 5 m

11 Wreck showing part of hull at chart datum.
12 Sandy shore.
13 Depth contours indicate gradient.
14 Buildings.
15 Fort with flagstaff 31 m high.
16 Rocky bottom.
17 Light beacon flashing every 5 secs, 6 m elevation, luminous range 5 mls.
18 Light beacon flashing red every 5 secs, 9 m elevation, 8 mls luminous range.

elevation luminous range 5 mls. Marks a shoal with 5.5 m over it. Useful day mark.
3 Mud.
4 Coral and shell bottom. 16.6 m charted depth.
5 A patch of shallow water.
6 Beacon with quick flashing light. Useful day mark.
7 7–10 m contour.
8 Wharves.
9 Church.
10 Flagstaff on coal wharf building.

Cr.	Creek
Pass.	Passages
Chan.	Channel
Appr.	Approaches
Apprs	
Anch.	Anchorage
Hr.	Harbour
P.	Port
Lndg.	Landing place

⚑ Oil/Gas platform

⚓ Light ship

📮 *Jade* ▲ *No 5*
R   B

Names, numbers and colours of buoys are shown as above

◉ RC

Non-directional radio beacon

◉ RD   RD 269°30′

Directional radio beacon

◉ RG

Radio direction-finding station

◉ R

Coast radio providing QTG service

3

Coast Radar Station providing range and bearing on request

✳ Rock awash at level of chart datum *(Masts)*

⊞ Wreck on which masts only are visible

(15) *Wk*
Unsurveyed wreck; exact depth unknown; considered to have safe clearance at depth shown.

(7₃) *Wk*

Wreck over which the depth has been obtained by sounding, but not by wire sweep.

(5) *Wk*

Wreck which has been swept by wire to the depth shown.

+++
Wreck over which exact depth is unknown but thought to be over 28 m.

Overfalls and tide-rips

Eddies

Kelp

Traffic separation scheme: one-way traffic lanes (separated by zone)

19 Coral reef.
20 20 m contour.
21 Flashing beacon marking a shoal.
22 Black and red buoy, flashing red every 1.5 secs. Marks a patch with 8.3 m over it.
23 Bearing line.

Sounding the depths

Knowing the water depth, especially when used in conjunction with other information, can be valuable in many circumstances at sea, such as clearing a danger or making a landfall. Where the bottom configuration is distinctive or displayed on the chart as depth contours, a line of soundings can help to determine the boat's position.

Echo sounders give a continuous record of depth within the range of the instrument. An acoustic signal is transmitted to the sea bed by means of a transducer fixed to the ship's bottom, and the reflected signal received is converted into depth by measuring the time interval between transmission and reception – the average speed of sound through water being 4,925 ft/sec (1,500 m/sec). The display of depth can be presented in a number of ways: digitally, as a trace reproducing the bottom profile, on a cathode-ray tube or as a flash on a circular scale.

An echo sounder with a graphic read-out is best suited to running a line of soundings, since dramatic changes in the water depth are immediately apparent. In very cold or fresh water, sound travels more slowly, so allow extra clearance since the actual depth will be shallower than indicated.

To get a position fix from a line of soundings, plot the course-made-good on the chart and mark dead reckoning positions along it at convenient intervals, corresponding to, say, every 15 mins. Then draw to the same scale a similarly marked line on a sheet of tracing paper and place the soundings at each of the time intervals alongside them. Remember to reduce each sounding to chart datum by subtracting the height of the tide. Overlay the tracing paper on the chart in the vicinity of the plotted course and adjust to fit the soundings on the chart. (It will be useful to have a meridian marked on the tracing paper for this operation.)

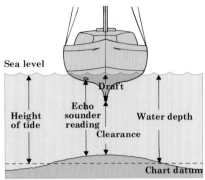

Sea level

Draft

Height of tide | Echo sounder reading | Water depth

Clearance

Chart datum

The depth of water on charts is given in fathoms and feet or in metres below chart datum, which is now usually the lowest predictable water depth. To estimate the clearance beneath a boat's keel, take the height of tide and deduct the measured depth to give the actual depth. Deduct the draft of the boat below the water surface, to give the distance between the keel and the sea bed.

Depth alarm

Hull transducer

The latest electronic echo sounders display depth up to 600 ft, 100 fms and 200 m in a clock-face display and/or LED read-out. The problem of weather-proofing is largely overcome by using a repeater in the cockpit, so allowing the main system to be sited in a sheltered position. An alarm, set to operate at any chosen depth up to 30 m, is useful in poor visibility, shallow water or at anchor.

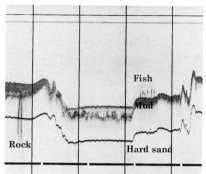

Rock Fish Mud Hard sand

Unlike the digital sounders, the more elaborate graphic recorder provides a permanent depth record by tracing the contours of the sea bed with a stylus on a moving, sensitized-paper roll. It gives detailed information of the nature of the bottom; mud, hard sand and rock are clearly defined. Shoals of fish are indicated as weaker signals.

Digital repeater metre

A transducer fitted to the ship's hull transmits the sound signal; although normally mounted on the outside of the hull, some models can be fitted inside to avoid cutting holes in the hull. Most give out an arc of sound over 45°, so if the boat heels more than about 22°, the signal will not aim directly at the sea bed. This produces a false reading. The solution for most cruising boats which are likely to heel more than 20° is to fit twin transducers, one for each tack, preferably with an automatic gravity switch. Position them forward of the keel and away from any areas of turbulence. If they are mounted too close to the keel the sound may be obstructed. Remember to calculate the vertical separation between the transducer and the bottom of the keel. This must be subtracted from the sounded depth to give depth below the keel.

Sounding Leads
The traditional way of sounding at sea is with the sounding lead: a leaden weight, generally 'armed' with tallow to collect bottom samples, attached to a marked line. The hand lead is still widely used. The markings on the line, widely adopted with metrication of British Admiralty charts, are as follows:

Metres	Markings
1,11,21	1 strip of leather
2,12,22	2 strips of leather
3,13,23	blue bunting
4,14,24	green and white bunting
5,15,25	white bunting
6,16,26	green bunting
7,17,27	red bunting
8,18,28	blue and white bunting
9,19,29	red and white bunting
10	leather with a hole in it
20	leather with 2 holes in it
0.2	a piece of mackerel line

Using a depth sounder
In thick fog or off low-lying coastlines, a depth sounder can be invaluable. It can be used to confirm an estimated position and to indicate position by successive soundings, with or without a bearing. It can also serve to guide the boat into a harbour entrance or to a given destination by following a line of soundings. Choose a contour line on the chart and take continuous soundings, having confirmed that no underwater dangers lie along the route. Soundings are, however, often difficult to interpret, and should be treated with caution.

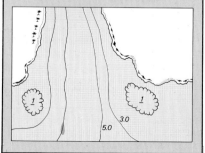

Timing the tides

The tides are caused by the difference in the gravitational pull of the sun and the moon on the rotating Earth. The effects are two-fold – a vertical pull which is opposed by the Earth's gravity and a horizontal pull which causes the waters to move across the Earth's surface and is responsible for the tides.

The moving water itself is referred to as the tidal stream and the change in depth as the water piles up as the tide. A tidal day corresponds to the period of rotation of the Earth with respect to the moon, which is about 24 hrs 50 min. Tides may be divided into three main categories: **1**, semi-diurnal with two high waters and two low waters each tidal day; **2**, diurnal with one high water and one low water each tidal day; and **3**, mixed tides which vary from essentially diurnal to essentially semi-diurnal in character.

The seaman's principal interest in tides is in how to predict the times and heights of high and low water and the rate and set of the tidal stream. Tide tables give the times and heights above chart datum of high and low water for various Standard Ports and time differences for Secondary Ports, also a means of determining heights at intermediate times.

Tidal streams, a coastal phenomenon caused by the vertical rise and fall of the tide, normally change direction every six hours. Their direction and strength are given in tidal stream atlases for both spring and neap tides, with a means of interpolating between them according to the range of the tide. Tidal stream information also appears on charts.

Meteorological conditions can have a pronounced effect on both tides and tidal streams. A prolonged strong on-shore wind will increase the height of the tide and an offshore wind decrease it and the tidal streams will be affected accordingly. A very high barometric pressure will lower the tidal heights.

Charted depths on modern charts are given in metres below (and drying heights in metres above) chart datum, which is usually the lowest astronomical tide. Older charts show depths in fathoms, usually below mean low water springs (MLWS). The height of the tide is the distance between chart datum and sea-level, and the range is the difference between the height at high water and the height at low water. This range is greatest at spring tides, two days after a full and a new moon, when the sun and moon are in conjunction or opposition. When the sun and moon exert a right-angled force on the oceans, the water displacement, and thus the tidal range, is least.

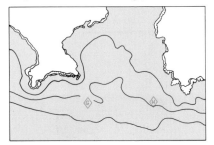

Diamonds marked on the chart indicate positions for which tidal stream data is available. The letter keys in with a panel on the chart where information for each of the six hours before and after high water, springs and neaps, is given.

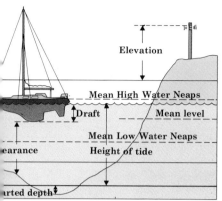

Mean high water springs (MHWS) is the average level of all high water heights and mean low water springs (MLWS) of all low water heights, at spring tides throughout the year. US charts use mean high water, the average level of all high water heights and mean low water, the average of all low water heights (both springs and neaps) over a 19-year period. Metric charts use a separate chart datum. The mean high and low water levels at neap tides fall within the range of the springs. Drying heights covered at high tide, but not at low, are measured above chart datum and underlined on the chart, to distinguish them from soundings.

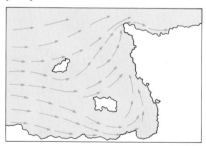

The tidal atlas of a given area indicates the direction of the tidal stream and its rate in knots. Pairs of figures, e.g. 10.24, give the rate at neap and spring tides respectively. The atlas contains 13 chartlets one for each of the six hours before and after high water, and one for high water itself.

Tidal predictions
To find the height of tide at a particular place, consult the tide tables to discover the most recent high or low water at the nearest Standard Port, and its height. If you are nearer a Secondary Port, check the tables for the tidal time differences between the two. For example, if high water occurs 20 min later at the Secondary Port add 20 min. Work out the tidal range by subtracting the height at low water from the height at high. Note the difference between the time of the nearest high water and the time you require, to give the interval (number of hours) before or after high tide. Turn to the tidal curve diagram for the Standard Port and with reference to time between high and low water select the appropriate curve. Read off the factor where the interval cuts the curve. Multiply your tidal range by the factor to give the height of the tide above low water. Add this to the low water height (already gathered from the charts) to then obtain the height of the tide above chart datum at the time required. If times given in tide tables are in Greenwich Mean Time, when necessary, allow for Daylight Saving Time or British Summer Time or other time changes.
Twelfth's rule, *below,* gives a rough guide to the change of depth in a 6-hr tide.
The rate of rise or fall is:
1st hour – 1/12 of range (10%)
2nd hour– 2/12 of range (15%)
3rd hour – 3/12 of range (25%)
4th hour – 3/12 of range (25%)
5th hour – 2/12 of range (15%)
6th hour – 1/12 of range (10%)

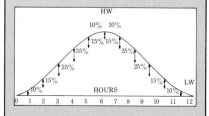

Logging your speed

The difficulty in measuring distance travelled at sea is that the medium in which the craft moves is itself moving with respect to the Earth. Distance over the ground can be measured directly between fixes but otherwise must be deduced from measurements of speed or distance travelled through the water.

A log is a shipboard device for measuring speed or distance through the water. In the towed, or taffrail log, a rotator is towed behind the vessel and turned by the flow of water past it as the vessel proceeds. The distance run, mechanically derived from the number of revolutions, is recorded, usually in miles and tenths of a mile, on a dial fixed to the taffrail. In spite of its simplicity, it remains one of the most reliable logs.

The principle of deriving speed from a rotator is also used in an electronic log. Here the rotation of a small impeller projecting through the hull, or towed on a cable astern, generates an electric current, the frequency of which will be directly proportional to the speed of the vessel. Such logs are highly sensitive and are often integrated with other sensors that measure sailing performance.

In a pitot-static log, a pitot tube projecting through the hull detects the dynamic pressure in undisturbed water and, from this, the speed through the water is recorded automatically on a dial. The pitot log is apt to be unreliable at low speeds. Another way of deriving speed from dynamic water pressure is by means of a small strut, usually raked aft and found in a number of yachts' logs.

The electromagnetic log, housed beneath the hull, uses the principle of magnetic induction to detect the movement of the magnetic field as the vessel moves through the water. It is extremely accurate over a wide range of speeds, but may be affected by turbulence.

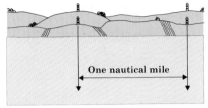

One nautical mile

Logs fitted to the hull should be calibrated by checking the recorded speed over a measured mile with a timepiece. Various measured distances around the coast are marked by transits and shown on charts. Several runs in both directions need to be made under power at a constant speed, and at right angles to the transits.

Line

Rotator

Fish

One of the most robust, reliable and inexpensive logs is the 'Walker' taffrail log. The rotator is streamed behind the boat on the end of a line. The inboard end is attached to a register which converts the number of revolutions into nautical miles on

Autopilot Radar scanner
Radio earth RDF Loop
Compass plate Electronic log

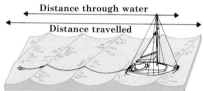

Echo sounder

The positioning of hull fittings for electronic equipment is important. Echo sounders and log transducers should be in the middle section of the boat to avoid turbulence but forward of the keel. Avoid using different metals together under water.

Checklist

1 If you suspect the log's accuracy, check that the impeller, rotator or pitot tube is not fouled by seaweed. Also check the power supply.

2 One knot equals one nautical mile per hour. Speed in knots equals distance in nautical miles divided by time in hours. Time in hours equals distance divided by speed. Distance equals speed multiplied by time in hours.

3 The Dutchman's Log requires no equipment and gives a rough speed guide. Throw any floatable object well ahead of the bow and start the stop watch as it passes the boat's stem. Stop the watch as it passes the stern. Speed in knots is length of boat (distance) × 3,600 (seconds in an hour) divided by time in seconds × 6,076 (feet in a nautical mile).

Distance through water

Distance travelled

Logs are prone to give false readings for various reasons. In heavy weather, a towed log will over-read by 2% in a fresh breeze, 4% in a strong wind and 6% in a gale. Likewise, an unsteady course will increase the distance travelled in relation to the intended course. Since the log reads the boat's speed or distance run through the water, the tides and currents must be allowed for, to determine the speed or distance-made-good over the ground.

Chip log

A good 'home-made' log is the 'chip' log – a weighted triangle of plywood, approximately 6 in (17.7 cm) across. A towing line is attached to the top corner and short lines running from the bottom two corners are clipped to it with a clothes peg. The towing line, always measured metrically, consists of 61 m (200 ft) of soft cord, knotted at 7.7 m (25.3 ft) intervals, starting some 30 ft (9.1 m) up the line. Drop the triangle over the stern and, using a stop-watch, count the number of knots which run out in 15 seconds to check your speed. (1 knot of speed = 7.71 m/15 sec).

the dial. Towed logs can be calibrated by altering the length of the log line. If fouled by weed the rotator can be hauled on board and cleaned. Remember to recover it before coming into port, or it may become fouled or severed when the engine is put astern.

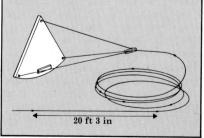

20 ft 3 in

The reason for Radar

The size and weight of modern radar equipment makes it practicable for boats as small as 25 ft (7.6 m) overall. It can be used day or night and in fog as both a navigational aid and a collision avoidance device. It detects the range of an object by timing the interval between the transmission of a radio wave and the return of its echo.

The bearing of the object is determined by the direction of the antenna or scanner and the information is translated on to a map on the screen – a cathode-ray tube plan position indicator (PPI), usually fitted by the chart table. In most yachts the PPI is a 'head-up' relative display with the boat stationary at the centre and the head pointing to the top. The shore, anchored ships and buoys thus appear to move past as the boat follows its course towards the top of the screen. Larger vessels generally have a true-motion display on which vessels move and static objects do not.

The most usual use of radar for position fixing is by comparing the radar picture with the chart. But considerable caution is necessary since the echoing characteristics of points of land are not always obvious from the chart. A radar fix can be obtained from the ranges of two or three objects, the bearings of two objects, or a range and bearing of a single object. Visual bearings are more accurate than a radar bearing and are often used in conjunction with the radar range to produce a more reliable fix.

Radar transponder beacons, called Racons, are used to enhance the echoing characteristics of seamarks and landmarks around the coast, such as light-vessels and lighthouses, and are marked on the chart. Since there is a slight delay in the signal, however, the boat's real distance from the Racon is slightly less than that indicated on the screen. Racons are used primarily for identification and generally have a range of about 10 nautical miles.

Solid objects, such as ships, buoys, beacons and land, show up as lighted areas on the screen and the water as dark. High cliffs and even distant hills may be visible before an approaching fishing vessel or low-lying beach. So choose prominent objects as marks for coastal navigation. Remember that underwater dangers will not be picked up on the screen.

7

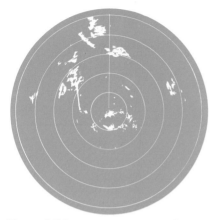

Radar reflectors
To alert other vessels to its presence, a boat needs a good radar reflector to boost any radar signals which bounce off it. The reflector works as a prism, presenting a series of right-angled corners to trap the signals and bounce them straight back, with as little loss in other directions as possible. It needs to be accurately constructed, strong, rigid and not less than 18 in (45 cm) across the diagonal. Even a small increase in size dramatically increases the echoing area.

To establish your position by radar, refer to the local chart. Buoys marking a channel are often fitted with reflectors and look conveniently similar on the screen and chart. Radar beacons, marked on the chart as Ramark, appear as a line on the screen. Ships, islands, etc., often appear wider than they are, and a harbour entrance may only show up at close range. Consult the chart regularly for underwater hazards.

Modern radar
sets for yachts are operated from controls on the display unit. These include range selection, **1**, tuning, **2**, anti-rain and sea clutter, **3**, for bad weather and a switch for range rings, **4**. In addition, an illuminated rotating cursor can be operated to align with an echo, **5**. Its bearing relative to the ship's heading can be read off the graduated bearing scale, **6**, surrounding the screen. It reads 0°–180°, both port and starboard, and is adjusted by the bezel, **7**.

Site the reflector
at least 15 ft (4.5 m) above sea level. Mount a bracket at the masthead, spreaders or on twin triatic or backstays for a permanent fitting. To hoist temporarily, secure with shock cord or use a flag halyard to the spreader or up the backstay.

The octahedral-shaped reflector
must be hoisted in the 'catch rain' position, *not* point up. It is cheap, easy to stow, but loses efficiency when the boat heels.

The Firdell Blipper,
which consists of a five-fold array of corners, accepts angles of heel up to 30° with little loss of echo. Light-weight and sealed in a plastic case, it will be picked up by most vessels at a good range; this depends on its size and height.

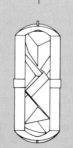

Radio direction-finding

Radio direction-finding equipment (RDF) is compulsory for vessels over 1,600 tons. For smaller craft it remains one of the simplest and most useful aids, although its effective range is generally less than 50 nautical miles and it is subject to a number of errors.

In good conditions a skilled operator with a good set can probably achieve bearings to within $\pm 2°$. The accuracy decreases rapidly with the distance from the beacon, the quality of the compass and the movement of the boat. Bearings taken when the beacon is at more than its listed range should be treated with caution.

RDF bearings are also subject to quadrantal errors (at a maximum on the bow and quarter), due to magnetic interference within the ship, which distort the radio signal. For this reason it is essential to calibrate the set. The magnetic compass in the antenna unit will also be subject to deviation, so bearings should always be taken from the same position. Errors are introduced by having a continuous metal lifeline round the craft and this should be broken by a nylon spacer or lanyard.

Radio beacons are usually arranged in groups sharing a common frequency, each transmitting in a fixed sequence within the cycle. They are listed with their frequencies, range and call signs in the *Admiralty List of Radio Signals*, Vol. 2: and the US Coast Guard *Light List* or *Eldridge*, and in various almanacs. The bearing of the station is established by the null or minimum signal.

Equipment varies considerably, but a typical small-craft set would comprise a receiver with headphones. A small ferrite rod antenna and a compass will have been incorporated into the receiver.

Although considerably more expensive, an automatic direction-finder removes the problem of finding the null aurally.

The most suitable RDF set for cruising consists of a fixed radio receiver, a portable compass, **1**, incorporating a ferrite rod antenna **2**, and headphones. The receiver is adapted to receive the beacon bands on very long wavelengths as well as ordinary broadcasts. The frequency can be pre-set or selected with a digital keyboard, **3**, and appears on a liquid crystal digital display, **4**. The headphones, **5**, are

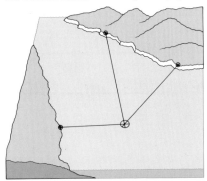

To take a direction bearing of an RDF beacon, tune in to the listed frequency and turn the aerial on a vertical axis. When the signal is loudest, the ferrite rod in the boat's RDF antenna will be at right angles to the beacon. As soon as the signal becomes null it will be pointing either directly towards or away from the beacon. Read the bearing off the compass. Repeat several times.

used for audio tuning and to detect the null

signal. In addition, the precise point at which the signal becomes null is indicated on the frequency display unit, **4**, on the receiver.

Cost comparisons
The cost of RDF equipment ranges from £45 ($90) to over £1,000 ($2,000) and, in general, price reflects accuracy and reliability.
1 Simple hand-held sets with a compass on top, such as Seafix, cost between £45 ($90) and £100 ($200).
2 More sophisticated versions of the hand-held unit, such as Lokata and Aptel, lie in the £200–250 ($400–500) bracket. The signal is stronger, frequency location easier and compass reading more accurate.
3 Other sets double as a normal radio and receive ordinary broadcasts on short and medium waves as well as RDF longwave signals. The price, however, leaps to £400–500 ($800–1,000). The most sophisticated, Brookes and Gatehouse's Homer 5, offers nine general purpose frequencies and storage and recall of six RDF frequencies for £1,000 ($2,000).
4 Automatic direction finders cost £800–1,000 ($1,600–3,200), but usually give very accurate bearings.

Radio waves are refracted by high ground and off cliffs and so will give inaccurate bearings. Whenever possible, therefore, choose a radio beacon whose signal will not have to cross land before

reaching the boat's aerial, unless it crosses the coast at right angles, not obliquely.

Buoyage systems

The buoyage system now being introduced worldwide is the IALA (International Association of Lighthouse Authorities) Maritime Buoyage System. There are two regions, A and B, in which the marks are identical. The colours, red and green, however, are used in region A to indicate respectively, the port and starboard lateral limits of a channel, whereas in region B they indicate the reverse. Region B comprises the USA, Central and South America, Japan and the Phillipines; region A, the rest of the world. Implementation should be complete by 1990. There are five types of mark: lateral, cardinal, isolated danger marks, safe water marks and special marks. During the day, they are identified by the colour and shape of the buoy and topmark and at night by the colour and rhythm of lights. Lateral marks indicate the port and starboard limits of a channel.

Cardinal marks, 4, are black and yellow with black double-cone topmarks to indicate where navigable water lies. If north, 5, the cones point up; south 6, down; west 7, inwards; east, outwards 8. At night Cardinal marks exhibit quick or very quick flashes of white light: north, uninterrupted; east, groups of three; south, groups of six and a long one; west, groups of nine.

IALA Maritime Buoyage System for region A

The port-hand lateral markers have a red can, 1, or spar-shaped, 2, base with a can-shaped top. The starboard markers are conical green with pointed topmarks, 3. At night they flash red or green, respectively.

Isolated danger marks 9 are striped red and black with two round black topmarks, and can be passed either side. At night they emit groups of two flashes. Special marks are yellow, with yellow lights.

Safe water marks 10 are striped red and white with a round red topmark, and at night exhibit an occulting white light. Uncharted dangers are shown by cardinal or lateral marks.

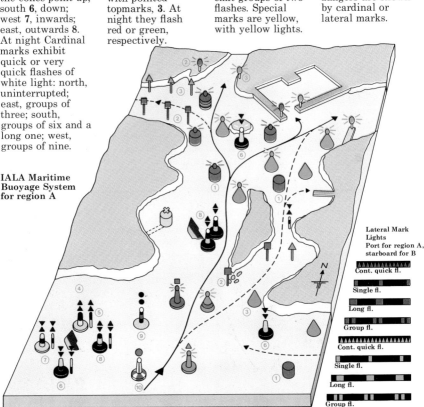

Lateral Mark Lights
Port for region A, starboard for B
Cont. quick fl.
Single fl.
Long fl.
Group fl.
Cont. quick fl.
Single fl.
Long fl.
Group fl.

Cardinal marks generally draw attention to shoal water, and the shape and colour of the topmark indicates the side on which it is safe to pass.

Isolated danger marks are positioned above isolated shoals, rocks or wrecks surrounded by navigable water. Safe water marks indicate that surrounding water is navigable. Special marks identify military, recreational and traffic separation zones, as well as instruments or pipelines.

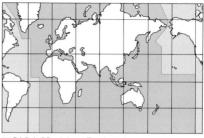

☐ IALA Maritime Region A
☐ IALA Maritime Region B

The United States, parts of Central and South America and Japan, comprise region B, where the system will be gradually introduced to remove the confusion caused by the variety of traditional systems at present in use. The marks for regions A and B are almost identical, except that region B uses red to indicate the starboard side of a channel and green to show the port side.

IALA Maritime Buoyage System for region B

The conventional direction is clockwise – north along the Pacific coast, south along the Atlantic, north and west along the coast of the Gulf of Mexico and in the Great Lakes except L. Michigan where it is south.

A preferred channel may be indicated by a modified lateral mark – red with a green stripe if the preferred channel is to port, **11**, green if it is to starboard, **12**. (The reverse for region A.)

Special marks, yellow in both regions, sometimes with a yellow X topmark, mark forbidden zones, such as cables, military areas and spoil grounds.

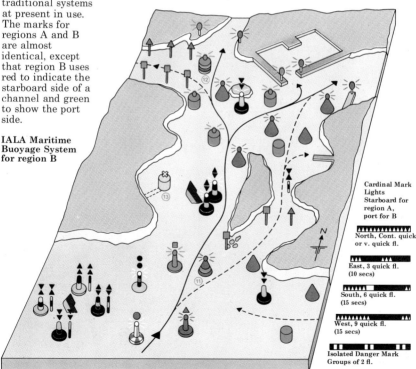

Cardinal Mark
Lights
Starboard for
region A,
port for B

North, Cont. quick
or v. quick fl.

East, 3 quick fl.
(10 secs)

South, 6 quick fl.
(15 secs)

West, 9 quick fl.
(15 secs)

Isolated Danger Mark
Groups of 2 fl.

127

Navigating by the stars

Offshore, astronomical navigation provides the most generally available form of position-fixing. The apparent position at any moment of all visible heavenly bodies as seen from the Earth is tabulated in the *Nautical Almanac* and can be used in conjunction with a sextant and timepiece to establish position.

The coordinates given in the almanac are declination (Dec), which is analagous to latitude, measured north and south of the celestial equator, and Greenwich hour angle (GHA), measured westward through 360° from the Greenwich meridian. Time needs to be within about 1 sec since, at the Earth's rate of rotation, an error of 1 sec can produce an error in position of a quarter of a mile.

The fixed parts of the sextant are the frame, graduated arc, telescope and horizon glass, which is half silvered so that the horizon can be viewed through the unsilvered part. The instrument should always be picked up by the frame, never the arc, and the delicate mirrors should never be touched except for cleaning.

The word sextant is derived from the arc which is 60°, one-sixth of a circle, but the mirrors double the reflection so angles can be measured up to 120°.

When the movable index arm is at zero the index mirror should be precisely parallel to the horizon glass.

The sextant altitude of the observed body must be corrected to obtain the true altitude. First, the observer's height of eye produces a dip or depression in the horizon and a correction must be made. Second, atmospheric refraction of light introduces an error; this is especially marked at low altitudes, and observations of less than 12° are usually ignored.

Third, when one or other of the body's limbs, rather than its centre, is observed (as with the sun or moon), a correction of half the diameter is necessary.

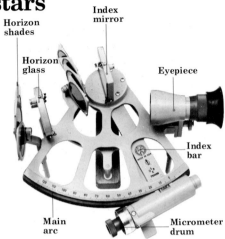

To take an observation, view the horizon glass, and move the index bar along the arc until the body is visible. Turn the micrometer drum until the lower limb touches the horizon. Sway the sextant gently sideways through an arc about 20° either side of the line of sight to ensure that the exact point of contact is vertically below the body. The precise time to the nearest second is recorded, usually in GMT. The angle between the horizon, the line of sight and the body is read on the arc for the degrees and on the drum for the minutes, read to the nearest half minute.

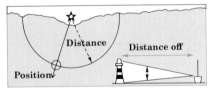

Distance-off can be measured by vertical sextant angle, if the height of an object, such as a lighthouse, is known. Given height of eye and the height of the object, Distance-off Tables or a calculator will give the object's distance. A bearing taken at the same time gives an accurate position fix. Ensure that the reading is corrected for any index error.

DECLINATION (15°-29°) SAME NAME AS LATITUDE

N. Lat. { LHA greater than 180°...... Zn=Z
{ LHA less than 180°...... Zn=360−Z

LHA	15° Hc	d	Z	16° Hc	d	Z	17° Hc	d	Z	18° Hc	d	Z	19° Hc	d	Z	20° Hc	d	Z
0	61 00	+60	180	62 00	+60	180	63 00	+60	180	64 00	+60	180	65 00	+60	180	66 00	+60	180
1	60 59	60	178	61 59	60	178	62 59	60	178	63 59	60	178	64 59	60	178	65 59	60	178
2	60 57	60	176	61 57	60	176	62 57	60	176	63 57	60	176	64 57	60	176	65 57	59	176
3	60 53	60	174	61 53	60	174	62 53	60	174	63 53	59	174	64 52	60	173	65 52	60	173
4	60 48	60	172	61 48	59	172	62 47	60	172	63 47	60	171	64 47	59	171	65 46	60	171
5	60 41	+60	170	61 41	+59	170	62 40	+60	170	63 40	+59	169	64 39	+59	169	65 38	+60	169
6	60 33	60	168	61 33	59	168	62 32	59	168	63 31	59	167	64 30	59	167	65 29	59	167
7	60 24	59	166	61 23	59	166	62 22	59	165	63 21	58	165	64 19	59	165	65 18	59	165
8	60 13	58	164	61 11	59	164	62 10	59	163	63 09	58	163	64 07	58	163	65 05	59	163
9	60 00	59	162	60 59	58	162	61 57	58	162	62 55	58	161	63 53	58	160	64 51	58	161
10	59 47	+58	161	60 45	+58	160	61 43	+57	160	62 40	+58	159	63 38	+58	158	64 36	+57	158
11	59 32	57	159	60 29	58	158	61 27	57	158	62 24	57	157	63 21	57	156	64 18	57	157
12	59 15	58	157	60 13	57	156	61 10	57	156	62 07	56	155	63 03	57	154	64 00	56	156
13	58 58	57	155	59 55	56	155	60 51	57	154	61 48	56	153	62 44	56	152	63 40	56	154
14	58 39	56	153	59 35	57	153	60 32	56	152	61 28	55	151	62 23	56	150	63 19	55	152
15	58 19	+56	152	59 15	+56	151	60 11	+55	150	61 06	+55	149	62 01	+55	149	62 56	+55	150
16	57 58	55	150	58 53	56	149	59 49	55	149	60 44	54	148	61 38	55	147	62 33	54	148
17	57 36	55	148	58 31	54	147	59 25	55	147	60 20	54	146	61 14	54	145	62 08	53	146
18	57 12	55	147	58 07	54	146	59 01	54	145	59 55	54	144	60 49	53	143	61 42	53	145
19	56 48	54	145	57 42	54	144	58 36	53	143	59 29	53	142	60 22	52	142	61 15	52	143
20	56 23	+53	143	57 16	+54	143	58 10	+53	142	59 03	+52	141	59 55	+52	140	60 47	+52	142
21	55 58	52	141	56 50	52	141	57 42	53	140	58 35	52	139	59 27	51	138	60 18	51	140
22	55 29	53	140	56 22	52	139	57 14	52	139	58 06	51	138	58 57	51	137	59 48	51	139
23	55 01	53	139	55 54	51	138	56 45	52	137	57 37	50	136	58 27	51	135	59 18	50	138
24	54 33	51	137	55 24	51	137	56 15	51	136	57 06	51	135	57 57	49	134	58 46	50	137
25	54 03	+51	136	54 54	+51	135	55 45	+50	134	56 35	+50	133	57 25	+49	132	58 14	+49	135
26	53 33	50	135	54 23	50	134	55 13	50	133	56 03	50	132	56 52	53	131	57 41	48	133
27	53 01	51	133	53 52	49	132	54 41	50	131	55 31	48	130	56 19	49	130	57 08	47	132
28	52 30	49	132	53 19	50	131	54 09	48	130	54 57	49	129	55 46	47	128	56 33	48	131
29	51 57	49	131	52 46	49	130	53 35	49	129	54 24	47	128	55 11	48	127	55 59	46	

Sight Reduction Tables for Air Navigation Ap 3270 (=HO249)

are the most suitable for small craft: Vol II covers latitudes 0°–39° and Vol III, 40°–89°. To work up a sight, choose a position near your DR such that the latitude is a whole degree and the longitude, when combined with the Greenwich hour angle (GHA), will give a whole degree of local hour angle (LHA). Enter the tables at the page indicated by the latitude and declination of the body. Extract the calculated altitude **Hc** and azimuth z. Then correct Hc for the odd minutes of declination **d** and compare it with the true altitude.

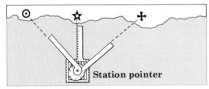

Station pointer

A Horizontal

sextant angle will provide an extremely accurate position fix. Three objects must be visible and the angle between them measured by holding the sextant horizontally. The easiest way to plot the bearings on the chart is to use a station pointer, the three arms of which are set to produce the two angles read off the sextant. The pointer is then moved around the chart until the three arms cut the three objects and the fix is at the centre of the plotter. Tracing paper can be used.

Sight reduction

The leap from a sextant observation to a position line is performed by means of sight reduction tables or a dedicated calculator. Declination and hour angle are both translated by means of the tables into altitude and azimuth. The difference in nautical miles between tabular and true altitude is the intercept. This is plotted from the assumed position along the line of azimuth towards the body if the observed altitude is greater than the tabular, and away from it, if it is less. A line perpendicular to the intercept represents the position line.

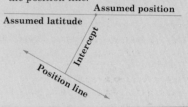

Noon sight

The simplest form of sight is the meridian altitude or noon sight, when the sun or moon lies due north or south of your position. The position line at right angles to the sun or moon's bearing thus defines a parallel of latitude, so no plotting is needed. The calculation involves finding the zenith distance, which is the angle the body is observed away from 90°, and adding or subtracting the declination to find the latitude. The sun's declination (angle from the Equator) may be north or south, depending on the time of year. In the northern hemisphere, if the declination is north (northern summer), latitude is zenith distance plus declination; if south, declination is subtracted. To find the time (GMT) of the sun's meridian passage at your own longitude, consult the almanac for time on the prime meridian. Convert the longitude from arc into time (1° = 4 min) and add, if west of Greenwich or subtract, if east.

Collision regulations

Every seaman should be familiar with the International Collision Regulations which apply to all vessels on the high seas and the navigable waters connected to them. The following steering and sailing rules are of particular importance to small craft.

Risk of collision exists if the compass bearing of an approaching vessel does not appreciably alter.

Action to avoid collision should be taken in good time and be bold enough to be obvious to the other vessel.

In narrow channels, vessels should keep to the starboard side. A sailing vessel should not hinder a vessel which can navigate safely only within the channel. No vessel should anchor within a narrow channel.

Traffic lanes should not normally be crossed; if they have to be, the crossing should be made as close as possible to a right angle. A sailing vessel should not hinder a vessel under power following a traffic lane.

When there is a risk of collision between two sailing vessels: (i) the vessel with the wind on the port side keeps clear; (ii) when both have the wind on the same side the windward vessel keeps clear; (iii) a vessel with the wind on the port side keeps clear of another, if there is a doubt as to which side the other vessel has the wind.

An overtaking vessel keeps clear of the vessel being overtaken. When two power-driven vessels meet head on, each alters course to starboard. When two power-driven vessels are crossing, the vessel which has the other on her own starboard side keeps clear. The give-way vessel must take early and substantial action to keep clear. A stand-on vessel keeps her course and speed but she may take action if a collision appears unavoidable.

A power-driven vessel gives way to a sailing vessel. A sailing vessel keeps clear of a vessel not under command, or restricted in her ability to manoeuvre, or fishing.

Manoeuvring and Warning Signals

●	I am altering course to starboard
● ●	I am altering course to port
● ● ●	I am operating astern propulsion
▬ ▬ ●	I intend to overtake on your starboard side
▬ ▬ ● ●	I intend to overtake, port side
▬ ● ▬ ●	I agree to be overtaken
● ● ● ● ●	I do not agree to be overtaken, I doubt you will avoid a collision
▬▬▬	Warning signal and reply when approaching a bend.

Shapes

Shape	Meaning
▼	Vessel motor-sailing
⧓	Vessel engaged in fishing
▲	Fishing nets extending more than 490 ft (150 m)
◆	Vessel towing if length of tow exceeds 650 ft (200 m)
●	Vessel at anchor
● ●	Vessel aground
● ● ●	Vessel dredging or conducting underwater operations. Pass on the side of the diamonds

Sound Signals in Fog

▬	Power vessel making way
▬ ▬	Power vessel under way but stopped
▬ ● ●	Vessel not under command; restricted in ability to manoeuvre; constrained by draft; a sailing vessel; vessel towing, pushing or fishing
▬ ● ● ●	Vessel under tow
🔔🔔🔔🔔	Vessel at anchor. If more than 100 m long, bell is followed by 5-sec gong

At night and in poor visibility, every power vessel under way must display port, starboard, stern and masthead lights. The legal distances from which the lights must be visible depend on the length of the boat. When entering foreign customs ports, check that your boat is equipped with the required lights for customs clearance. British customs, for example, request an all-round red light no more than 6 ft (2 m) above a white light.

Yachts under 7 m (23 ft): must display all-round white light in time to prevent a collision.

Yachts under 12 m (40 ft): may combine stern and side lights in a tricolour masthead light.

Yachts over 12 m (40 ft) must carry stern and port and starboard lights. No masthead light.

Yachts over 12 m (40 ft) may carry an all-round red light above an all-round green.

Power-driven vessels under 7 m (23 ft) carry white, all-round masthead light above a bicolour light.

Power-driven vessels under 12 m (40 ft) display white masthead and sternlight and sidelights.

Power-driven vessels under 20 m (65 ft) carry a white masthead light above a bicolour, also a sternlight.

Power-driven vessels may have a second, higher masthead light aft.

Vessels at anchor display all-round white light, visible from 2 mls (3.2 km)

When aground, two all-round red lights are shown below an all-round white light

Vessels not under command display two all-round red lights and, if making way, side- and sternlights

Vessels restricted in manoeuvrability carry a white mast-head, three all-round lights, side and sternlights.

When trawling, fishing vessels display an all-round green light above an all-round white.

When hauling nets, fishing vessels add to the trawling lights one white light over a red.

When fishing, other than trawling, vessels carry a red above a white all-round light.

When towing, vessels show two masthead lights forward or three, if the tow exceeds 200 m (657 ft).

131

Electronic and satellite navigation

Navigation involves conducting a craft safely and speedily to its destination and position finding is only one part of it. The danger of relying on electronic navigation is the tendency to equate good navigation with accurate position fixing. In fact, the good navigator is the one who makes best use of the information available, rather than the one who obtains the most accurate information.

With the explosion in electronic technology, however, the amount of information derived from position is increasing. The Decca Yacht Navigator, for example, displays not just latitude and longitude but the course-made-good over the last 10 mins. The Brookes and Gatehouse Hercules marine data system processes a wide range of inputs to give not only position but speed-made-good to windward, tacking performance, the wind speed etc. The limitation of all such systems is the reliability of the information fed into them.

To reduce such shortcomings, combination sets are appearing. The Satnav/Omega set, for example, derives an accurate but periodic fix from a satellite, and Omega uses the data to give a more accurate position.

It is interesting to speculate on the long-term effects on navigation of a completely reliable and highly accurate position-fixing system with worldwide coverage, such as Navstar GPS, assuming it eventually becomes commercially available. Logs, compasses and most other sensors could be rendered obsolete, since all navigational information could be derived from accurate position data. Such a development would introduce a revolution in navigational methods as profound as the introduction of the magnetic compass in the twelfth century and of the chronometer for establishing longitude in the eighteenth. But it would do nothing to lessen the need for good navigation.

■ **Decca full coverage**
▨ **Night coverage**

The Decca Navigator System covers most of western Europe and parts of Canada, Australia, South Africa and Japan. Its range varies from 175–350 n. miles from the station, and accuracy can vary from a few metres to a few miles at the limit of the coverage. A land-based master and two slave stations transmit signals which are radiated as hyperbolic lines. The Decca receiver on board compares the differences in phase and displays numbers corresponding to the hyperbolic position lines overprinted on the chart; where two such lines cross is the position. Recent displays give a latitude and longitude read-out.

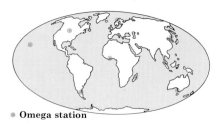

◉ **Omega station**

Since it operates on very low frequencies, Omega has worldwide coverage. Its accuracy, however, is limited to 1 ml during the day, and 2 mls at night. It transmits from eight stations set up in Trinidad, Hawaii, Japan, North Dakota, La Réunion, Argentina, Norway and Liberia. Unlike Decca and Loran, each station operates singly so that any two can be used to establish a position. If the boat's position is fed into the receiver on departure, it will give a continuous digital read-out of the hyperbolic lines being crossed, which, when plotted on the lattice chart, give the position.

■ Loran C coverage
▨ Skywave

Loran C, which is gradually replacing standard Loran, covers most of the United States, the North Atlantic and the Mediterranean. It has a range of about 1,500 n mls by day and can be accurate to 150 yds (136 m) when 1,000 mls (1,600 km) from the master station. The Loran receiver measures the time lapse between signals from the transmitters to calculate the position. This is displayed either as position lines to be read off the lattice chart or in terms of latitude and longitude. At long range, signals are received from sky waves and need correction.

Satellite navigators at present use the US Navy Navigation Satellite System. The installation consists of a masthead aerial receiver and computer. Several satellites orbit the Earth at 85 mls (1,100 km) up and are told their position by four tracking stations on Earth. They transmit their orbital position data every 2 mins. A satellite passes overhead 15–20 times a day for a period of 6–18 min, and at each pass the computer calculates latitude and longitude with an accuracy of 20–30 mls for a single pass or 5 mls for 25 passes. The computer then updates the position fix by dead reckoning until the next pass.

Choice of equipment

1 Decca, which is particularly useful for sailing in the North Atlantic and off the coasts of North-west Europe, needs no special expertise. Hitherto somewhat bulky for small vessels and only available on hire, compact sets are now on the market for around £1,000 ($2,000).

2 Omega lends itself to long-distance and world cruising. A big investment at £5,000 ($10,000), it is none the less the only hyperbolic system with worldwide coverage to give constant fixing ability.

3 Loran C is useful for cruising off the US coasts and in the Mediterranean. It costs about £1,200–3,000 ($2,400–6,000) and, unless it has an automatic latitude/longitude readout, requires skill for fast, accurate readings.

4 Satellite navigation sets compare well with other systems at a cost of £1,000–5,000 ($2,000–10,000).

The future

The future of electronic position finding probably lies in satellite navigators. The current transit system, which provides two- or three-hourly fixes with dead reckoning updates, will be superseded by the Navstar Global Position System (GPS), which promises continuous and highly accurate fixing, worldwide. A new direction for shorter-range and less-expensive direction-finding equipment may be VHF radio. Five VHF radio lighthouses are in operation experimentally around the British coast, and at Calais in France. A beacon transmits an audio VHF directional signal, rotating at a rate of 4° a second, identified by half-second beats equivalent to 2° of rotation. The bearing of the station is obtained by counting the number of beats between the start of the transmission and the passage of the null radial when the tone disappears. Special tables give the bearing.

Weather patterns

The sailor's greatest friend, and enemy, is atmospheric pressure. It not only causes daily fluctuations in wind and weather but remains the most accurate source of weather forecasts. The standard pressure at sea level is 1013.2 millibars (29.92 inches of mercury on the barometer) and it falls with altitude so that at about 20,000 ft (6,100 m) up it is approximately half that at the Earth's surface.

Variations in the standard pressure occur at the surface because cold air is more dense and sinks, while warm air is buoyant and rises. Cold air from high, polar latitudes and warm, subtropical air meeting in the temperate latitudes are distorted by the Earth's rotation to form high-and low-pressure circulations – the anticyclones and depressions – with their associated fine and unsettled weather conditions respectively.

Warm air holds more invisible water vapour than cold air and cooling causes moisture to condense into cloud, rain or fog, or, if the air is very cold, into snow or hail.

When pressure falls, air expands and cools, thus increasing the amount of cloud. If the fall continues cloud may lower and thicken enough to produce rain. When pressure rises, the air is compressed and warms, and cloud cover breaks up. If it continues to rise, becoming anticyclonic, subsidence of the air results in haze.

Wind is air moving from higher to lower pressure – or from a cooler to a warmer place. However, it does not blow directly from one to the other since it is deflected by the Earth's rotation – to the right in the northern hemisphere.

Circulation around a low is anticlockwise, so when facing into the wind, pressure will be lower to the right. In the southern hemisphere the situation is reversed, producing eastward-moving fronts, and clockwise-circulating winds.

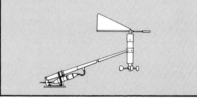

Cirrus cloud gives advance warning of low pressure moving eastwards across the Atlantic, *above.*

Cirrus, the prophet of unsettled weather, forms at great heights from ice crystals. If it does not spread and thicken, the bad weather is passing to one side. Small or shapeless cirrus may accompany anticyclones, and pose no threat.

Reading the weather

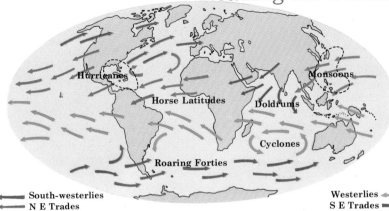

Hurricanes

Monsoons

Horse Latitudes

Doldrums

Cyclones

Roaring Forties

← South-westerlies
← N E Trades

Westerlies ←
S E Trades →
Typhoons

Wind is air moving from high to low pressure. It does not blow directly from one to the other as it is deflected by the Earth's easterly rotation. The north-easterly and south-easterly Trade winds blow in towards the low-pressure doldrums at the equator. High-pressure belts either side bring light, variable winds. In the past, becalmed ships offloaded their livestock cargo in these 'Horse Latitudes'. The poleward winds, bent by the globe's curve, become westerlies – stronger in the southern 'Roaring Forties' than in the depression-laden northern Forties. Land masses complicate wind systems and annual variations in temperature bring seasonal winds. Monsoons blow from sea to warm land in the summer and from land to warmer sea in winter. Tropical revolving storms, known as cyclones, hurricanes or typhoons, occur in the early autumn.

Drizzle and thick stratus accompany the warm front. The following cold front brings heavy rain and heaped clouds.

'Cotton-wool' cumulus clouds indicate fine weather. They spread and flatten in moist air, and thunderheads may develop if the air is unstable. Forming early in the day over land, they signal the likelihood of sea breezes.

Squalls and unexpectedly strong winds may follow the cold front, after a short period of clear sky. Prepare for rain.

Squalls, often accompanied by local rain and hail, may occur when cumulus develop in unstable air after a cold front. The cloud grows fast, drawing in local air. This causes strong, gusty winds to blow from different directions.

135

Interpreting the forecast

Use all the forecast information available: national and local radio, television and daily newspapers. Carry a barometer or, better, a barograph, and set an alarm to catch the shipping forecasts. The times and radio frequencies of offshore forecasts vary all over the world and must be found out locally. Ask the coastguards for more precise and up-to-date actual details of weather in their own locality.

The shipping forecast may begin with a summary of gale warnings, issued if the mean wind speed is expected to rise to Force 8 (34 kn) or if Force-9 (43-kn) gusts are anticipated. When described as *imminent*, the gale is expected to arrive within six hours, *soon* means it may come within 6–12 hrs and *later* indicates the possibility of gale-force winds in more than 12 hrs. Storm cones or flags are hoisted at coastguard stations and harbours to warn of gales.

A general synopsis follows, giving details of the current position and direction of movement of High- and Low-pressure systems. If the pressure is above 1020 millibars (mb) and steady, the weather should be settled for the next 24 hrs, except for sea fog. A rapid fall of 10 mb in three hours shows worsening weather with backing (anticlockwise shifting) and strengthening winds, or a gale soon; a steady fall indicates less imminent bad weather. A rapid rise brings clearing skies and a veering (clockwise shifting) wind, but often a strong short blow; a steady rise means better weather is on its way. The speed of each weather system is described as: *slowly* (0–15 kn), *steadily* (15–25 kn), *rather quickly* (25–30 kn), *rapidly* (35–45 kn) or *very rapidly* (over 45 kn).

Visibility is described as: *good* (more than 5 mls or 8 km), *moderate* (2–5 mls or 3–8 km), *poor* (1,100 yds–2 mls or 1097 m – 3 km), *fog* (less than 1,100 yds or 1,097 m).

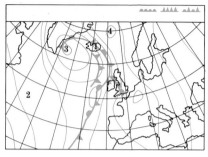

Isobars close together indicate strong winds, **1**; widely spaced over a large area they indicate slack pressure and small weather changes, **2**. After bad weather, watch for a small but vicious low forming on the trailing cold front of a large depression, **3**. A ridge of high pressure, **4**, often gives a single day (or night) of good weather between depressions. As it approaches, the wind veers and drops; there is less cloud. When it passes, the wind backs and freshens, and high cloud appears.

Plotting a weather map
Weather centres and chandlers usually supply maps of different sea areas with a plotting form on the back. Record the shipping forecast on tape and write down every detail in shorthand on the form. Then transcribe the information on to the plotting map (see back of jacket) using symbols, *right*. Locate centres of Highs and Lows, plot reported pressures and join lines of equal pressure (isobars). Plot reported wind, rain and fronts and add, in another colour, forecast winds and weather to show the movement of earlier systems. The symbols in one area may read:

meaning, wind south-westerly 4, becoming westerly 5 or 6, rain then showers, visibility good, 1024 (pressure) falling then rising. Note time and date of forecast.

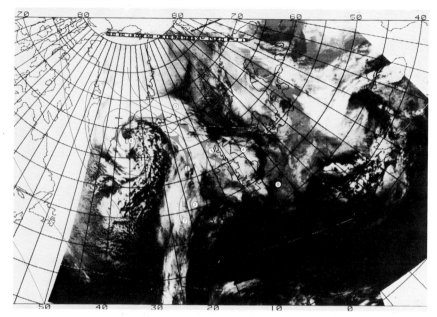

This is an old, decaying Low, **1**. The cold front has caught up with the warm front and is now occluded, **2**. Cloud is still thick in the north, **3**, drizzle mixing with heavier rain.

As a warm front approaches, cloud steadily thickens and lowers with drizzle, or sleet preceded by snow in winter. Here the front is weakening with the cloud breaking up, **4**.

Cold fronts move faster than warm, and a new, active cold front can be vicious, with heavy rain. Here a second and more active cold front, **5**, has developed behind the original one, on which cloud evaporates as it weakens. Note the sharp clearance behind the following cold front, then a band of clear sky before showers or squalls develop (likely before midday).

A trailing cold front may spawn a small, fierce, secondary Low, **6**. This can move fast, with strong, gusty winds rapidly changing direction cyclonically, and can be dangerous, if not expected. Note cloud forming. Farther south, another secondary is in its early stages, **7**, and will move around the circulation of the original low.

The high-pressure area **8**, is almost free of cloud, and partly responsible for the decay of the warm front now in its influence. If a High is large and well established, approaching fronts pile up and decay. The weather stays fine though the wind may freshen.

Use these symbols when taking down the radio forecast. Arrows indicate the direction and force of the wind and any expected changes. Arrows fly with the wind; a whole barb is added for two Beaufort forces; half added for one.	✓ **Visibility Good** — **Moderate** = **Poor** ≡ **Fog** ⊕ **Overcast**	∞ **Haze** ✳ **Snow** △ **Hail** ✳ **Sleet** ○ **Blue sky** ◐ **Partly cloudy** ❜ **Drizzle**	• **Rain** ⋮ **Heavy rain** ⋎ **Squall** ▽ **Showers** ⎦ **Thunderstorm** < **Lightning** ▽ **Thundery showers**

The visual clues

To benefit from a forecast and to check its accuracy, it is important to observe and recognize what you see in the sky. It can reveal all you need to know for the next 4–5 hrs over a distance of 30–50 mls. Coastal winds may differ from those generally forecast.

When there is good convective heating over the land, a sea breeze develops. This pulls in cool air from the sea as early as mid-morning.

Along the coast, the sea breeze is more likely to change the direction of the prevailing wind than increase its force. However, if big cumulus clouds grow over the land in the afternoon, the sea breeze may increase to as much as Force 6 or 7 in estuaries.

However, if the prevailing wind is already from seaward, it will be intensified by the sea breeze without much change in direction. If the wind is from the land, any existing cumulus will drift out over the sea. These will clear from seaward with the approach of the sea breeze. If the land wind and sea breeze converge, a line of cloud with a ragged, wispy base may form along the junction of the opposing winds. The wind often drops before the sea breeze arrives. Sea breezes occur less frequently in the late summer when the sea is warmer.

Heat thunderstorms grow mainly in the afternoon over land, but may drift out over coastal waters. If the air is hazy, towering cumulonimbus cloud developing over the land may not be observed. The wind blowing out from the storm following the calm is often gusty and cold, bringing sudden heavy rain or hail.

If a thundery low is forecast this may produce extensive cloud of variable thickness, some rumbling and poor visibility.

When a warm front approaches, with thick cloud and drizzle, the air blowing up over cliffs will be cooled so that orographic cloud forms, often obscuring the cliffs from seaward.

Fog

Fog develops more rapidly over salty than over fresh water.

Sea fog forms when moist air moves over cold water or when cold air cools the surface of warmer water. Since the saturation or dew-point is reached earlier in cool air than in warm, the moisture is condensed into fog.

Coastal fog may occur when sea fog is carried in by a sea breeze or when warm oceanic air blows across cold coastal water.

Action: Slow down, use your fog horn, radar reflector and navigation lights. Keep a good all-round lookout and listen. Keep a close check on your position, and avoid sailing near shipping lanes.

Wind increases around prominent headlands and eddies may form on the lee side. Pass a few miles to seaward. Large coastal features will distort the strength and direction of the sea breeze.

An apparently sheltered cove may suffer from sudden powerful gusts pouring over the cliffs. At night, cool air may flow down from higher land causing a katabatic wind.

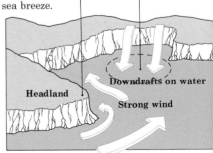

Downdrafts on water

Headland

Strong wind

If the contrail from a jet is thin and evaporates quickly, the upper air is dry and settled. If it spreads and lingers, watch for signs of change.

A large, 22° halo with red inside it, around the sun or moon, means high ice-crystal cirrus and a distant low. A red corona shows with water-droplet cloud.

Sea types

Waves are generated by gusts of wind pushing into the surface of the water, and the energy transfers from wave to wave like a ripple down a rope. Waves take time to gather momentum and their height is only partly determined by wind strength. A long swell, produced by waves formed a long way away, local wind waves and surface ripples, can cause a confused sea when they meet at different angles. when all the crests of several wave systems coincide, a 'rogue' wave may result. At the coast, tides, coastal features and water depths complicate the sea. In deep water, **1**, the energy of the waves has room to dissipate, but in shallow water, **2**, the waves are forced to rise and break. Water thus becomes turbulent over shoals and sand-bars, **3**.

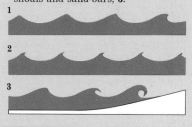

Steep cliffs may block the sea breeze, which develops around mid-morning, causing it to become intermittent or erratic.

The risk of sailing along a steep–to lee shore in a strong wind may be less than passing to windward of a shallow bank or shoal which causes approaching seas to heap up into steep waves.

Wind against tide creates choppy water. At a shallow harbour entrance, particularly with a bar, high, breaking waves are a hazard. Ensure there is adequate depth in the wave troughs.

Air always takes the easiest route and will funnel down river valleys. The Mistral, which blows down the Rhône valley, exemplifies the strong winds which may result.

Sea breeze

Inshore passage and lee shore

Shoal water

Tide

Steep waves

Estuary

Wind

Equipping for safety

The safety equipment on any yacht depends on where it sails, its size, and the likelihood of being out in bad weather. It is rare for a new boat to come complete with equipment and even a second-hand boat, supposedly fully equipped, may in fact be fitted with time-expired or outdated safety apparatus.

The first thing an owner must do is to assess where he thinks the dangers lie, then spend a day delving into the interior of his boat checking the fuel, water, gas and electrical systems.

A visit to any chandler will reveal a complexity of so-called 'essential' safety equipment. But, unfortunately, much of the apparatus creeping in under this guise is electronic and, apart from VHF radio or an EPIRB, of no practical use in an emergency.

When planning your list of essentials, start with the headings: Personal, Group/Crew and Boat; and the attitude that once at sea you should be totally self-sufficient, with adequate training and knowledge to cope with most emergencies. This leaves the real accident, medical emergency or situation caused by gear failure, grounding, hull damage or inextinguishable fire for outside assistance.

Personal safety of each member of the crew starts with an awareness of the types of emergency that can occur, knowledge of where all safety equipment is stowed, and how it works. Personal equipment includes appropriate clothing to combat heat and cold; safety harness to prevent falling overboard and a life-jacket in the event of abandoning ship. If the Group/Crew act responsibly, aware that a thoughtless action may endanger others, a corporate safety umbrella is set up.

As with all safety precautions, prevention is better than cure, and a regular checking and maintenance schedule of properly installed systems should prevent accidents.

Minimum safety requirements for coastal cruising boats (A) and ocean-going yachts (B) are:

	A	B
PERSONAL (for each crew member)		
1 Warm clothing, oilskins, seaboots, life-jacket, safety harness	*	*
GROUP/CREW		
1 Liferaft for all crew		*
2 Horseshoe life-belt, drogue and self-igniting light	1	2
3 Buoyant heaving line	*	*
4 Dan buoy		*
5 Hand-held VHF/CB radio (EPIRB for B)	*	*
BOAT		
Means of propulsion:		
1 Storm try-sail or reefed mainsail and storm jib	*	*
2 Independent battery or hand start for engine	*	*
Anchors		
1 With appropriate chain	1	2
2 Strong mooring point on foredeck	*	*
Bailing and Bilge Pumping		
1 Buckets with lanyard	2	2
2 Bilge pumps (1 electric, B)	2	2
Detection		
1 Radar reflector, fixed navigation lights, foghorn, powerful torch/lamp	*	*
Flares		
1 Hand-held: 4 red, 4 white	*	*
2 Hand-held smoke signals: 2 orange	*	
3 Buoyant smoke signals: 2 orange		*
4 Red parachute rockets	2	4
Fire-fighting equipment		
1 Fire blanket	*	*
2 1.5 kg dry-powder extinguishers	2	2
Radio		
1 For shipping forecasts	*	*
Navigational equipment		
1 Adequate charts, tide tables, almanac, pilots, etc.	*	*
2 Steering compass, hand-bearing compass	*	*
3 Drawing instruments, barometer, lead and line, echo sounder, watch or clock	*	*
4 Radio direction finder	*	*

Safety at sea

Two horseshoe life-belts, 1, should be stowed in quick-release holders on the guard rails within easy reach of the helmsman. House the top and bottom parts of the dan buoy pole in two short lengths of tube lashed to the backstay or in a tube glassed into the stern of the boat. A stern boarding-ladder, **3,** makes it easier to recover anyone who may fall overboard.

Stow the liferaft on deck, just abaft the mast, **4,** or in a deck locker where it is accessible in an emergency. Liferafts are packed either in rigid containers with quick-release straps or in soft, easily-carried bags. The painter triggers the inflation device, so secure it to a strong point.

For stability, freshwater tanks, **5,** should be located low down. Clean them often and check for contamination. Ensure that sea-cocks to galley, heads and engine, **6,** are always shut after use or when leaving the boat.

A wet, slippery deck is dangerous when doing deck work. There should be non-skid strips, **7,** at least on the foredeck and coach/cabin trunk roof. Netting attached to the lifelines, **8,** will stop a foresail or even a child from going over the side.

All fuels are fire hazards, so site the fuel tank, **9,** as far as possible from the engine and hot exhaust pipe. Keep fire extinguishers handy – one just inside the forward hatch, another by the main hatch, **10,** or in a cockpit locker, **11.**

Engine spaces, 12, must be clean and well vented. All fuel pipes should be copper, and drip-trays large and deep enough not to overflow when heeling.

Secure the gas bottle inside a cockpit locker, **13,** with a drain directly through the topside. Turn off the gas at the bottle as well as at the cooker. A gas detector in the bilges, **14,** will give added security.

The electrical system is a source of heat and sparks which could cause an explosion, so cables must be adequate for the load, and fuses, insulation and earthing efficient. Batteries should be sited close to the engine starter motor in an easy-to-reach, vented box, with an acid-proof tray beneath them, **15.**

Signalling for help

Distress signals should not be used unless the situation justifies it. At the same time, as an emergency is developing, it is impossible to know what the outcome will be. Fortunately, the majority of rescue services would rather you advised them early than late, particularly since they may take some time to reach you.

VHF radio is now emerging as the foremost safety aid to the average yachtsman. Its greatest asset is that it enables you to speak directly to other vessels and shore stations, giving precise details of the emergency and your estimated position. Its greatest drawback is that many people do not know the correct procedures for using it.

Check that the radio is switched on, transmitting on maximum power and tuned to Channel 16, the International Distress Safety and Calling frequency. Send the International Distress Signal MAYDAY (from the French *m'aidez*) only if your boat or a person is in serious or imminent danger and immediate assistance is required. It takes priority over all other calls.

Give the name and estimated position of your boat, the nature of the distress and the help required, and if you have time, any other information which might aid rescue vessels or aircraft. If no one answers within 30 secs, check the controls, and repeat the message at regular intervals. If there is still no reply change to Channels 6 or 8, which are ship-to-ship and within the US Coastguard frequency.

In mid-ocean, make a call on VHF or on 2182 kHz on the MF band. If there is no response from shipping, switch on your EPIRB and hope that overflying aircraft will pick up the signal.

Use the urgency signal PAN PAN, when safety of the boat or a person is a priority but no immediate aid is needed. In a medical emergency use PAN PAN MEDICO, but ask to be switched to a working channel away from Channel 16.

Choice of radio

VHF radio is the workhorse, with a range of 15–30 miles (24–28 km) and 55 Channels. Its main uses are to link up with the telephone system via coastal stations, to contact harbour authorities and to alert search and rescue services. MF with a range of around 350 miles (560 km) is effective in near offshore areas and gives a better chance of contacting a ship. EPIRBs are a most effective way for search and rescue aircraft to find and keep track of a liferaft or casualty in the sea. Their range is 150–250 miles (200–400 km) and they will send out signals for 36–96 hrs.

Antennae are usually masthead mounted. A whip antenna on the stern ensures radio contact if the mast breaks.

Visual distress signals

There are some commonly accepted distress signals which are independent of radio or flares. Morse Code in any form – blinker light, sound or visual signalling – is international; SOS is the distress signal.

Visual signals include:
Standing up and slowly raising and lowering your arms.
Thick black smoke, as from burning oily rags in a bucket on deck.
The ensign hoisted upside down.
A square flag with a ball or anything resembling a ball above or below it.
A piece of clothing attached to an oar or spar held up in the air.
International code flags include:
F   I am disabled
V   I require assistance
O   Man overboard
W   I require medical assistance
AN I need a doctor
Aids to identification from the air:
Dye marker in the sea.
A piece of orange cloth with a black square and circle on it.

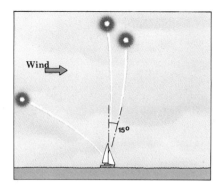

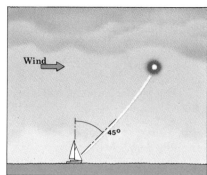

Rockets turn into the wind, so aim them vertically, or 15° downwind in strong winds. Hold handflares downwind to avoid dropping burning particles on clothing or on to a liferaft.

Beware loss of night vision when using a white collision flare; shield the eyes while it is burning. When using short-burning flares, fire two with an interval of about one minute.

In low cloud fire rockets at a 45° angle downwind, so that the flare is visible under the cloud. In poor visibility do not fire all your flares at once; keep some until conditions improve.

Flares have a life of 3 yrs if well stored. Inspect them twice a year for signs of deterioration and replace any which are suspect. Replace all flares by the expiry date on the label.

Flares have two functions: to draw attention to the boat and to pinpoint its position. The flares you should carry depend on your cruising ground. Minimum requirements are: *Inshore:* 2 red handflares, 2 hand-held orange smoke signals – use in bright daylight and light wind. *Coastal:* 2 red parachute rockets, 2 red handflares, 2 hand-held orange smoke signals. *Offshore:* 4 red parachute rockets, 4 red handflares, 2 buoyant orange smoke signals. All boats at sea at night should carry 4 white handflares for collision warning.

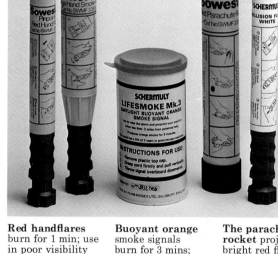

Red handflares burn for 1 min; use in poor visibility and high wind. Hand-held orange smoke signals burn for 40 secs.

Buoyant orange smoke signals burn for 3 mins; use to signal to aircraft. White handflares burn for 50 secs.

The parachute rocket projects a bright red flare to a height of more than 1,000 ft (305 m) which burns for over 40 secs.

Recovering a man overboard

Man overboard is, without doubt, the most frightening situation that can face any crew member, especially if it is the skipper of a family-crewed boat who falls overboard.

The subject of 'Man overboard' has been written about so often that it is in danger of falling into the category of, 'I know that bit so I'll move on to the next chapter.' But before you do – are you quite sure that, as the skipper of your family or racing yacht, you have equipped your boat and trained your crew sufficiently well for them to pick *you* up at night in freshening conditions of Force 4, gusting 5?

When any person falls into the water they are visibly immediately reduced to the size of a football, say 14 in (35 cm) high, and the truth is that none of us, even the most experienced of skippers, can guarantee to find, let alone pick up, a person who has gone overboard in poor conditions. Go overboard, even in a moderate breeze, and you run the risk of not being picked up; at night in a blow, death is almost a certainty.

Established, safe working routines go a long way towards keeping the crew where they belong – on the boat. Safety harnesses used in conjunction with deck-mounted jackstays are the surest safety devices. Life-jackets or buoyancy aids, worn whenever there is the likelihood of falling or being swept overboard, ensure that a person will stay afloat.

The problem is when to insist on such routines. On a hot sunny day, running under spinnaker or boomed out genoa in 20 kn of wind, your crew would not bless you for disturbing their sunbathing. Yet if one of them fell overboard, it would take all of five minutes for the average family or 'guest' crew to get the boat under control so that they could motorsail back to the MOB. Maybe a rope trailed astern would be the average skipper's compromise.

ACTION when someone falls overboard:
1 Whoever sees the incident shouts 'Man overboard', and points to him.
2 The person nearest the dan buoy and horseshoe life-belt throws them over, shouting 'Life-belt clear'.
3 The helmsman shouts 'Time' and 'Log'. Everyone not involved notes the time and one person notes the distance on the log and the course steered in subsequent manoeuvres.
4 The skipper takes charge of the rescue operation, leaving the steering to the helmsman who was steering at the time, and the navigation to the navigator. On a family boat the skipper may have to do both jobs.
5 The skipper's first priority is to stop the boat's progress away from the MOB and to return by the most direct route. Unless he plans to sail back, headsails and spinnaker should be lowered and lashed to the guard rail and the engine started.

Surviving in the water
A good life-jacket should have at least 35 lb (16 kg) of buoyancy. The type with permanent buoyancy is bulky to wear and to stow and most people prefer the type inflated by an inbuilt CO_2 cylinder. An insulated life-jacket will also help to retain body heat, especially if a person adopts the heat escape lessening posture, or HELP. Holding the arms tight against the sides of the chest and pressing the thighs together and raising them to close off the groin area will significantly reduce heat loss from these critical areas.

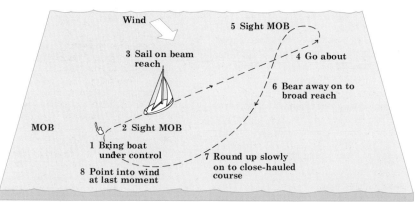

Wind

5 Sight MOB

3 Sail on beam reach

4 Go about

6 Bear away on to broad reach

MOB

2 Sight MOB

1 Bring boat under control

7 Round up slowly on to close-hauled course

8 Point into wind at last moment

If you have to pick up a MOB under sail, carry out **1–4** in ACTION and place the boat on a beam reach at 90° to the wind. Sail for 30 secs then go about on a reciprocal course. Identify the MOB; bear away on to a broad reach, round up so the MOB is on the windward beam; secure him with a rope.

The simplest way to recover a MOB is by means of a ladder, but if he is wearing a lifejacket or safety harness, you can attach a halyard and winch him up.

Alternatively tie a bowline in a halyard, put the loop under his arms and winch in; lash a half-inflated dinghy alongside, and get him into that first.

The answer to the problem of how to find a MOB and keep him afloat lies in the dan buoy, or safety

Bright light

Strips or narrow flags rather than large flag

pole with an attached horseshoe life-buoy, and drogue to retard drift. The pole is 8–10 ft (2.5–3 m) long, weighted at the bottom to keep it erect, and with a float 3–5 ft (1–1.5 m) from the bottom.

Thin fishing rod to offer least resistance

Drogue

6 m floating line

Bridle on float

Light activated by sea water battery in float

Horseshoe life-buoy with light

Large-diameter plastic pipe with flooding holes; bottom filled with lead

Steering failures

Inability to steer may well endanger the boat and the lives of all on board. It is essential, therefore, to plan ahead so that in the event of loss or damage to the steering gear, you have on board the wherewithal to make up some form of emergency rig.

On most modern designs, the fin and skeg or spade-rudder configuration results in increased windward ability, but if the steering fails the boat is virtually unmanageable. It is almost impossible to repair or replace a spade-rudder while at sea, but it is not too difficult on most boats to fit an outboard rudder on the transom, and it may be as well in this type of boat to carry one. The traditional long-keeled yacht with a transom-hung rudder is in a much better position.

If the rudder becomes jammed and cannot be freed immediately, it is essential to stop the boat making way by lowering sail or stopping the engine and heaving to. If the rudder is free it is usually possible to steer a small boat temporarily with an oar. Self-steering gear which uses even a small auxiliary rudder may be used in an emergency in light weather, with reduced sail. When it is not possible to make any progress under sail, try the engine alone, using the emergency steering rig to counteract the turning movement of the propeller.

Tillers usually break when conditions are boisterous. Surprisingly, it is often difficult to find a substitute and there is the added problem that most tillers are attached to the rudder stock with a special metal fitting. If about 1 ft (30 cm) remains it may be possible to lash the broken piece to it and to steer with rope taken to winches, but the lesson would seem to be to carry a spare tiller and rudder-head fittings.

There is no substitute for thinking ahead, so be prepared with some plan for emergency steering and test it out beforehand.

Keel configurations

When the rudder post breaks below deck level, but the rudder is still in place and moves freely, a keel-hung rudder, 1, can be operated by ropes attached from the after end and led to the cockpit. A spade-rudder, 2, is much more difficult to rig this way, since the ropes must be brought quite far forward through blocks on the gunwales and back to the cockpit. Prepare for this by having a hole drilled in the rudder.

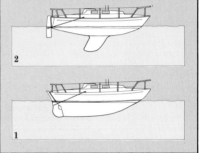

Wheel steering

With wheel steering you need a quickly rigged emergency tiller. The wheel drives a sprocket, 1, which moves a chain, 2. The wires are attached to the chain and thence to the quadrant, 3, via a number of pulleys, 4. If the wire is too slack and slips off a pulley it can jam. In this event, fit the emergency tiller, release the wires, remove the pulley and extract the wire – refit.

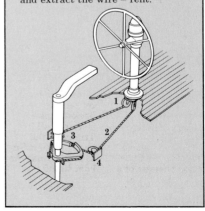

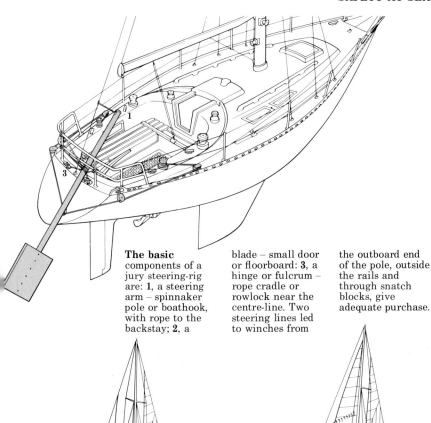

The basic components of a jury steering-rig are: **1**, a steering arm – spinnaker pole or boathook, with rope to the backstay; **2**, a blade – small door or floorboard: **3**, a hinge or fulcrum – rope cradle or rowlock near the centre-line. Two steering lines led to winches from the outboard end of the pole, outside the rails and through snatch blocks, give adequate purchase.

Boats which have divided rigs can be steered with sails alone simply by trimming or slackening sheets. The best rig for a sloop consists of a large jib to supply power and hold the bows off and a large riding sail set on the backstay as a steering sail. Trimming the sheet of the riding sail will cause the boat to luff, slackening it will let her fall off.

Some steering control is obtained by towing a small tyre which can be shifted from side to side by using a steering bridle, attached to the tow line with rolling hitches. The farther sideways the drag can be moved, the more effective it is. So lead each end of the bridle through blocks at the ends of a spar, lashed across the stern, which extends outboard on each side.

147

Rigging failures

Standing rigging is carefully designed to support the mast from the minimum number of directions; once a single part of it fails, the mast is in danger of breaking through bending.

Inspect the rigging frequently, keeping an eye open for worn threads on screw fittings, missing or worn clevis pins and frayed wires, and replace or repair the part as soon as a weakness is spotted. If you notice a weakness when under sail, put the boat on the point of sailing which minimizes the stress on that area until repairs can be made.

Broken shrouds and stays can often be replaced by spare halyards, if the mast is intact, and it is a good idea to carry a spare flexible 7×19 or 7×7 wire for the longest stay which can be cut to any required length.

No two masts break in the same way; the only general advice, therefore, is to rescue as much of the rig as possible: halyards, shrouds, sails and pieces of the mast. If you are lucky enough to have a break above the lower shrouds you have the basis for a workable jury rig.

Masts which bend or break should be secured to the deck quickly. Retrieving the mainsail is often the principal problem because, if it runs in a groove, it will be securely held at the break or bend. Try to open up the ends of the track with a hammer and screwdriver so that the sail can be edged through and lowered. If it is attached with slides you may have to cut them off the sail.

When the mast goes over the side, it is usually to leeward and the first priority must be to avert further damage by ramming padding between the spar and the hull. You can then decide how to cope with the tangled mass of wire, rope and submerged sails, and how to haul the mast out of the water and secure it to the toe rail, while working out a satisfactory jury rig to get you home.

Jury rigs

If you have material for spars on board, you can jury rig the boat and get it sailing again. Where the lower part of the mast is intact you can gain height by using the gunter rig, often found on small dinghies. Use the spinnaker pole, boom or top section of the mast to form the gaff and lash the top part of the mainsail to it. The sprit rig also increases the sail area, but uses the lower part of the mainsail. Stitch a loop to the leech of the sail to take the top of the sprit; you may be able to use the cringle of the top reef. The bottom end of the sprit should be adjustable so you can tension it.

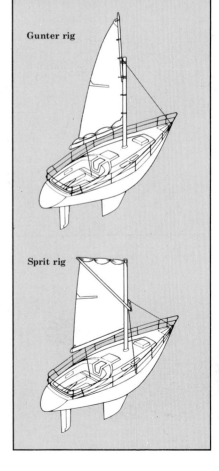

Gunter rig

Sprit rig

Attaching ropetails
A broken wire can be utilized by attaching a rope tail to it. Either make a loop and secure it to the wire with bulldog clips or make a tuck splice, using a hollow fid, 1, and knot the end of the rope. A tail can be added to a halyard with a knot such as anglers use to tie on their hooks, 2. Knot the end of the rope, and pull the whole thing tight with pliers.

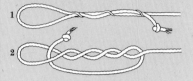

Dismasting checklist
1 Do NOT start the engine. Stray ropes could foul the propeller.
2 Do NOT rush around on deck. You run the risk of tripping overboard.
3 Get some sort of padding between the mast and the hull.
4 Get the mast alongside.
5 Get the sails off the mast to prevent tearing; they will be needed.
6 Cut only those wires and halyards which restrict the mast's retrieval.
7 Haul the mast up out of the water. Drain the water out of an open-ended metal mast by raising the head to deck level first.
8 Lash the mast along the deck.

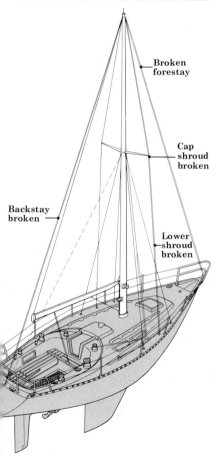

Broken forestay

Cap shroud broken

Backstay broken

Lower shroud broken

If the forestay snaps, the whole rig will sag back a little. Release mainsheet tension as you bear away on to a broad reach or run. Spare jib and spinnaker halyards can be rigged to the forestay anchorage, bow cleats or sampson post to provide emergency guying.

If the backstay breaks, you may lose the whole rig over the front of the boat. If it is a failure of wire splice or rigging screw/turnbuckle, the rig may survive. Steer on to a close reach and tighten the mainsheet. This enables the boat to fit nicely into the waves without causing the rig to sway about. Rig the topping lift or a spare halyard to a stern cleat or backstay.

The shrouds prevent the mast bending sideways. If any of them breaks under load it is most likely that the mast will also break. If it does not, tack at once so that the wind blows on the other side. When a cap shroud breaks, the mast usually snaps off just above the attachment point for the lower shrouds. If one of these breaks, release all tension in the rig – kicking strap, halyards – as soon as the boat has turned on to the other tack. Rig a sheet to duplicate the broken wire, leading it to a winch via a deck-edge snatch block.

Fire hazards

Fires and explosions are the principal causes of damage to pleasure craft and of personal injury. Most sailors are aware of the hazards and emergencies associated with the sea, and their boat's equipment reflects this knowledge: shelters from rain and spray, large efficient bilge pumps, reliable diesel engines. Most owners are, however, lamentably ignorant of fire prevention and fire-fighting methods and equipment, especially of how to fight different types of fire.

The main danger areas are the cooker and its fuel system, the engine and its fuel system, batteries and smokers – whether of pipes or cigarettes.

Cooker fuels include alcohol, paraffin/kerosene and bottled gas. All but bottled gas should be stored in leakproof containers whose contents must be poured into the small tank on the cooker via a funnel. Bottled gas must be stored outside the cabin space and connected to the cooker by seamless copper and flexible piping. Being heavier than air, any gas which leaks will lie in the bilges, pervading the whole boat; if exposed to naked flame .it will ignite, and the resulting explosion demolish the boat. Always ensure that the boat is left well-ventilated and hand-pump or bail the bilges as soon as you come on board.

More common and less disastrous is a fire in the galley, which should be smothered with an asbestos fire blanket (kept handy to the cooker and reusable) or even a wet bunk blanket, or by using a dry-powder extinguisher. Never use water on burning fuel or oil, it will only spread the flames.

Some skippers will not allow smoking below decks because of the risks involved and smokers must be exceptionally careful. Ashtrays must be emptied often – overboard to leeward – and only safety matches should be used aboard, since the other type can ignite by friction.

Engines and fuel systems
Modern diesel engines have a high safety record. The fuel is less volatile than petrol/gas and exhaust systems are efficiently cooled with water, but once alight it burns fiercely. Petrol engines need much more care: they should be fitted with flame traps on the carburettor, drip trays, and vent pipe; at least two 'on/off' taps on fuel lines and a fuel filter. The filler tube has to be connected to the fuel tank and the tank to the engine, with an electric bonding cable to earth it, and the engine compartment vented with a flameproof fan.

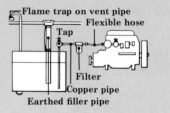

Flame trap on vent pipe
Flexible hose
Tap
Filter
Copper pipe
Earthed filler pipe

Fire extinguishers
Dry-powder extinguishers, *left*, eject chemical powder under great pressure. They can be used on all types of fire and douse flames quickly. The type with a controllable discharge enables you to hold some in reserve in the event of the fire rekindling. The BCF, *right*, is a compound liquid for killing fires in engine compartments or for fighting fuel or engine fires in the open only, since the vapour and fumes are toxic.

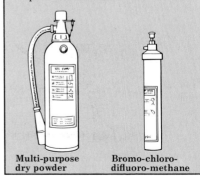

Multi-purpose dry powder

Bromo-chlorodifluoro-methane

The recommended minimum number of fire extinguishers which should be carried is:
Auxiliary craft up to 30 ft (9 m) LOA Three extinguishers of the largest size which can be accommodated, but never less than 3 lb (1.4 kg) capacity, dry powder or BCF.
Auxiliary craft over 30 ft (9 m) LOA Three dry-powder extinguishers, one of at least 7 lb (3 kg) capacity, and the other two of at least 3 lb (1.4 kg) capacity.
Motor cruisers with powerful engines and carrying large quantities of fuel. Two dry-powder extinguishers of 7 lb (3 kg) capacity; three if more than 30 ft (9 m) LOA.

If you discover a fuel or gas leak:
1 Turn off engine, stop smoking, put out all naked flames, switch off electrical appliances.
2 Turn off fuel and gas at source.
3 Open all hatches and portholes and air the boat thoroughly before making repairs.
If a fire occurs:
1 Raise the alarm – shout 'FIRE'.
2 Use the fire blanket to smother the flames or to protect yourself.
3 Attack the fire with an extinguisher, aiming at the source of the flames.
Never use water on electrical, fuel or galley fires. Use only on fires in wood or to cool down a burned area.

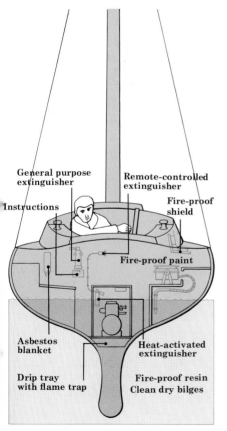

General purpose extinguisher

Instructions

Remote-controlled extinguisher

Fire-proof shield

Fire-proof paint

Asbestos blanket

Heat-activated extinguisher

Drip tray with flame trap

Fire-proof resin
Clean dry bilges

The best fire protection is given by a fixed remote-controlled system, backed up by portable fire extinguishers, a fire blanket and heat-proof shield by the galley, fire-proof bilge paint and a warning device.

Bottled gas and petrol systems should be fitted with solid state sensors or warning devices of the type where an alarm is triggered by a change in air pressure, caused by the presence of a gas heavier than air on one side of a porous membrane. Another type of detector rings an alarm when a gas lighter than air (hydrogen in a battery locker) causes a platinum or palladium filament to change its electrical resistance.

Carbon dioxide extinguishers release an oxygen-smothering gas that replaces air, does no damage, and leaves no residue. CO_2 is excellent for use on inflammable liquids and on electrical fires, but should not be inhaled.

A remote-controlled carbon dioxide installation is particularly suitable for use in both engine and fuel tank compartments. It consists of a CO_2 gas cylinder with a lever-type piercing head, which releases the gas when operated by cable from the cockpit.

Abandoning ship

The Fastnet Race of 1979, when 15 people lost their lives through failure or capsize of their liferafts, showed emphatically that unless your boat is actually sinking underneath you, the last thing you should do is abandon it.

On the credit side though, liferafts have saved the lives of many crews and aided the survival of others, some for long periods of time.

Much recent research has been done into all aspects of their construction and design, and manufacturers are improving their liferafts in light of this research.

Most liferafts are made from natural-rubber-coated nylon fabric, although recently new synthetic coatings have come into use. They normally consist of two independent buoyancy tubes, one above the other, which are automatically inflated by CO_2 and/or nitrogen when the painter/lanyard which activates the mechanism is jerked. Most manufacturers offer a double floor which gives better insulation.

Stability is provided by ballast pockets which hang down underneath, but it can still prove a problem with lightly loaded liferafts. Recent research has shown that an efficient sea anchor on a long line is the primary instrument in preventing capsize.

Most liferafts have self-erecting canopies which afford protection from cold, wind and sun. These have a variety of zips, velcro fastenings and ties with which to keep the door closed; some also have a window to make it easier to keep a lookout.

All manufacturers provide survival packs with their liferafts, but the quality of items and their usefulness tends to vary. Check what is provided and make good the deficiencies in your own specially prepared survival pack.

Finally, make sure that your liferaft is carefully looked after and goes back to the manufacturer for inspection annually.

Abandoning ship routine
1 Send out a final MAYDAY call. Give boat's name, estimated position and number of crew and state that you intend to abandon ship.
2 Crew to put on life-jackets before coming into the cockpit.
3 Check the liferaft painter is secured to a strong point on the boat.
4 Launch the liferaft, make sure it is fully inflated and bring it alongside the cockpit.
5 If there is time, bail out any water.
6 Cut lifelines so that crew can step off rather than climb over.
7 Load and secure flare pack, emergency clothing, food and water, navigation pack, radio, EPIRB, survival bags and two long warps.
8 Put the strongest crew member into the raft first to hold it steady and catch other members.
9 Cut the painter only when it is no longer safe to stay attached.

Getting into a liferaft from the sea.
Ideally you should be able to board the liferaft directly from the deck of the foundering boat, but it does not always work out in this way. Occasionally a liferaft will capsize when it is launched or will inflate upside down. The best way to right it is to get into the water, stand on the gas cylinder and heave on the righting line or straps. This is quite a difficult job even in practise conditions, and a hard struggle in severe ones, so a practical way of getting on board from the sea is an important feature of any liferaft.

Good handholds made from heavy webbing are as essential as good lifelines on the inside of the raft. The design of the boarding ladder, too, is critical. Too short and it is difficult to get your foot up to the bottom rung – too long and your legs are swept underneath the liferaft. The right length is one that brings your waist about level with the top of the buoyancy tubes, enabling you simply to roll aboard.

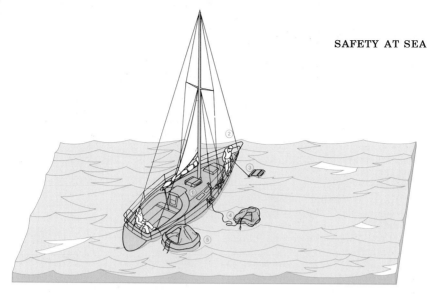

Before launching the liferaft, **1**, check that the painter is tied to the boat, **2**. Then release or cut the lashings and throw the liferaft over to leeward, **3**. Pull out all of the painter and jerk hard to fire the CO₂ cylinders, **4**. Allow the raft to inflate fully and vent, away from the side of the boat, **5**. If time allows, bail out the water. Load survival gear and board the raft from the cockpit. Cut the painter only when it is unsafe to stay attached.

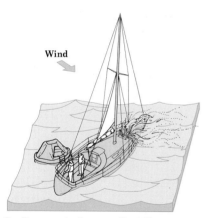

Wind

In the event of fire, launch the liferaft to windward to keep it out of smoke and flames. You may have to cut adrift before all the crew are aboard. If you do have to jump and there is burning oil on the water, shed heavy clothes, swim underwater as long as possible, then spring above the flames, take a breath, sink and swim again.

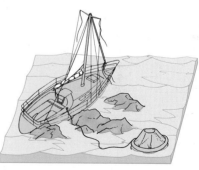

You may decide to abandon the boat, if she runs aground. A liferaft should survive a trip through breakers to a sandy beach, but the crew must inflate their life-jackets before entering the surf. If the coast is rocky tie the crew together and the raft to the boat, which will act like a drogue. The raft should make the tideline, but you will probably need the crew's combined strength to get ashore.

153

Survival in the water

From the moment the liferaft is cut away, the aim of each individual must be to survive. A state of shock exists, and someone must take charge to break the almost hypnotic effect of lethargy that shock induces.

No one must be permitted to sleep in the early stages of being cast adrift. Drowsiness is the first sign of capitulation and the crew must be forcibly kept awake by singing and exercising. Everybody should take a turn at being the lookout because it is a constructive action of hope, and gives a chance to breathe fresh air which, in turn, will help, with pills, to combat seasickness. The main threat to survival will almost certainly be from exposure and hypothermia.

It is very unlikely that many ordinary sailors will have to remain in a liferaft for long. Unless you are in the middle of the ocean, far from shipping lanes, you can expect rescue within a day or two at most. Never attempt to sail away from the area where your boat has sunk. Although wind and tide will make your liferaft drift, search and rescue craft will be aware of this and will be able to calculate your likely position.

When rescue arrives, allow your rescuers to dictate the transfer of survivors to the rescuing craft. A big ship will probably launch a lifeboat and then transfer you to the ship's side, where you will be helped up a ladder or a scrambling net. Coastal lifeboats are purpose designed to rescue and care for survivors; once aboard you will be in good hands. Aircraft are playing an increasing part in search and rescue operations and it is quite likely you will end up being winched aboard a helicopter.

Whatever the mode of rescue, it is essential that all survivors, whatever their apparent condition, should have skilled medical attention as soon as possible to ensure that their recovery is monitored and complete.

Helicopter rescue
If your mast is still standing the winchman may tell you to jump into the sea so he can get close enough. Usually a winchman will place each survivor in the strop. If only a strop is lowered slide the toggle up towards the wire, place both arms up through the strop so the loop rests in the centre of your back; slide the toggle down to your chest, hold your arms out wide and signal to the winchman to haul you up.

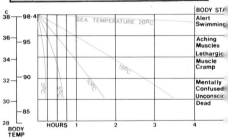

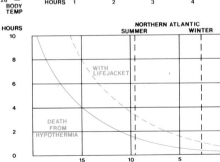

Unconsciousness occurs when the deep-body temperature falls from the normal 37°C to 32°C. At 30°C, death is caused by heart failure. In the northern summer, this takes 2–4 hrs in 5–10°C water.

Immediate action on boarding the raft
1 Check for leaks, top up buoyancy tubes. Stream the drogue.
2 Secure survival pack and radio or EPIRB.
3 Issue seasickness pills. Treat all injuries, even minor ones.
4 Post a lookout and gather any useful wreckage.
5 Make sure nothing with sharp edges – knives, shackle keys – can make holes in the raft.
6 Dry out the raft, using bailers, sponges. Wring out wet clothes. Get into plastic or foil survival bags.
7 Start a routine of bailing, lookout, exercise, etc.
Special action in cold climates
1 Close the raft entrance securely.
2 Keep as warm and dry as possible. Cover yourself, including your head (an area of great heat loss), with any spare clothing.
3 Huddle together, but be careful not to upset the stability of the raft.

4 Keep moving toes, fingers, hands and feet. Clench fists and stretch limbs to aid circulation.
5 Avoid exposure: face, ears and hands are quickly affected by frostbite. Lookouts must wrap up well.
6 Issue sugar or glucose and frequent small snacks, if you expect early rescue. Otherwise establish a ration of food and water.
Special action in hot climates
1 Avoid all unnecessary exercise, and exposure to sun. Use sunburn cream for protection.
2 Open liferaft entrance fully for air. In the daytime, deflate floor for cooling effect of sea underneath.
3 Keep outside of the canopy wet with sea water to reduce inside temperature.
4 Keep all clothing wet by day. Clothing and raft floor must be dry by sunset; it can be cold at night.
5 Catch all rainwater or dew you can – an inflatable life-jacket will hold 27 lb (12 kg) water.

Without a life-jacket, either tread water, 1, to keep afloat or try 'drownproofing', 2. Float restfully with the lungs full of air and face in the water. Every 10–15 secs, raise the head and breathe. Both techniques result in far more rapid body cooling than holding still with a life-jacket on.

Swimming ability, amount of insulation and water conditions will affect your decision to swim for shore. Tests show that in water of 10°C, people wearing standard life-jackets and light clothing can swim just over $\frac{3}{4}$ ml (1,200 m) before being incapacitated by hypothermia.

The body cools more quickly in water than in air of the same temperature, so it helps to keep out of the water. If possible get on top of an over-turned boat or other floating wreckage. This is particularly important for children with their rapid rate of cooling.

Hypothermia means lowered deep-body temperature. The external tissues cool rapidly; it takes 10–15 mins for the heart and brain to cool. It is a great threat to survival: always suspect crew who are seasick, tired, clumsy or shiver violently, or whose skin goes grey, and treat at once.

1

2

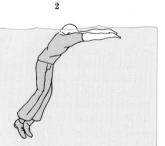

Medical emergencies/1

First aid afloat falls into two distinct categories: life-saving and keeping the patient comfortable until expert help can take over. As skipper, it is in your interest to have someone on board capable of delivering first aid, mouth-to-mouth resuscitation and heart massage. The last thing you want to see, as you suffer your first heart attack from worrying about all the things that can go wrong on a boat, is a member of your crew thumbing through the almanac saying, 'I'm sure I saw a section on first aid somewhere.'

If a crew member collapses, is severely injured in a fall, or by being hit by, say, the boom, you must check that he is breathing, by placing your ear close to the mouth or by watching the chest for movement.

If he is not breathing your first priority is to get air into the lungs at once by artificial respiration and if the pulse in the neck indicates that the heart has stopped, to try to trigger the heart into action with external heart massage. Once you have the patient breathing and heart ticking, the blood will flow around the body and you have to check for leaks!

To prevent burns, anyone using the cooker should protect their legs and chest. All burned and scalded areas should be immersed in cold water for at least 10 mins. Minor burns can be left open, but major damage should be kept germ free by covering with a sterile dressing or even a newspaper. Elevate the burn to minimize swelling and insist that the patient drinks plenty of water. If the burned area is large, seek medical help at once.

A broken limb must be immobilized with splints and bandages, or an inflatable splint, but ensure that the flow of blood to other parts is not restricted. If toes or fingers go white or blue, loosen the splinting.

If the spine is damaged the patient should be placed in the coma position in warm surroundings.

First aid kit

The size and contents of the first aid box should relate to the number of crew and length of the voyage. Carry a first aid manual on board. The box itself should be waterproof, with a captive lid. Keep a waterproof contents list and instruction sheet attached inside the lid. Most items deteriorate with time, so carry small quantities, if they can be easily replaced.

Medicaments

60 gm	Antiseptic cream
60gm	Antihistamine cream
35 gm	Calamine cream
1	Bottle sunburn lotion
100 gm	Kaolin powder
2 × 15	Throat lozenges
25	Aspirin and Paracetamol
24	Laxative tablets
50 gm	Ultraviolet filter cream
5 gm	Ultraviolet lip salve

Only available from a chemist

24	Kwells or Stugeron tablets
50	Antacid tablets
1	Small phial eye drops

Dressings

3	Triangular bandages
2	Large wound dressings
3	Medium wound dressings
3	Conforming bandages
1	Crêpe bandage 7.5 cm
1	Roll 2.5 cm adhesive waterproof strapping
1	Large box assorted plasters
1	Eye pad and cotton wool
10	Sachets antiseptic wipes
1 pkt	Sterile suture strips
2 pkts	Single sterile gauze swabs
10	Kerosene gauze dressings
1 pr	Scissors and tweezers
10	Protected safety pins
2	Fingerstalls – size 3 and 8

On private prescription (long trips)

20	DF118 tablets (for pain)
30	Lomotil tablets (diarrhoea)
30	Penicillin tablets
30	Stemetil suppositories
1	Thermometer
1	Foil survival blanket
2	Hot water bottles

Begin artificial respiration with one long blow into the patient's mouth. When this air is exhaled, take a breath and repeat quickly five or six times, then settle into a breathing rhythm. If, after six more blows, the patient's face does not turn from grey to pink the heart may have stopped. If so, deliver a sharp blow to the lower breastbone. Then breathe into the lungs six more times.

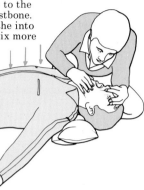

Flex the elbow over a pad to stem the flow from a forearm cut.

To stem the flow of blood from a wound, Pinch it together and apply pressure. Do not release for at least 10 mins, even to see if it is working! If possible, raise the wound above heart level. Bleeding from a cut palm is stopped by gripping a roll of clean cotton.

If breathing has stopped the first priority is to get air into the lungs at once. Clear the mouth of obstructions, including false teeth, rotate the head back to open up the airways. Pinch the patient's nose, take a deep breath and blow hard into his mouth until you see the chest rise. Gravity will then force air out of the lungs.

Head tilted back

Clear airways

Pressure applied to one of the pressure points around the body should stop almost any bleeding, if direct pressure does not work. Using a pad, press firmly on the point nearest the wound, on the heart side, to block off the flow of blood. As the bleeding slows down, the pressure can be slightly relaxed but not removed until a clot has formed.

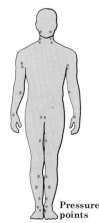

Pressure points

To treat a cut, remove obstructive clothing, clean the area with an antiseptic wipe and apply antiseptic cream. Draw the lips of the wound together, **1**, and apply sterile suture strips, **2**, without touching the inner surface. When the bleeding stops, bandage firmly from below

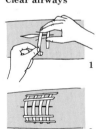

1

2

up. If injury is to a limb, raise it. If the wound swells, administer antibiotics.

Medical emergencies/2

Injuries are easily understood because they can be seen, but if a crew member collapses, complaining of internal pains or develops internal bleeding, expert medical help is needed. Divert to the nearest port, call PAN MEDICO or, if the radio is not working, indicate that you require medical assistance by flag or Morse Code or the International Code Signal W (Whiskey). As a last resort, reach for your comprehensive first aid manual.

Symptoms requiring medical aid include: *Chest pains* – severe pains radiating to the neck or arms suggest heart disease; *unconsciousness*; *abdominal pains* – especially if accompanied by vomiting, clamminess of the skin, rapid pulse, and severe tenderness of the abdomen. (Suspect internal bleeding, especially if the patient has fallen heavily, or appendicitis if the patient has not had an appendectomy); *burns* – large burns need medical attention; *severe pain* – try to alleviate with pain-killers and reassure the patient; *insulin starvation* – if this happens to a member of your crew it shows negligence on your part. You should ask everyone if they have adequate supplies of regular medication with them.

If a severe accident occurs when you are two or three days from land try to establish contact with a ship. It may be able to relay messages to shore stations and even contact the patient's own doctor.

If the patient is unconscious for more than 24 hours he must be given water to drink or by drip.

Anyone just recovered from the sea risks hypothermia. Strip off his wet clothes, protect him with a blanket or sleeping bag and rush him below into a bunk, preferably warmed by someone else. In a liferaft, replace wet clothing with dry, place the casualty in a large plastic bag and surround him with other people. Watch his heart rate and breathing.

Unconscious recovery position
After artificial respiration or heart massage, or when a wound has been dressed, lay the person in the coma position at once. Turn him face down, head to one side, pull up the leg and arm on this same side, push the chin up and pull out the elbow of the other arm to prevent him rolling over. Anyone who loses consciousness should be put in this position immediately, if breathing is normal. Put someone suffering from shock flat on his back with feet slightly raised. If breathing is laboured raise the head. Injury often results in a drop in body temperature, so cover with a blanket.

External heart massage
If the heart has stopped and the patient does not respond to artificial respiration, begin cardiac massage immediately.
1 Lay the patient out, face up.
2 Cross your hands over the breast bone and press firmly, depressing it about 1 in (2.5 cm) and release suddenly. Children need less pressure.
3 Repeat every one to two seconds, establishing a rhythmic pattern.
4 Stop every 15 secs to blow into the lungs.
5 Check the patient's colour or pulse every 2 or 3 mins.
6 Check the eyes. If the pupils contract when the eyelid is open, consciousness is returning.

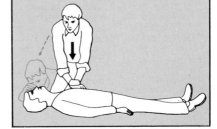

Heat exhaustion and sunburn
When sailing to sunny waters, guard against sunburn and heat exhaustion; wear a hat and avoid prolonged exposure. Sun filter creams with a graded protection factor block out harmful ultraviolet rays and should be applied regularly, especially to extremities. To treat sunburn, apply calamine cream to the skin, take Paracetamol for headaches and drink plenty of water. Heat exhaustion is caused by loss of salt and fluid from excessive sweating, often aggravated by a stomach upset. Symptoms include cramp, headaches, dizziness, clammy sweat and sudden fainting. Keep the patient cool and, if conscious, give cold water and salt. The coolest place in most yachts is in the airstream abaft the genoa. If the symptoms persist, seek medical advice.

Seasickness
Seasickness can often be prevented by avoiding excessive alcohol and strange or rich food, and by taking at least two doses of seasickness tablets, at the prescribed interval, before leaving. It is worth experimenting with a variety of pills until you find one which suits you. Stugeron proves effective with many people and the normal side effects of drowsiness, lethargy and a dry mouth are minimal. Boredom and tiredness often provoke seasickness and it sometimes helps a sufferer to take the helm and fix the eye on the horizon. Anyone suffering from seasickness should be secured to the boat with a safety harness. After vomiting, keep warm below and try to drink a little water. When recovering, take light, dry food, water and more seasickness tablets.

1 To remove a **foreign body** from the eye, try to flush it out with tepid water. If no success, pull upper lid over lower. If all fails, soothe with eye drops, use an eye pad and seek medical aid. If the eye is inflamed due to wind or glare, use simple eye drops and wear dark glasses.
2 **Violent choking** can be stopped in two ways. First try lying the patient face down over a table with his head hanging over the edge; deliver a series of quick hard blows between the shoulder-blades to dislodge the obstruction. Alternatively,

grasp him round the stomach, from behind, and jerk your linked fists into a sudden squeeze, then release. The offending blockage should then pop out of the throat.
3 Never treat a **fractured skull** with drugs. Lay the patient down with head raised, keep warm and soothe. Do not try to stop bleeding from the ears unless excessive. Check bleeding from the bruise without putting too much pressure on the brain. Put cold cloths on the head. If the patient is unconscious, put him in the coma position and monitor his pulse and responses.
4 To remove a

fishhook from a finger, paint exposed part of hook with iodine, push right through the flesh, cut off the eye and draw the hook free. Make the wound bleed, apply antiseptic cream and dress.
5 **Food poisoning** can be identified by stomach cramps, nausea, vomiting and diarrhoea. Dilute the poison by administering large quantities of water. Induce vomiting and keep patient warm.
6 If **appendicitis** is suspected, put the patient to bed, call for medical aid, and do not give a laxative or food.
7 **Pulled muscles**, torn ligaments or

joint pains should be rested. Apply ice packs or cool, wet cloths and administer pain-killers. If a fracture is suspected, immobilize the limb.
8 **Toothache** should be treated with pain-killers, and antibiotics, if the jaw is swollen. If there is a cavity fill it with damp cotton wool to prevent air reaching the nerve.
9 **Frostbite** must never be treated with direct heat or friction. Warm the affected part gently under the armpit or in cool water, then wrap up in a blanket.

Rules of the sport

Yacht racing began in the sixteenth century in Holland, the birthplace of sailing as a sport. The word yacht comes from the Dutch word *jacht* or 'hunter', the name they gave to the small craft they built for pleasure. Racing these *jachts* was an inevitable development, but it remained a uniquely Dutch sport until the restoration of the monarchy in Britain in 1660, when Charles II, who had spent his exile in Holland, brought the sport back with him.

Although cruising rather than racing was the main preoccupation of the first yachtsmen, races were organized by the early clubs such as the Royal Cork and Royal Thames Yacht Clubs. However, most races were the result of wagers between owners of yachts, who would race boat-for-boat.

Yachting began its international expansion in the long period of peace after the Napoleonic wars, from 1815 onward. The boat-for-boat races eventually proved unsatisfactory to the racing enthusiasts, so primitive systems for matching boats for racing began to appear.

One of the earliest attempts to provide a handicap system was the Thames measurement in 1854. It is still used today to indicate a vessel's size.

(Length-Beam) × Beam × $\frac{1}{2}$ Beam ÷ 94 = Tonnage

This measurement penalized beam and encouraged the design of very narrow boats, but in 1886 Dixon Kemp produced a better system which lasted well into the twentieth century.

Waterline Length × Sail Area ÷ 6000 = Rating

In 1906, with the formation of the International Yacht Racing Union, came the development of the first international rating system which gave a boat's class in metres.

There have been other rating systems, but in 1969 the International Offshore Rule (I.O.R.) was introduced and accepted on a world-wide basis, and although it is frequently revised, it is, today, the principal rule in use.

Unlike other sports, sailing races are not umpired by referees, so it is up to competitors to enforce the rules, and to maintain a sense of fair play. Fouls, usually collisions, are dealt with by an independent committee after the race, unless the guilty helmsman takes a voluntary penalty. A boat that retires receives a slightly better score than a

Wind

Boat on starboard tack

Boat on port tack

The boat on the port tack should keep clear of the boat on the starboard tack.

Windward boat

Leeward boat

When two boats on the same tack are overlapped, the leeward boat has right of way over the windward boat.

Boat on a tack

Tacking boat

A boat which is tacking or gybing/jibing should keep clear of one that is not. When two boats are tacking at the same time, the boat on the port side should keep clear. A boat should not tack into a position that will give her right of way if it causes another boat to alter course.

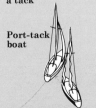

Port-tack boat

Starboard-tack boat should not alter course

A boat which holds right of way, must not alter course to hinder another boat which is keeping clear.

The great races

disqualified boat, but worse than the last boat in the race. Time penalties are sometimes used, in which the rule-breaker must drop down the finishing order. This has the advantage of allowing all boats to complete the race. The rules apply worldwide and are slightly modified, from time to time, to accomodate ambiguities brought out in various appeal cases. The rules come into force five minutes before the start of the race and continue until boats have crossed the finishing line. When long-distance racing offshore, racing rules apply only during daylight; at night normal Collision Regulations are in force.

Outside boat must keep clear

When rounding a mark or avoiding an obstruction, the outside boat must leave room for the inside boat. When two boats are on opposite tacks, the tacking boat must keep clear.

A boat which gains right of way must do so far enough from other boats to give them the opportunity to keep clear.

Leeward boat

A leeward boat has the right to protect her wind by luffing to windward. This is not allowed once the helmsman of the windward boat is forward of the mainmast of the leeward boat.

A boat clear astern of another should keep clear of the one ahead. When rounding a mark, the boat clear astern should not luff to prevent the boat ahead from tacking.

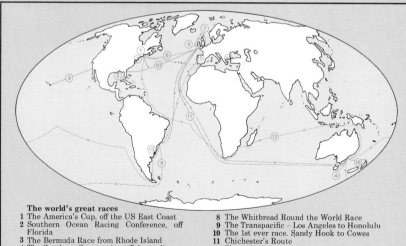

The world's great races
1 The America's Cup, off the US East Coast
2 Southern Ocean Racing Conference, off Florida
3 The Bermuda Race from Rhode Island
4 The Southern Cross series, off Australia
5 The Admiral's Cup series, off SW Britain
6 *The Observer* Single-handed Transatlantic Race
7 The Round Britain and Ireland Race
8 The Whitbread Round the World Race
9 The Transpacific – Los Angeles to Honolulu
10 The 1st ever race. Sandy Hook to Cowes
11 Chichester's Route
12 Slocum's route
13 Buenos Aires to Rio de Janeiro
14 Athens to Rhodes
15 Lisbon to Madeira
16 Trans-Tasman race

The America's Cup

In 1851 the American schooner *America* won the 100 Guinea Cup for a race around the Isle of Wight. The Cup was later presented to the New York Yacht Club as a prize to be contended for by the holders and any foreign yacht club.

Seventeen years later James Ashbury, Vice Commodore of the Royal Harwich Yacht Club challenged, and so started what has become the most prestigious and expensive sporting event ever. Ashbury lost against fourteen yachts, after which the rules were changed to make the challenge a match race. In 1871 Ashbury was back with *Livonia* and lost the series 4 to 1, but there was an argument about the second race, the first of many disputes in its history that were to bedevil the challenge.

The most famous challenger was Sir Thomas Lipton, who between 1899 and 1930 made five challenges with his *Shamrocks*. The closest he ever came to winning was with *Shamrock IV*, in 1920, which took the first two races in a best-of-five series.

In the 1930s the races were sailed in the glorious 'J' class boats. Sir Thomas Lipton's *Shamrock V* lost to *Enterprise*, after which Sir Thomas Sopwith took up the challenge with *Endeavour*, which might have won the cup from *Rainbow*, if her crew had not gone on strike. In 1937, the last pre-war series, *Endeavour II* was trounced by *Ranger*, a radical new 'J' class yacht designed by W.S. Burgess and Olin Stephens.

Since 1958, the first post-war challenge, the America's Cup race has been sailed in 12-metre yachts, and the most persistent contestants have been the Australians. However, other countries have now entered the ring and there are no fewer than six challengers for the Cup in 1983. The elimination trials which precede the final race promise to give the challengers the match-racing experience that has, so far, given the American defenders the edge.

In 1870, after the Cup had been presented to the New York Yacht Club, the race moved to the New York Coast. Since 1920, it has comprised a Gold Cup course of about 24 mls off Newport, Rhode Island. The race is without handicap and the course is set according to the wind. The match winner is the first yacht to win four races.

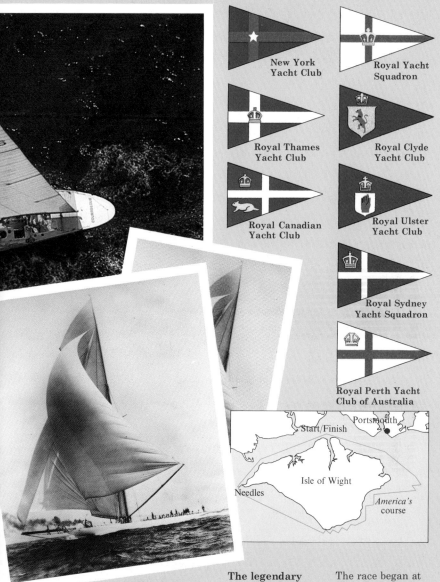

New York
Yacht Club

Royal Yacht
Squadron

Royal Thames
Yacht Club

Royal Clyde
Yacht Club

Royal Canadian
Yacht Club

Royal Ulster
Yacht Club

Royal Sydney
Yacht Squadron

Royal Perth Yacht
Club of Australia

Portsmouth

Start/Finish

Isle of Wight

Needles

America's
course

The superior sail and spar design of *Courageous*, *top*, and slick crew work was responsible for America's victory in 1974 and 1977.

1903's winner, *Reliance*, *above*, was the ultimate racing machine of its day. The bronze paragon designed by Nat Herreshoff, carried 16,160 sq ft (1,500 sq m) of sail.

The legendary schooner *America* changed the face of yachting history when it stormed over the finishing line after the first 100 Guinea Cup challenge round the Isle of Wight.

The race began at West Cowes and just over 10 hrs later the schooner had usurped British supremacy of the racing world.

SORC, The Onion Patch and Bermuda

In 1906, T. Fleming Day, the Editor of *Rudder* magazine and a vigorous exponent of the seaworthiness of small boats, organized a race from New York to Bermuda, a distance of 635 mls (1020 km), to prove that small yachts could race so far in safety. The race was highly successful and was repeated each year until 1910. In 1923 the race was re-started, and the organization passed to the newly formed Cruising Club of America.

While the prevailing wind is usually south-westerly, the vagaries of the Gulf Stream, which has to be crossed to reach Bermuda from Newport where the race now starts, mean that the race is not just a question of boat speed. Since 1964, the Bermuda has been a part of a series of ocean races known as the Onion Patch.

The other major American series is the Southern Ocean Racing Conference. The origins of this series date back to 1930 when a race was held from St Petersburgh, USA to Havana. In 1934, a second race was run from Miami to Nassau, and soon other races were added to make up the series. The modern series has changed slightly because yachts have not been able to visit Havana since the Cuban crisis of 1959. The St Petersburgh race goes to Fort Lauderdale instead and there are a number of smaller races, the Ocean Triangle, the Anclote Key Race and the Lipton Cup. The Miami to Nassau Race is still in the series, followed by a short race for the Nassau Cup.

Unlike other series, the SORC is spread out around Southern Florida, providing foreign yachtsmen with an exciting winter series and the USA with a series during which they can choose their team for the Admiral's Cup. The Gulf Stream is as important to the competitors as the wind. It sweeps round the southern tip of Florida and then north up the east coast into the Atlantic, occasionally reaching speeds of six knots.

The SORC, like other great competitive events, has been the catalyst of countless new developments, designs and techniques. 1977, for example, produced a medley of ambitious new designs, including *Imp, above*, which used welded hollow tubular frames to support the rigging and reinforce the hull. This reduced weight, without weakening the structure, and proved highly efficient, if demanding on the crew.

Botera

The Onion Patch Series, named after Bermuda where the last race finishes, offers the forceful challenge of the Gulf Stream – unpredictable, meandering and, when combined with the spring weather, often threatening. The series begins with the 175-ml Astor Trophy race from Oyster Bay to Newport. A succession of racing weekends follows, leaving the week-days free, unlike the European races.

Two major innovations arrived on the scene for the 1926 Bermuda race. Radio was used aboard racing boats for the first time, which was to stimulate the new marine electronics industry and so more accurate navigation. And *Jolie Brise, above,* having won the first Fastnet race, sailed the Atlantic to become the first entry from Britain. Ten years later, *Jolie Brise* rescued ten of the crew from *Adriana* which burned and sank in the exceptionally heavy seas.

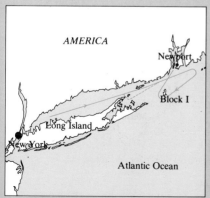

AMERICA

Newport

Block I

Long Island

New York

Atlantic Ocean

Newport

AMERICA

Rhumb Line

Successful track

Cape Hatteras

Bermuda

Gulf Stream

Atlantic Ocean

The Southern Cross Series

The Southern Cross Series, based in Australia, has become the most important international sailing series in the southern hemisphere. It uses the same format as the Admiral's Cup: three short inshore races, one intermediate 200-ml (320-km) race from Sydney to Flinders Island and back, and the long Sydney to Hobart race.

Like most of the other major ocean racing series, teams of three are selected from each of the competing nations, which in this instance also includes teams from the Australian states. The points system is the same as for the Admiral's Cup, and the series usually hinges on the last, treble-point Sydney to Hobart race.

Like the Fastnet Race, this has become a classic event. Started in 1945 by the Royal Yacht Club of Tasmania, it takes place just after Christmas (midsummer in Australia) and runs from Sydney Harbour straight down the coast and past the Bass Strait to Hobart in Tasmania, a distance of just over 600 mls (1,000 km).

Although the course is direct, the weather conditions can vary dramatically. Lightish north-easterly winds are usual down the New South Wales coast, but once the boats emerge into the exposed eastern approaches to the Bass Strait, depressions sweeping eastward in the Roaring Forties can produce wind strengths up to Force 10, and abrupt changes in wind direction and speed. Weather-watching, therefore, is crucial. Before the depressions arrive, a light northerly wind is common, but as the fronts go through, the wind backs round to a south-westerly and rises in force. A boat caught well east of the rhumb line when this happens is faced with a hard beat to the finish. This was particularly true of the 1977 race when three boats lost their masts and 15 out of 82 boats were forced to retire, while those inside the rhumb line were sheltered from the gruelling south-westerlies.

Usually a speedy downwind contest, the Sydney-Hobart tests the strength of both spinnaker and crew to the maximum. Blown-out spinnakers have become an accepted part of competitive sailing in Australia. The crucial decision is whether to follow the shore or the rhumb line.

The sunny, Boxing Day start to the Sydney-Hobart race, *above*, draws nearly 100 competitors every year, from all over the world.

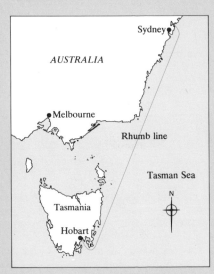

Pacific Ocean

AUSTRALIA

Track
8 miles

Sydney
Harbour

Olympic course
area

Southern Cross

The Southern Cross, like the Admiral's Cup series demands a versatile crew and a responsive boat. A good grasp of tactics and rules as well as slick crew work are the winning qualities for the three short, round-the-buoys, inshore races, while the longer courses rely more on correct trim of the sails, tuning of the rigging and reading of the weather. The nature of the series has influenced local design and techniques. Australian yachts now carry heavyweight storm spinnakers of 3-5 oz (85-140 gm) with a short foot which is strapped firmly to the deck to reduce rolling and the threat of a gybe/jibe or broach.

The Admiral's Cup Series

In 1957 the Admiral of the Royal Ocean Racing Club, Sir Myles Wyatt, presented a Cup to be raced for internationally by teams of three boats from each country. The Cup is awarded to the team gaining the most points in a series which now consists of three inshore races of about 30 mls (48 km), the Channel Race of 230 mls (370 km), and the Fastnet of 605 mls (1000 km).

The positions of individual boats in any of these races, which are run under the IOR handicap system, decides the number of points gained. If there are 45 boats in the race, the first boat receives 45 points, the second 44 and so on. The Channel Race earns double points and the Fastnet treble.

The series takes place during Cowes Week every odd-numbered year, starting with an inshore race, then the Channel Race, followed by two more inshore races and finally the Fastnet. Because of the points-scoring system, no team can be sure of winning until the end of the Fastnet race, which maintains the suspense until the last day of the series.

Unlike most other international competitions, the Admiral's Cup always takes place in British waters and has become the most prestigious of the international offshore series. Five teams took part in 1957, but by the 1970's fifteen nations was an average entry; and the numbers continue to rise as new contenders, who have only recently taken up ocean racing, such as Japan, become regular participants in the race.

The Fastnet Race is one of the oldest and most notorious ocean yacht races and first took place in 1925, when a converted Le Havre pilot cutter, the *Jolie Brise*, won. Every other year the race attracts an international fleet of up to 250 yachts. It takes the fleet from Cowes, out into the Western Aproaches, to the Fastnet Rock off the south-west Irish coast, and back to Plymouth, often in gale-force winds.

The Admiral's Cup is one of the most fiercely contested offshore races and has attracted keen international competition. Germany, Argentina, Poland, France and Spain now pose a potential threat to the British, American and Australasian stranglehold on ocean racing.

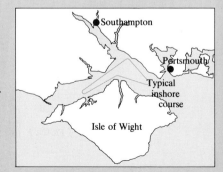

Southampton

Portsmouth

Typical inshore course

Isle of Wight

Daily Mail

WEDNESDAY, AUGUST 15, 1979

9p

MONEY MAIL

30 lives feared lost... 21 boats missing as a near hurricane hits yachtsmen

FASTNET RACE OF DEATH

DISASTER AT SEA

Weather and crew are the main ingredients for success in the series. The swirling tides of the Solent, the subtle shifts of wind and the shoals need a highly tuned crew to turn them to advantage.

The freak conditions of 1979 provoked long-overdue research into safety equipment and procedures. Trysails and VHF and SSB radio are now compulsory for the Fastnet Race.

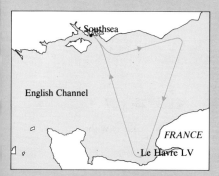

Southsea

English Channel

FRANCE

Le Havre LV

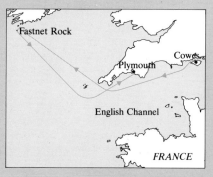

Fastnet Rock

Cowes

Plymouth

English Channel

FRANCE

The single-handed transatlantic

In the 1950s a retired Royal Marine, Lieutenant-Colonel 'Blondie' Hasler, wrote and published the rules for a single-handed transatlantic race. He had taken up single-handed sailing to avoid the problems of finding crew, and hoped that a race would lead to developments to help single-handers. By 1960 four other single-handers had responded; a club, the Royal Western, had been found to organize the race; and *The Observer* newspaper emerged as a sponsor. So OSTAR, the *Observer* Single-handed Transatlantic Race, was born.

The 1960 race was won by Francis Chichester in the 39-ft (12-m) *Gypsy Moth III* in a time of 40 days – then a very fast passage for a single-hander. The race was considered so successful that it became a regular four-yearly event. The 1964 race attracted sixteen starters, and was won in a new record time of 27 days by a young French Naval Lieutenant, Eric Tabarly. In 1968 Geoffrey Williams cut the time to 25 days 20 hrs.

Alain Colas brought the time down to 21 days 13 hrs in 1972 in the first multihull to win, beating a 128-ft (39-m) monohull. But monohulls were back in 1976 after a storm decimated the fleet, and Eric Tabarly won again in *Pen Duick VI*, a 73-ft (22-m) monohull, beating the 236-ft (70-m) *Club Méditerranée* by 7 hrs.

This was the last race with no size limits. Two hundred and thirty-six feet of boat, sailed single-handed, presented a risk to other vessels, and in response to this threat, a top limit of 56 ft (17 m) was imposed. The 1980 race was won by Phil Weld's trimaran *Moxie*, establishing a new time of 17 days, 23 hrs, 12 mins, less than half the time of the first race.

'Blondie' Hasler's concept has lead to dramatic changes in the design of boats and in what is considered to be humanly possible within them – but the story is far from over.

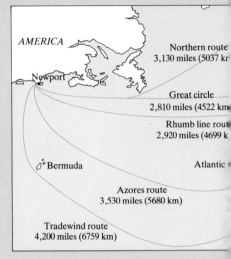

AMERICA

Newport

Northern route
3,130 miles (5037 km

Great circle
2,810 miles (4522 km

Rhumb line rout
2,920 miles (4699 k

Atlantic

Bermuda

Azores route
3,530 miles (5680 km)

Tradewind route
4,200 miles (6759 km)

The Transatlantic Race has become the testing ground for both advanced yachting equipment and innovative hull designs. Solar panels, wind generators, self-steering gear, furling sails and self-tailing winches have developed, side by side with such imaginative hull designs as *Club Méditerranée, below,* with its 'tennis court' dimensions.

THE GREAT RACES

Since 1960, OSTAR has grown from a friendly wager between four pioneers to a fierce contest between hundreds.

FRANCIS CHICHESTER

VAL HOWELLS

DAVID LEWIS

The lone yachtsman must weigh up the risks and choose his hazards; slow but sure, or fast and frightening.

Taunting calms, sudden storms, fog, icebergs and loneliness lie in wait.

ERIC TABARLY ON 'PEN DUICK VI'

171

Round Britain and Ireland

The first two-handed Round Britain and Ireland Race, sponsored by *The Observer* and organized by the Royal Western Yacht Club, took place in 1966. It was conceived as a test of stamina, seamanship, navigation and seaworthiness and is open to all boats, whether monohull or multihull, but limited to a two-person crew.

Sailing close to a coastline requires constant alertness from a crew, and to reduce the risks from fatigue, four compulsory stops are included in the race, at Crosshaven near Cork in Southern Ireland, Castlebay on the island of Barra in the outer Hebrides, Lerwick in the Shetland Isles and Lowestoft, with Plymouth witnessing the start and finish of each race. The boats must wait 48 hrs at each stop before going on, to give crews time to rest and to make any repairs which may be necessary.

The winner of the first race was the trimaran *Toria*, crewed by Derek Kelsall and Martin Minter-Kemp. In 1970 the race was won for the first and only time by a monohull, the 71-ft (21.6-m) ketch *Ocean Spirit*, crewed by Robin Knox-Johnston and Leslie Williams. In 1974 Knox-Johnston with a different crew, Gerry Boxall, won in record time in the 70-ft (21-m) catamaran *British Oxygen*. 1978 saw the trimarans back again in the form of *Great Britain IV*, crewed by Chay Blyth and Robert James. And in 1982, James and his wife Dame Naomi set a new record sailing time of 8 days, 15 hrs and 3 mins, in their lightweight trimaran *Colt Cars GB*.

This 2,070-ml (3,345-km) race has become one of the most popular short-handed sailing events, attracting competitors from all over the world every four years. The weather conditions encountered round the British Isles, from misty calms off the north of Scotland to gales in the English Channel, are so varied that every aspect of a boat and the crew's ability are put to the test.

The infinitely variable wind and weather around the British and Irish coasts adds spice to an already challenging race. The hazardous coastline, with its rocks, oil rigs and strong tides calls for deadly accurate navigation, and the patchy calms and gales need a steady nerve.

The question which preoccupies all contestants before the race is mono- or multihull. In light winds, catamarans, trimarans, proas and lightweight monohulls are faster, particularly downwind. In rough weather, monohulls have greater stability and can sail closer to the wind which can be an advantage when beating against the mixed winds encountered around Britain.

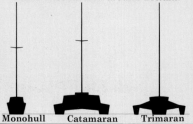

Monohull   Catamaran   Trimaran

Robin Knox-Johnston's 70-ft (21-m) catamaran, *British Oxygen*, proved the superior speed of larger, lighter designs in 1974 when it knocked a day and a half off the previous record. Since then, the limelight has been mainly focussed on the trimarans. In spite of these ocean 'giants', the Round Britain remains a 'friendly race', attracting plenty of amateurs with yachts of less ambitious dimensions.

It was victory for the trimarans again in 1982 when husband-and-wife team, Naomi and Rob James scooped up the trophy in their 60-ft (18-m) *Colt Cars GB*, below.

COLT CARS GB

Binatone

ROUND BRITAIN & IRELAND RACE '82 PLYMOUTH

Round the world

In 1898, Joshua Slocum, a retired American sea captain, completed the first voyage around the world in a yacht, and he did it alone. Although he called into many ports, he proved that it was possible for a man to manage a small boat at sea for long voyages. In the following 70 years, nearly 20 people sailed round the world, but in 1966, Francis Chichester set out from Plymouth and set a new record by stopping only once at Sydney, Australia. The following year Alec Rose completed a similar voyage, but with two stops.

The next step had to be a single-handed non-stop circumnavigation, and in 1968 nine boats sailed from Britain to attempt the 'Everest of the Sea'. In the event, only one man completed the voyage, Robin Knox-Johnston in his 32-ft (9.8-m) ketch *Suhaili*, and he won the *Sunday Times* Golden Globe for the achievement. Of the other eight, Nigel Tetley nearly completed the trip in his trimaran *Victress*, Donald Crowhurst disappeared at sea, Bernard Moitessier decided not to return to Europe and went round again to Tahiti, and damage forced the rest to pull out before passing South Africa. Two years later Chay Blyth completed a similar voyage the other way round, against the wind, in *British Steel*. It was to be another ten years before the first woman entered the arena, when Naomi James from New Zealand completed the voyage with just two stops.

In 1973 the first fully crewed Round the World Race took place, sponsored by Whitbread the famous brewing firm. It covered 27,000 mls, had three compulsory stops and was so successful that it was repeated in 1977 and is now scheduled as a four-yearly event.

1982 saw the birth of a similar race for single-handed sailors from Newport in the USA. Sponsored by the British Oxygen Co. there were seventeen boats at the starting line.

Round the world records

1 1898 Joshua Slocum completed the first single-handed voyage.

2 1966 The first single-handed circumnavigation with a single stop, Sir Francis Chichester took 274 days.

3 1968/9 The first non-stop single-handed trip round the world. Robin Knox-Johnston alone completed the *Sunday Times* race in *Suhaili*.

4 1968 The longest single-handed circumnavigation, when Moitessier passed the Cape of Good Hope and Tasmania a second time.

5 1970 The first east-to-west circumnavigation. Chay Blyth took on the major winds in *British Steel*.

6 1973 The first fully crewed race around the world.

7 1977 Dame Naomi James became the first woman to sail single-handed round the world.

8 1982 Fastest circumnavigation. *Flyer* took only 120 days.

Until Robin Knox-Johnston sailed into Falmouth harbour in April 1968, no man had ever sailed solo round the world without a port of call. He nursed the 32-ft (9.7-m) *Suhaili* through shattering storms in the South-east Trades and South Atlantic, undefeated by leaky bilges, sharks, serious damage to the self-steering gear, a split spinnaker, a broken tiller, boredom and loneliness.

Robin Knox-Johnston's route
The Whitbread Race route

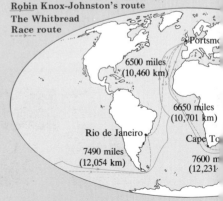

Portsm

6500 miles
(10,460 km)

6650 miles
(10,701 km)

Rio de Janeiro

7490 miles
(12,054 km)

Cape To

7600 m
(12,231

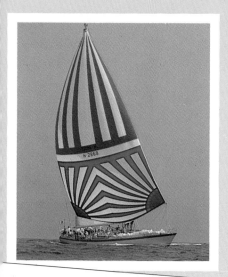

The Whitbread Round the World Race and the BOC Challenge have become the ultimate racing experience. It challenges the mental and physical strength of all who take part as much as the structures, rigging and equipment they need to rely on. The route is based on the wool-clipper races of old, except that three stopovers, at Cape Town, Sydney and Rio de Janeiro, are included to help the crew. There must be a minimum of five crew and the major prize goes to the fastest corrected time, regardless of size or rig. Handicaps allow a wide range of yachts a chance of winning. In March 1982, Dutchman Cornelius von Rietschoten set a new record of 120 days, 6 hrs, 34 mins, 14 secs in *Flyer*, *left*, knocking two whole weeks off the 1978 record.

THE FORCE TEN APPETITE

DAILY MIRROR, Wednesday, April 23, 1969   PAGE 19

Robin sails in to enjoy a nice big juicy steak

The finish. . . . *Suhaili, sails billowing bravely, is escorted over the line by an armada of boats.*

By DOUGLAS SLIGHT, RONALD RICKETTS and KENELM JENOUR

ONE sailor Robin Knox-Johnston sailed in yesterday to a hero's welcome, a pint . . . and a big juicy steak.

HIS SOLO VOYAGE 'WAS A HOLIDAY'

LAND AHOY!

Sydney

Sleep

Lone sailor Robin Knox-Johnston laughs with delight as he prepares to attack the steak supper he has been dreaming about for so long.

175

Hulls/1

Introduction

There is no such thing as a maintenance-free boat, and care and repair are much more complicated than they seem. The whole structure of a boat is in a damp and usually salt environment and much of the cabling or pipework is hidden behind linings. Boats moored or secured at a jetty are vulnerable to chafe from ropes or chain or the jetty itself, as well as damage due to collision with passing craft.

Sunlight attacks fabrics and dark GRP gelcoats, wind causes chafe with loose halyards or covers slapping against spars or deck fittings, while underwater growths try to eat into the hull. Below decks, if ventilation is inadequate, mould grows and rots fabrics. If there is a slight discharge from the electrical system the battery will be flat when you come aboard, and if there is a gas leak you may blow yourself up when lighting the cooker.

All these problems are avoidable, but looking around any marina or mooring area, or listening to the flapping halyards on a windy day, it is clear that the majority of boats need and deserve more care and attention than they get.

It is important to remember that timely maintenance, as well as being cheaper than repairs, is much more economic than a high depreciation in price before resale. In this section, the particular areas at risk are pointed out and suggestions made for maintenance and repair. The basic principle is that immediate boat maintenance leads to reliability. This is particularly true over the long-term, as complicated components go out of production and leave you with the problem of finding an alternative solution.

Damage

Regardless of the construction of the hull, the first priority after damage, however it is caused, is to stop the water getting through and possibly sinking the boat. The second priority is to stop water causing damage to the hull fabric, and the third is to preserve the boat's appearance.

Below-water leaks

Whatever the hull structure, the action is virtually the same and must be swift. If at all possible, something must be put over the outside of the damage. Ideally, a fabric sheet should be used, but this can be very awkward to manoeuvre into position owing to pressure of water and the difficulty of moving the fabric. A berth cushion is stronger, and although it probably fits less closely to the hull, it might succeed because at least it can be placed correctly. Another solution is to carry a Subrella which can be pushed through the hole and opened outside. Of course, success with this relies on having access to the inside of the damage, but it is worth trying. All boats should carry soft-wood plugs, which may not sound much good but, if nothing else can be done, a number of these hammered into a hole, side-by-side, reduces the volume of water coming in.

Another idea worth considering, to restrict the flood in to one compartment only, is to have panic boards, with strong backs and bolts and soft rubber gasket material upon the board, to place across doorways or gaps in bulkheads.

All boats should carry quick-hardening, two-part epoxy putty which can be used to fill holes, particularly the gaps between soft-wood plugs in a split. Epoxy has better mechanical properties and lower shrinkage than polyester resin. It is easy to apply and some types will set under water.

Assuming that the boat is saved, or that the hole is above the waterline, the next thing is to consider the actual repair.

GRP hulls – holes

The ideal procedure is to match the curve of the damaged area, either by using a piece of plastic laminate or by taking a mould off an undamaged hull of the same design. Use this as though it was part of the original mould, that is, mould-release agent, gelcoat, laminate of matt and rovings, and lay it up over a large area of the interior.

If the job has to be done from outside it is normal to use a piece of expanded metal mesh to support the new laminate inside the hull, securing the mesh to the hull with wires round strongbacks on the outside. Once this first layer has hardened, the wire can be removed and lay-up completed from the outside. It is harder to get a fair surface from the outside by this method, but with patience and skill it can be done.

Delamination

This can happen as a result of a collision and is typified by the sight of individual fibres or groups of fibres protruding from the main laminate. All the loose material must be chiselled away and the surrounding area sanded back to allow the new laminate patch to adhere both to the original deep material and to those areas near the surface. Build up the thickness, using successive layers of glass cloth to give a smoother surface, and sand again. Apply gelcoat, assuming that the surface is now level with the original – more glasscloth if it is not – and cover with Melinex, aluminium foil or plastic laminate, both to give a surface for the gelcoat to harden against and to try to get the correct shape of the curves. Finally fill, sand and polish until you are satisfied with the result.

If the area is below water, the colour does not matter, and it is easier to replace the gelcoat with epoxy paint which will also give the laminate better protection.

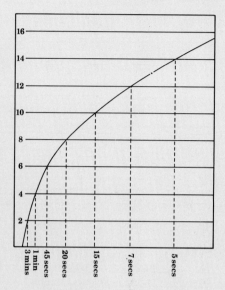

The graph, *above*, shows how long it would take a 30-ft (9-m) boat to sink. The size of the hole (given in the vertical column in sq in) determines the rate of flow. If, for example, the boat sustains a hole of 8 sq in, it will sink within 20 secs. With a hole as small as 2 sq in, the boat has a mere 3 mins before submerging, since 1 gallon of water weighs more than 10lbs.

GRP Repair kit

Pre-accelerated polyester resin – 2 litres
Catalyst paste (safer than liquid organic peroxide) – 6 tubes
Chopped strand mat – 2 sq yds (1.6 m)
Resin putty with hardener – 2 lb (1 kg)
Measure for resin – small polythene bucket
Paper cups (not polystyrene) – 10 and stirrers (ex-lolly sticks)
Resin brushes (Strand Glass) – 10 or cheap paint brushes – 1 in (2.5 cm)
Masking tape, plastic bags, clean rags (wet and dry), hand creams, rubber gloves
Acetone in metal container – ½ litre
Pre-accelerated gelcoat resin, topsides colour, or International Gelcoat tubes, or Plastic Padding Epoxy Gelcoat
1 tube water-curing polysulphide caulking compound
Sandpaper

Hulls/2

Curing time

A boat cannot be taken to sea immediately after repair. The laminate needs time to cure; how long will depend partly on the weather conditions and the temperature in which the job is done and partly on whether any accelerator has been put into the material. Basically, the longer the job is left the better, and this will depend very much on the size of the hole. However, assuming the latter is about the size of your hand, it should be quite safe to move in two or three days in normal weather.

Splits, cracks or scrapes

These must be opened out enough to take putty, annoying though it is to make a small blemish bigger. A router or chisel is the best tool to use, and the putty should be a mixture of gelcoat and filler, pressed firmly with a putty knife. Cover the area in the same way as before, and then polish once the gel has hardened.

Scuffs

Some of these will clean up with fibre-glass cleaner, and more difficult ones with car cellulose rubbing-compound. If this fails then the damage must be serious enough to justify applying gelcoat.

Do not delay this sort of apparently trivial task: any opportunity for water to get through the protective gelcoat and soak into the laminate can be the beginning of real trouble and high repair bills.

Osmosis

This word, dreaded among GRP boat owners, refers to the seepage of water through the gelcoat into the laminate. It then produces bubbles in the gel, which may burst as blisters or may be pricked to reveal liquid spreading thinly down to the hull bottom. It is more prevalent in fresh water than salt, and in warm water than cold –

even swimming pools suffer from it. Quite often bubbles will appear in anti-fouling, possibly due to reaction between the primer and gelcoat, so ensure this is not the simple cause before assuming the worst. Even if you can prick the bubbles and produce the ominous dampness and smell of styrene, your boat is not doomed: many boat owners are blissfully unaware of the problem.

A professional surveyor will check and give sound advice, which may well be to leave the dreaded 'pox' until it has finished emerging. If only a small area has appeared there is probably more to come and an immediate repair may need further treatment in due course. Osmosis repairs are just possible for the keen owner, but are much better undertaken by professionals, under a surveyor's supervision if necessary. Nowadays, however, it is possible to avoid this expensive situation altogether. A two-part epoxy paint is the most waterproof barrier for boats yet discovered and it is becoming commonplace to paint the gelcoat with this when the boat is new. It should also be satisfactory to paint a used boat. A less drastic (and less effective) precaution is to allow the boat to dry out thoroughly for several months each year, but this is largely self-defeating because it denies you the use of your boat.

Wooden boats

Holes and splits should be repaired by replacing damaged planks, using a template to shape the wood. Each case is different. Short-term repairs – crucial to ensure that water does not penetrate into the grain – can be carried out with epoxy putty or by mixing epoxy glue with filler. However, this is unlikely to provide a satisfactory permanent repair because of subsequent movement in the surrounding timber and eventually a proper repair will become necessary.

Rot

This is generally caused by neglect or poor ventilation, either of which allow the wood to become damp. Neglect in this case means that the film of protective paint, varnish, deck-sealing compound or caulking is broken, and water is allowed to get in. Luckily, owners of wooden boats, or boats with wooden decks, fittings, or cabin tops, usually appreciate that a large part of the attraction of their craft is a well-maintained and gleaming appearance.

Metal hulls

These dent quite severely before actually splitting. Once again the 'get-you-home' technique is epoxy putty in the split, with the surplus material adhering to a patch placed inside the hull. It may be possible to repair a split by straightforward welding, possibly with a patch fixed on the inside. Alternatively, a piece must be cut out and a new plate rolled and welded into place. Before doing any sort of repair to a split, it is worth drilling a hole at each end of it, thus reducing tension in the metal and also the risk of the split spreading.

Ferroconcrete

The essential thing here is that the water must not be allowed to get to the reinforcing metal mesh, or hull weakness will result when it rusts, thus reducing support to the concrete. Again, therefore, use epoxy putty for quick remedial action.

If severe damp occurs, so that the mesh is exposed, it must be cut back where it is bent or broken, the concrete cleaned off, and replacement pieces of mesh attached. This forms the basis for new cement applied, ideally, on the inside against a piece of plastic laminate clamped outside. Once the material has cured (and the surface must be kept damp during this time), the outside surface can be faired, using a belt sander.

When choosing an adhesive, make sure that any to be used on the hull are waterproof. Consider the materials of the two surfaces, the setting time of the glue and its resistance to moisture, heat, stress and mould. Always read the manufacturers' instructions before opening the tube.

Adhesives

EPOXY RESIN (Araldite, Borden Superfast Power Pack, Twinbond, Bostic 7, Aerodux 500)
A strong, versatile and durable glue, it is excellent for general repairs. It is a two-part compound which has to be mixed before use. It is resistant to damp, mould and heat and takes 6 hrs to set.

PLASTIC PADDING
Suitable for mending rusted holes and gaps in any material.

PLASTIC ALUMINIUM
Good for repairing sumps, pipes, tanks, casings. It sets hard and can be drilled.

RESORCINOL and FORMALDEHYDE (Aerolite, Cascamite, Welwood plastic resin glue)
Excellent for bonding wood to wood. Resorcinol types are highly water resistant and durable and popular for boat building. Both types need mixing and need to be clamped for 3–10 hours while setting.

PVA ADHESIVES (Duralite, Unibond, Sears white glue, Titebond, Bondcrete, Bostic carpentry glue, Dufix)
Universal bonding agent, which is particularly good for wood repairs below decks. Always remove all trace of the old glue before re-bonding. Although strong, it is not very stress or weather-resistant.

MASTIC ADHESIVES (Secomastic, Evomastic, Weblex 200, Ruscoe Pan-L-Bond)
Ideal for caulking, bedding door frames, roof lights.

CONTACT ADHESIVES (Devco rubber, Sears Miracle Pliobond, Bostik 3, Durofast, Evostick Impact, Gloy Contact)
Good for general purpose use above waterline on interiors and on laminated plastics. It requires no mixing and is cheaper and more convenient than epoxy.

POLYSTYRENE FOAM CEMENT
Good for fitting tiles to bulk- and deckheads.

Seacocks and skin fittings

Although they are out of sight and difficult to get at, seacock and skin fittings need careful routine checking, say, every three months. Many, such as engine-cooling inlets and sink or cockpit drains, tend to be left open continuously, so the spindle may jam in the open position. Others, such as the heads pipes, which are often closed when not in use to prevent siphoning, quickly reveal any tendency to stick and sometimes leak. Finally, it is essential to inspect the bolts, withdrawing one from each cock every year, to ensure they are in good condition. Seacock-makers provide special grease to lubricate valve spindles: a much more efficient aid to water-tightness than over-tightening the spindle nut. The spindle is usually tapered, so too much tension on the nut can seize the whole unit.

Pipe clips

Normally pipes from seacocks are flexible plastic, and the pipe is held on to the seacock with some type of screw clip. This should always be of stainless steel since nothing else will resist corrosion as effectively. It is important, also, that there are two clips, so that if one works loose there is less danger of springing a leak. Also check periodically that these pipe clips are tight because loose clips are the most likely cause of an accident.

Pumps

Always carry spares for all pumps, whether bilge or domestic. A basic racing rule, and one that makes excellent sense for cruisers, is to have two manual bilge pumps, one of which can be operated from below decks, and one operated from on deck, with all hatches shut, including the cockpit locker lids.

Modern bilge pumps accept and pass all types of rubbish, but the careful owner still has an accessible strum box filter on the pipe inlet.

An automatic electric bilge pump is useful, both for normal use and when the boat is left unattended on the moorings, but float switches often stick and you could return aboard to find a burnt-out pump, due to lack of water, and a flat battery.

Engine-driven bilge pumps are good in a crisis, but extra pipe work is required, to provide a bypass system when there is no bilge to clear, or some sort of easy connection to bring the pump into use when you do require it. However, the pump can also be used to provide a useful deck or anchor-washing facility.

Keels

If a keel is externally bolted on, check its security. The first sign of trouble may be the breaking away of the stopping between the flange and the hull. Apart from simply checking that the bolts are tight, it is also possible to have them X-rayed. This is particularly suitable for the traditional type of keel where the ballast is the lower part of a wood or GRP fin, and the bolts are long and difficult to remove.

Rudder

Like keels, rudders tend to be neglected until something goes wrong. The most common problems with a transom-hung rudder are the pintles or gudgeons pulling out or breaking. With a through-hull rudder stock/post, the problems can include the tiller or steering quadrant working loose on the stick, the stock fastenings working loose in the rudder, and wear or stiffness in the bearings. The final disaster – the rudder blade breaking off – is normally a problem confined to spade or transom-hung rudders.

Periodical checking of gudgeon and pintle forgings, nuts and bolts and backing pieces will ensure that they are in good order, while any slackness between rudder stock/post and tiller should become obvious by feel and inspection. The stock should have tongues protruding into the body of the rudder, which, if necessary, can be opened up for securing by bolts or epoxy cement.

The tiller should have at least a keyway and, ideally, a tapered square on which a nut can tighten the tiller head. If the stock bearings feel loose it should be possible to replace the gland packing and to retighten the securing nuts; if the steering is stiff the packing and bearing require grease. The stock is best mounted in a tube until well above the waterline and a stuffing box gland used at the lower bearing. However, the tube, being full of water, will attract marine growths and the rudder should be removed annually for cleaning. If the rudder is hung on a skeg this will involve the removal of a bottom bearing, preferably during the winter when the boat is out of the water.

Electrolysis and galvanic protection

Salt water allows electric current to flow from anodic to cathodic material. Any two metals from two components, and their relative positions in the galvanic rating table, will determine which loses material (the anode) and which remains largely undisturbed (the cathode). The rate of wear is determined by the distance apart on the galvanic table of the two metals. Thus a sacrificial zinc anode is often fitted to the underwater area of a boat to attract any destructive currents away from bronze or steel propeller shafts, for example.

It is not enough to know that your boat does not suffer from electrolysis: a newcomer in the adjacent marina berth may start a too-friendly association with metal components on it. An easy place to fit an anode is on the propeller shaft, or covering the propeller nut. The anode should not be painted because this will only defeat the purpose.

To prevent electrolysis in sea water, the difference between the voltage of two adjacent metals should not exceed 0.20 V. Zinc and carbon steel, for example, used together, risk corrosion, while lead and active stainless steel are compatible. Metals with a high voltage corrode faster and need a larger area to diffuse the electrochemical reaction.

High Corrosion

Metal	Voltage
Magnesium Alloy	− 1.6
Galvanized Iron	− 1.05
Zinc	− 1.03
Aluminium 3003	− 0.94
Cadmium	− 0.80
Aluminium	− 0.75
Carbon Steel	− 0.61
Grey Iron	− 0.61
Lead	− 0.55
Type 304 Stainless Steel (active)	− 0.53
Copper	− 0.36
Admiralty Brass	− 0.29
Manganese Bronze	− 0.27
70/30 Copper–Nickel	− 0.25
Copper	− 0.24
Nickel 200	− 0.20
Silicon Bronze	− 0.18
Type 316 Stainless Steel (active)	− 0.18
Inconel alloy 600	− 0.17
Titanium	− 0.15
Silver	− 0.13
Type 304 Stainless Steel (passive)	− 0.08
Monel	− 0.08
Type 316 Stainless Steel (passive)	− 0.05

Low Corrosion

Bilge Pumping Equipment

1 Recommended for 18 to 45 ft (5.5 to 13.7 m) boats: 1, 2 or 3 bilge pumps and a strum box to prevent the pipe becoming choked. One pump should be kept by the helmsman and if two are fitted, another below decks. Pumps and strum boxes need to be overhauled before each voyage.

2 Recommended for boats under 18 ft (5.5 m): 1 bilge pump. It should have a non-choke diaphragm with a pumping capacity of 10 gals (45 l) per min. A strum box to keep the pump clear is a recommended accessory. The best position for it is bolted down near the helmsman. Alternatively, a portable pump which can draw water from the sea may be a useful fire-fighting tool. Overhaul before each trip.

Decks/1

There is no excuse for poor maintenance of deck gear and fittings. Everything is within reach, at sea as well as in harbour, and much of this equipment has a direct effect on your comfort and safety.

Hatches and boards
If these are allowed to leak even slightly they cause untold gloom, as well as danger, if the leaks are serious. Leaking rubber seals on hatches can be replaced, but this is unlikely to be needed for several years, and the good types are adjustable at the hinge to ensure parallel matching of the hatch and frame. Sliding hatches normally open into a 'garage' which covers the complete unit and prevents spray finding its way under the hatch and then below. Some hatches, fitted externally without this cover, require a substantial lip inside, plus drains to ensure that water is kept out. A hose test will quickly show whether the hatch should be removed and the lip increased in height.

Hatch tracks also need drains. The vertical face of a hatchway is usually secured with two or three hatchboards, slotted in behind wooden or metal strips. Hatchways on European boats usually taper so that they are wider at the top than the bottom, which simplifies removing the boards; those on American boats normally have parallel sides which may be safer.

Hatchboards
At least two hatchboards are needed, with the lower one left in place to keep spray or rain out of the hatchway. Simply cut the board in half with a slanting cut which slopes down aft from the horizontal to ensure water cannot run into the cabin. Clear or tinted plastic boards give maximum light below deck. Boards provide a convenient location for a fixed and drip-proof ventilator. This can be easily made by fitting plastic panels inside and outside of a hole cut through the board, with the outer panel covering slightly more than the top half of the hole, and the inner piece slightly more than the bottom half.

Making hatchways safe
It must be possible to bolt each board in place, and to open it from either inside or out. The usual arrangement is to fit sliding bolts to each board except the top one, which is fitted with a lanyard led through it from inside to a clam cleat outside. If the inboard end of the line is also led from a clam cleat below the hatchway, either can be freed.

Another solution is to fit a bolt with its actuating lever running through the hatchboard, allowing it to be worked from inside or out. The same applies to the sliding hatch. Indeed, in this case, it is more important because a closed hatch should hold the uppermost board in place and so must be opened first.

Vents
Air flows in at the main hatch of the boat then forward and out of the forehatch or ventilators. Each compartment in the boat requires a fixed vent which operates continuously unless it is deliberately shut off. Forward, it is usual to fit low ventilators which rely on venturi action to pull air and smells out of the boat. Further aft, some sort of dorade vent – named after the yacht in which the idea was first tried out in 1931 – will allow in-or-out air movement. An offset draining trap stops water getting into the boat, so allowing the vent to face forward into wind and spray or rain, and driving volumes of air below, but no water.

The only maintenance required for a ventilator is periodic removal and resealing with silicone sealer. If it has corroded in the salt air the ventilator grid will need replacing.

Sheet tracks

Sheet tracks are a frequent cause of deck leaks, normally due to poor design or bad initial installation. Each hole for a securing bolt is a potential leak and a difficult one to deal with once cabin head-lining has been fitted. If you suspect a problem, remove the linings and take the boat on a good, hard-pressed punching sail to windward, making sure that there is plenty of water running down the deck. A thorough hosing in harbour somehow does not show up defects in the same way.

To cure this leak, first remove the old fitting and, to ensure a tight fit through the deck for the new one, fill the hole with an epoxy filler. Then redrill the hole to fit the bolt exactly, so that it can be tapped or screwed through the deck. A piece of backing timber will spread the load and take up any irregular under-deck shape (with the aid of bedding compound) and a large penny washer will help to spread the load of the securing nut across the wood. As a final precaution, apply silicone sealer to the bolt before tapping it home and tightening up the nut below.

Pulpit, pushpit and stanchion bases

These provide a more difficult version of the sheet track problem because the base must be bolted through. There should be no sandwich construction here, close to the deck edge, and the deck must be well reinforced because accidental heavy loads on the structure or stanchion will put severe twisting loads on bolts in the deck. A full-size metal plate under the deck provides extra support, but if it is not possible to use one, put extra-thick, penny washers below the pad piece. Stanchions are normally secured to their bases by split pins, so make sure that these are well protected to prevent damage to rope, sails or fingers.

Ventilation

1 For comfort, each person needs 14 cu ft (0.4 cu m) of air every minute, which means an air speed of about 3 ft/sec (90 cm/sec) in moderate temperatures.
2 In hot climates, an air speed of 5 ft/sec (150cm/sec) is more refreshing.
3 The engine needs approximately 2.5 cu ft (0.7 cu m) per horse power per minute of combustion.
4 Allow engine room ventilation. If the inlet is low speed and without a fan, an extra area of 1 in^2 (6.5 cm^2) per horse power will be needed, for sufficient air flow.

Ventilator Diameter	Cross Sectional Area
2 in (5 cm)	3 in^2 (19 cm^2)

Comments
Too small to supply adequate air flow, especially in calm weather.

3 in (7.6 cm)	7 in^2 (4.4 cm^2)

Comments
Well suited to small craft below 30 ft (9 m)

4 in (10 cm)	12.5 in^2 (81 cm^2)

Comment
The smallest standard-sized vent for all-round ventilation.

6 in (15 cm)	28 in^2 (181 cm^2)

Comment
The recommended size for boats over 40 ft (12 m).

Recommended air changes per hour

	Temperate Climate	Warm Climate	Hot Climate
	8 ch/hr	16 ch/hr	24 ch/hr
	1 vent for 2 people	2 vents for 2 people	3 vents for 2 people

Main Cabin
Wind scoops plus hatches and larger vents needed in hot climates.

Heads (6.5 cu ft–0.32 cu m)

15 ch/hr	25 ch/hr	30 ch/hr

Extractor fan with flow of 15 ft/sec (4.5 m/sec).

Galley

30 ch/hr	36 ch/hr	40 ch/hr

Extractor fan over cooker

Engine room
Inlet area should be 1.5 times exhaust plus 1½ in^2 (9.7 cm^2) per horse power of engine
Two cowls needed, one trunked to the bilge.

Decks/2

Deck fittings

The same technique should be used on other deck fittings where leaks are suspected. If the deck has a moulded upstand on which a fitting is placed, then the hole is somewhat elevated and the risk of a leak much decreased. It is sometimes worth mounting a fitting on a pad, though the pad must be well-varnished or protected to prevent water soaking into it and making an additional task later on.

Adding extra fittings

If the deck is of GRP sandwich construction it may not take the heavy compression loads of tightly fastened bolts without severe damage. If an extra fitting is to be added, the technique is to chop away some GRP inner skin and core and to replace the core with an area of plywood, larger than the bearing surface of the fitting. This can be fixed with epoxy to the underside of the deck itself and then the cutaway, inner skin of the deckhead can be glassed back into place. Bolts can then be fitted.

Cleats

These are usually fitted to coamings where through-bolting may be required. While this is straightforward, it is important to remember that there is a considerable twisting load on the bolts unless the cleat is properly positioned. This may be difficult to arrange if the cleat is needed for a number of tasks but, if possible, it should be fitted in line with the direction of greatest load. Taking a rope round the preferred winch, towards the intended position, will give a good indication of this line.

Guard rail wires

These need protection where they pass through stanchions. The wires are usually plastic covered, which gives a more pleasant feel and they should give few worries about out-of-sight deterioration, provided the holes in the stanchions are well protected so sharp edges cannot cut the plastic. However, even smooth plastic covering can chafe sheets at an alarming rate, so it is good policy to slide some additional, loose-fitting, tubing over the wire in areas where this might happen. Polythene or plastic tubing will do, but be prepared to change it each year since light makes some plastics tacky and unpleasant to touch and they will leave a dirty deposit on sails.

Guard rail ends are frequently secured with rigging screws/turnbuckles. This is satisfactory as long as the metallic connection is broken with an insulator at some point in the ring round the boat. Otherwise radio direction-finding bearings will be inaccurate owing to induced signals in the closed loop. A frequent solution is to fit plastic ferrules around the rigging screws; and shackle pins where they secure to pulpit or pushpit.

It is even simpler and cheaper to use a thin rope lanyard to tension the guard rails in the first place. This avoids the problem of mousing the shackles and screw fittings – essential for safety – and then taping them over to stop the seizing wire of the mousing tearing at hands and sails.

There is an added bonus. Should it prove useful to drop either lower or upper guard rails when recovering a man overboard, a lashing can be cut quickly – but make sure everyone realizes what you are doing or you could have more people overboard than left on board to recover them.

Jammers or stoppers

As it becomes increasingly fashionable (and convenient) to lead halyards and control lines aft, more stoppers and jammers are fitted on coach/cabin trunk roofs. The technique is the same as for adding other deck fittings, but remember that because greater loads can be exerted on a jammer assembly than on a single turning block, the reinforcing and bolts must be up to size. It is often necessary to fit a pad above deck as well, to give the rope an unbent, easy lead to the winch. Jammers should require little maintenance except for removing any accumulation of salt. Use fresh water, followed by WD40 or thin oil, if the jammer is plastic.

Winches

If you need to fit an additional winch the procedure is the same as for adding extra deck fittings. Normally, for reasons of economy, the technique is to add leading blocks so that an existing winch can be used for the additional task. Another possibility is to change the winch, replacing a basic single-speed model with a 2-speed or with a self-tailer. There is usually no problem with either of these tasks except that the bolt holes of the old and replacement winches may not match.

When fitting a winch, make sure that the drain hole in the side of the base is the right way for the deck or coaming camber and, if it is the self-tailing type, make sure that the lead on and off the winch makes sense; the stripper arm will be on a different position on each side of the boat.

When choosing a new winch, try to avoid one which uses dissimilar metals in its construction. Corrosion sets in with the aid of salt water, and this leads to worn, ill-fitting units and harmful deposits in bearings and gears. The best winches allow salt water simply to run through them. The next best construction is to have 'O' rings to keep the water out. The more bearings the winch has, the easier it will be to turn under load because the drum has more support. Although this will put up the price, you will benefit from the extra life of the unit.

WINCH SELECTION CHART

Boat length

	20/23 ft (6/7 m)	24/26 ft (7/8 m)	27/29 ft (8/9 m)	30/33 ft (9/10 m)	34/36 ft (10/11 m)
SHEETS					
Genoa	8:1	8:1/16:1	16:1/28:1	28:1/40:1	40:1
Spinnaker	8:1	8:1	8:1/16:1	16:1/28:1	28:1/40:1
Main	8:1	8:1	8:1	8:1	8:1/16:1
HALYARDS					
Genoa	8:1	8:1	8:1	8:1/16:1	8:1/16:1
Spinnaker	8:1	8:1	8:1	8:1/16:1	16:1
Main	8:1	8:1	8:1	8:1	16:1
Secondary	8:1	8:1	8:1	8:1	16:1

The chart, *above*, gives the recommended power ratio for winches for different tasks on five different sizes of boat. The correct size and strength of the winch, however, will vary with circumstances. If the crew is not strong or the boat is to be raced hard in heavy weather, a larger, more powerful winch will be needed. Multihulls also need a 20 per cent greater power ratio than monohulls. Many production boats are, unfortunately, equipped with inadequate winches. This ratio is calculated by dividing the radius of the winch handle by the radius of the drum and rope, then multiplying by the gear ratio.

Checklist

1 Make sure that all cleats, winches and blocks are firmly secured to the deck.
2 Check for dried-out sealant around bolts and screws, since it will lead to leaks.
3 Once a year, open each winch, wash off the salt, and oil the ratchets to keep the winch turning smoothly.
4 Always carry spare springs and ratchets.
5 Examine the guard rails, lifelines and stanchions and tighten the fastenings if they are beginning to work loose; replace lifelines at the first sign of fraying.

Standing rigging

The aluminium alloy of most modern spars needs careful preservation. The anodizing which protects it from salt and galvanic action is easily scratched and chipped, and it is worth spraying any damaged areas with a compatible metal spray to keep the material in good condition.

Some scratches, such as those caused by wire halyards when changing sails in bad weather, are unavoidable – others, such as those caused by halyards flapping in harbour, are inexcusable. At the end of each season it is also worth checking the spars to find where halyards leading from sheave boxes have caused chafe.

Small pieces of compatible metal can be secured with screws or epoxy glue, as protection. When putting screws into aluminium alloy, it is important to remember that galvanic action will start, if brass or even poor-grade stainless steel is used, and the metal will be eaten away so that the screw will fall out. Although wooden spars do not suffer in this way, chafe is just as big a problem.

Rigging terminals

Almost all masts are kept upright by rigging and, because it is out of sight and out of reach, the terminal on the mast is often neglected. Clevis pins must fit tightly in the tang or the strength of the unit is notably reduced. If it appears that the hole is becoming elongated, the mast-maker should be consulted. The clevis pin must also be well secured, usually with a split pin or ring. Although it is a natural thing to do, refrain from opening the pin wide, and ensure that it cannot catch halyards or sails.

Standing rigging

Modern standing rigging has swaged, permanently pressed-on end-fittings. They provide neat strong terminals and are very reliable. However, if the

rigging can vibrate at all, it may suffer fatigue where it emerges from the terminals so this area should be regularly inspected for broken wires.

The latest trend in mast-end terminals is for T-terminals, which are effectively hooked into the mast and supported by backing plates inside the spar. It is essential that the terminals lie parallel to the mast initially and then angle out the correct amount to give the wire a direct lead to the deck fitting. There is a much greater risk of failure where the wire emerges from the terminal.

Rigging screws/Turnbuckles

The same attention must be given to the rigging screw end-fittings. They must make a good fit on the clevis pin; a toggle, fitted between the lower part of the screw and the chain plate, allows for any difference in angle between the two.

Rigging screws should be $1\frac{1}{2}$ times as strong as the shroud they are connected to. The correct screw should be bought to fit the rigging terminal, chain plate, toggle, etc, to which it will be linked. Rigging screws work loose remarkably easily, and it is essential to stop this happening. The easiest solution with an open screw, is to pass seizing wire several times through the hole in the end of each screw thread and round one side of the frame.

Closed rigging screws have locking nuts on the end but these are rarely satisfactory, particularly since it is difficult to know how much of the screw thread is inside the closed bottle. The safest solution is to replace such screws with the open type.

When tensioning rigging, the screw may become strained by using large levers to force it tighter. If the thread is damaged in this way the screw is weakened and may well break particularly when heavy sailing loads are carried by the rig.

Setting up the rig

Assuming that the rig was properly adjusted at the beginning of the season, or the last time the mast was stepped, it is important to check periodically that all is still in order. The technique is broadly the same as for the initial setting up.

First check that the mast looks straight in harbour. To do this, hang a winch handle on the end of the main halyard. If the day is not too windy the handle should hang vertically, in line with the mast and about a foot abaft it.

If it appears to lean to one side remove the winch handle and adjust the main halyard so that its outboard end just touches the cap shroud chain plate when it is pulled tight. Now take the halyard end to the corresponding plate on the other side of the boat. Any discrepancy will be shown up and cap shroud adjustment will correct it. Having done this, adjust the lowers, if necessary, to get the whole mast straight. Check that corresponding stays each side of the mast are equally tight – pushing them to and fro simul-taneously at shoulder height to get a feel of the approximate tension – then take the boat for a windy sail.

Once at sea, get the boat sailing well on a close reach and inspect the mast again, looking for rake fore and aft. Then, by squinting up the luff track, check for sideways error.

Getting the fore-and-aft curve right is straightforward on a cruising boat, but if excessive tension is required to get a slight bend aft when the rig is loaded, it is advisable to get a backstay tensioner.

Sideways errors are more difficult to correct. Check for sag on each tack before making any adjustments, then check whether enough, or too much, has been achieved. On completion, secure the rigging screws/turnbuckles with seizing wire, tape over the wire and screw threads to guard against chafe, or fit plastic rigging screw boots. Despite its tough appearance, rigging wire stretches a surprising amount, so check the mast alignment every few weeks or whenever there is enough wind to show any stretch.

Breaking strength of wire rope
7 × 7 Construction

Diam. Inches	$\frac{1}{16}$	$\frac{3}{32}$	$\frac{1}{8}$	$\frac{5}{32}$	$\frac{3}{16}$	$\frac{7}{32}$	$\frac{1}{4}$	$\frac{9}{32}$	$\frac{5}{16}$	$\frac{3}{8}$	$\frac{7}{16}$
Galv. Plow Steel	—	—	—	—	—	—	4,200	5,300	6,570	9,270	12,400
Stainless Steel	355	780	1,150	2,000	2,750	4,000	4,800	6,100	7,500	10,600	14,200

7 × 19 Construction

Diam. Inches	$\frac{1}{8}$	$\frac{5}{32}$	$\frac{3}{16}$	$\frac{7}{32}$	$\frac{1}{4}$	$\frac{9}{32}$	$\frac{5}{16}$	$\frac{3}{8}$	$\frac{7}{16}$
Galv. Plow Steel	—	—	—	—	4,390	5,400	6,840	9,650	12,800
Stainless Steel	—	—	1,280	2,000	2,900	3,950	5,090	6,700	7,900	11,100	14,700

1 × 19 or 19-Wire Strand Construction

Diam. Inches	$\frac{1}{16}$	$\frac{3}{32}$	$\frac{1}{8}$	$\frac{5}{32}$	$\frac{3}{16}$	$\frac{7}{32}$	$\frac{1}{4}$	$\frac{9}{32}$
Stainless Steel	500	1,100	2,100	3,200	4,600	6,100	8,000	10,000

Running rigging

Running Rigging

Rope makes the most convenient halyard for a cruising boat because it is pleasant to handle. If chafe develops where the loaded halyards wear on the masthead sheaves it is possible to cut off the last 2–3 ft every year or so (provided the halyard was over-long to begin with). Finally it can be turned end-to-end, once it is down to its minimum length.

Pre-stretched three-strand terylene/dacron seems the obvious choice, but it kinks when wet and hard. If this happens where the halyard runs into the base of the mast it will jam while you are standing on the foredeck trying to pull the genoa down. Multiplait ropes are also very low-stretch and, since they are less prone to kinking, are better for halyards. Stretch is not too big a problem, if halyards are led aft, because they are then easy to adjust, and, indeed, adjustment is necessary as wind speed and relative wind angle change while you are sailing. Kevlar appears to be attractive for halyards because of its lightness and excellent stretch characteristics. However it has the disadvantage of being difficult to bend round a tight radius, which commonly makes for failures at the masthead sheave, and it is expensive.

If the boat is fitted with wire halyards, or your enthusiasm for stretch-free halyards is unwavering, beware of the splice joining the rope tail to the wire, for this is the most frequent area of failure. Galvanized wire is better for halyards than stainless steel because the latter does not wear well on sheaves. To keep galvanized wire in good condition for a long time, it should be soaked in boiled oil each winter.

Sheets are best made of multiplait terylene and simply turned end-for-end when they have chafed slightly, usually owing to a poorly angled sheet carriage roller. It is simple and safe to attach sheets to the clew of a headsail with a bowline, but make sure the knot is well tightened or it will shake loose when the sail flaps.

Such things as shackles should be made illegal on headsails. A small piece of metal, moving at high speed when the sail is released quickly, can do terrible damage to heads and eyes, but snap shackles are employed on spinnaker gear, because of the need for quick release.

The topping lift is a special case for running rigging. If it is shackled to the end of the boom mouse the shackle or the shaking of the slightly slack line will soon loosen it. In addition, the irritating noise of it chattering at the boom end, coupled with the desire to avoid the mainsail leech chafing, means it is common to move the topping lift aft to the pushpit. A snap shackle is needed to do this, plus some luck when refastening it to the gyrating boom before lowering the sail.

A better solution is to take up slack in the topping lift just above the boom by using a piece of shock cord to shorten it. Then, when the sail has been hoisted, ease the topping lift until the shock cord is nearly slack. When the sheet is pulled tight on the wind, the shock cord will be pulled taut, but the topping lift will lie quietly at the leech of the sail and cause little wear.

A topping lift of a fixed length, secured permanently at the masthead, is attractive in theory, particularly since it can be made of plastic-covered guard-rail wire which does not chafe easily. One of the side benefits of the topping lift is that it acts as a standby main halyard.

Short topping-lift strops fixed to the backstay are only useful as an extra, to stop the boom swinging and to pull it firmly to one side once the sail has been lowered. However, this type is useless when the topping lift is needed to support the boom when reefing.

Mast sheaves

These are divided between those under heavy load at the masthead, where halyards turn through 180°, and those lower down, where turns may be less than 90°. All of them should revolve on Tufnol or plastic brushes. It is important to check these for wear, the easiest way being to rock the sheave, making sure it cannot touch the walls of its box. If it can, the sheave is rubbing on the pin and the effort required to hoist or adjust the sail will quickly become excessive.

It can be difficult to remove the pins in masthead sheave boxes without dropping the latter inside the mast. It cannot be done with the mast stepped because the forestay blocks access, and even with the mast down, it pays to put a line round the sheave to ensure control of it.

Blocks

Running rigging blocks should last a long time provided they are properly treated. This means making sure that the block lines up with the load put on it by using a swivel or an extra shackle. Snap shackles themselves need to be lubricated, and the line which operates the release pin must be replaced, if it wears, or the snap can become painful and difficult to operate. This is often the forerunner to dropping it – inevitably over the side.

Going aloft

Hoisting a person aloft in a bosun's chair requires four people for complete safety. An easier alternative is to use a mast-climbing ladder which can be set up taut. The climber takes his own weight so no winching is needed, and only one other person is required to work a safety halyard attached to the climber. This can be a boon for family-crewed boats where the strong winch-winder is probably also the best person to the do the job at the masthead.

Guide to Rope sizes

The recommended sizes of rope for different tasks are given below. Anchor warps, for example, need a much higher breaking strain than, say, a halyard.

Approximate sail area in sq m

Length of boat in metres	6–8	9	10	11
Mainsail	12	16	19	22
Genoa/Jib	20	30	40	50
Spinnaker	45	56	65	90

Sheet sizes in mm diameter

Length of boat in metres	6–8	9	10	11
Main sheet	10	10	10	12
Jib sheet	10	10	12	12
Spinnaker sheet	8	10	10	10
Spinnaker guy	10	10	12	12

Halyard sizes in mm diameter

Length of boat in metres	6–8	9	10	11
Main halyard	8	10	10	10
Jib halyard	8	10	10	12
Spinnaker halyard	8	8	10	10

Mooring warps in mm diameter

Length of boat in metres	6–8	9	10	11
Approx. displacement in kg	2,000	5,000	5,000	6,500
Polyester/ Nylon	8–10	12	12	14
Polypropylene	10–12	14	16	18

Kicking strap in mm diameter

Length of boat in metres	6–8	9	10	11
Kicking strap	8	10	10	10

Anchor ropes in mm diameter

Length of boat in metres	6–8	9	10	11
Nylon	12	14	16	16
Polyester	14	16	18	18
Nylon (Kedge)	8	8	10	10
Bruce	5	7.5	10	10
Danforth & CQR	8	14	14	14
Chain	8	8	10	10

Sails

Although these are the primary driving force of a sailing boat, people often try to skimp when buying them and begrudge maintenance costs. But passage times depend on good, well-setting sails and a failure at a dangerous moment could be disastrous. The sailing boat and her crew are also much safer under sail in bad weather than when plunging and rolling under engine.

The first priority is to treat sails carefully on deck and when setting them, to ensure that they are not snagged. When in use, try, with the aid of binoculars if necessary, to spot areas of chafe or fraying stitching.

Devote a section in your maintenance jobs notebook to sail repairs, and jot down the whereabouts of a problem; for example, 'No 2 genoa, leech, four seams from the head, stitching frayed on leech tape.' Hoisting and lowering give opportunities to check for further defects.

When stowing, fold and flake the sails carefully to avoid damaging them. Try to vary the width of the flakes to prevent permanent creases forming. To remove creases, soak the sail in fresh cool water and hang it up to dry by the luff.

Maintenance is a simple task, if tackled promptly – the next time in harbour if the task is small, or to pass time on passage, if the problem is bigger or urgent. If it is left too long it will become a major, and probably expensive, repair.

If you do have to repair a tear the main concern is to retain the proper shape in the sail, partly to ensure it sets well and partly to stop the patch being strained and so pulling off. One method is to stick carpet tape along the split, taking care to match the torn edges of the fabric neatly. The tape can then be sewn into place, using a criss-cross stitching pattern. This will certainly save a larger problem developing and keep the sail working

until it can be repaired professionally.

The sail repair bag should include a variety of needles, kept in grease in a tube; stranded sewing thread that can be reduced to the number of strands required for the size of the job and the needle in use; beeswax to lubricate the needles and thread, and a sailmaker's palm for pushing the needle through the sail. Pliers will also be required to pull the needle through, and an upholsterer's needle, which is bent through a 90° curve, can be useful for many jobs.

If you find some area of a sail that is particularly prone to damage, such as the genoa leech where it may rub the spreader end, it is important to eradicate the problem. In this instance, protect the spreader end with a boot and also reinforce the sail. Pulpits, too, can cause bad chafing of the stitching of a low-cut genoa.

Mainsail luff slides should be supplied laced or taped on, not shackled, by the sail-maker. They should not have to be removed from the track when the sail is slab-reefed. If they are in the wrong place it will be impossible to get luff reef cringles on to the hooks at the gooseneck. It is worth correcting this fault, since replacing the slides in the track after shaking out a reef can be difficult. While the eventual solution is to move the eyelets holding the slides, for the rest of the season it should be possible to arrange for all slides below a reef line to be secured and tensioned with one lanyard and to use a different coloured one for the next group of slides, and so on.

It is important, when gathering up the folds of sail resulting from putting in a reef, that the line securing the reef points does not pull any tension wrinkles from the eyelets or they may easily tear. Ideally, the reef points should be secured with light shock cord, for this will stretch and even out the tension.

Sail Repair Kit

Needles – Nos 16–19, plus some domestic.
Hand-seaming twine – No 3, or 4–6 lb (2–3 kg).
Machine thread – general purpose Terylene/Dacron. Sailmaker's palm.
Several pre-cut patches of suitable sail cloth with heat-sealed edges. A few coloured squares for the spinnaker.
Spinnaker repair tape. (White is suitable for quick repairs on main and staysails.)
Lump of beeswax or candle.
Stitch-ripper or similar tool.
Insulating tape – plastic, not linen. Waterproof sail tape.
Two yds (1.8 m) of Terylene/Dacron woven webbing $\frac{1}{2}$ – $1\frac{1}{2}$ in (12–36 mm) wide.
Tubes of Clear Bostik.
Sharp knife, scissors, fid.
Double-sided adhesive tape.
Leather (raw hide, or chrome hide, from sailmaker).
Pre-waxed whipping twine.
Selection of sail battens (long – cut to length as required), piston hanks, slides, plus the necessary tape or twine.
Bosun's bag, measuring tape.
Sail shackles.

Removing stains

1 Oil and grease stains can be removed by rubbing Swarfega right into the weave, then washing in the normal way. Stubborn oil stains may have to be treated with white spirit before washing.
2 Tar may also be treated in this way, although you may need to resort to trichloroethylene. If so, do not smoke and work in a well-ventilated place.
3 If traces of paint or varnish find their way on to a sail, act immediately. Use white spirit, followed by Swarfega and wash in neat liquid detergent. If all else fails, try trichloroethylene, then an equal mixture of amyl acetate and acetone, then wash out.
4 Treat rust with 1 oz (28.35 g) of oxalic crystals dissolved in a pint ($\frac{1}{2}$ litre) of hot water. Wear rubber gloves.
5 Mildew will wash out, but air the sail thoroughly.
6 Household bleach will remove blood.
7 Treat bad stains as soon as possible and *before* washing the sail. First try the mildest cleaning agents and only experiment with stronger chemicals if all else fails. Always rinse out salt thoroughly.

Sailcloth weights for the 30-ft (9-m) cruiser

oz/sq yd (US)	oz/sq yd (UK)	gm/sq m
Mainsail:		
6.5	8.2	278
No 1 Light genoa (up to 12-knot wind):		
3.7	4.7	159
No 1 Heavy genoa (up to 20-knot wind):		
5.5	7	230
No 2 genoa:		
6	7.6	257
Jib:		
6.5	8.2	278
Storm jib:		
8	10.1	342
Spinnaker/Cruising chute:		
1	1.3	43

Washing sails

1 Sails must be washed at least once a year, since salt, dirt and stains weaken the cloth.
2 It is often easiest to wash sails in the bath. Use a mild soap and hand-hot water.
3 Scrub any persistent stains with soap and a nail brush, but be careful not to catch the stitching.
4 Rinse several times in clean water and hang up by the luff to dry.
5 When dry, repair any damage immediately. Fold carefully to avoid creasing the leech and stow in a cool, dry place.
6 Do not put sails in the tumble drier or iron them, since the heat may cause shrinkage.

Engines

Care of a boat engine is remarkably similar to that of a motorcar engine. Before starting up, check that there is sufficient fuel and that the oil is at the correct level on the dip stick. Ensure that fuel filters are clear and that the water-inlet strainer is clear of weed. Once the engine is running, check that water is coming out of the outlet and that the engine sounds right for the revolutions you are obtaining.

If petrol/gasoline engines refuse to start they are likely to be suffering from electrical problems due to salt air and damp. Diesel engines, however, need only fuel, compression and heat to get them to start. If a diesel will not start check that the fuel is passing right through the system to the injectors. If you have checked that the water strainer is clear, but there is no water coming out with the exhaust when the engine is running, there is the possibility that the engine suction has pulled a piece of a floating plastic bag on to the water-cooling inlet. When the engine is stopped, the plastic will probably fall away and there will be every sign that the inlet is clear. One way to check is to remove the strainer and turn on the seacock in the hull a little to ensure the water does actually come in at that stage. Polythene may also foul a propeller, in which case it will not break clear and considerable power loss can result.

Check periodically that the alternator and waterpump belts are both in good condition, and always carry a spare water pump impeller. Ensure that the alternator will not suffer from damp or salt water being sprayed on it by a belt, if the bilge is deep. If necessary fit it with some sort of spray guard.

Propeller shafts

It is important that the stern gland through which the propeller shaft leaves the boat is well lubricated to safeguard against heating of either the shaft or the gland, also to stop water getting in. This is done by a grease gun connected to a copper pipe, which forces grease around the shaft inside the gland. However, overgreasing the gland is almost as serious as not greasing it enough, so it is important that the grease gun is only turned enough to take up the slack in the thread, and not forced farther once back pressure is felt. It should be necessary to do this only every hour or so when the engine is running.

It is a good practice, on arriving in harbour, to check that there are no drips of water coming through the stern gland because they will slowly fill up the boat. If the packing around the gland is in good condition and the grease gun has not been wound too far, there should be no grease coming out of the gland into the boat. If the gland packing becomes worn, when the boat is next out of the water the gland nuts can be undone on the inboard side, slid back up the propeller shaft, and a replacement piece of packing fitted.

The outboard end of most modern propeller shafts is water-lubricated through a rubber or neoprene bearing.

It is important to make sure that the propeller is kept clear of weeds and free from damage by passing débris. Should the propeller hit the bottom, put the boat where it will dry out, and check the propeller for dents or bending. File the blade tips, if necessary, to remove any small blemishes. A chipped propeller will prove surprisingly inefficient.

Sail drives

It is important to ensure that the neoprene gasket around the sail drive remains in good condition, or a leak will develop which could cost you your boat. It is also important that water and grit do not get inside the leg of the sail drive, otherwise the gears at the bottom will be damaged and may prove expensive to repair.

OVERCOMING ENGINE FAILURES

Petrol/gasoline engine
When the starter will not turn the
engine over, first look at the electrics,
and check and tighten all connections in
the starting circuit.

1 Begin by pulling the H.T. lead out of
the distributor. Hold it a few centimetres
away from the engine block and turn the
engine on. If a blue spark jumps the gap,
battery ignition switch, points,
condenser and coil are in working order.

2 Check the spark plugs by removing a
lead and replacing the plug with a new
one. Rest the new plug on the engine and
if a blue spark leaps out when you turn
on the engine, the plugs are fine.

3 If there is no spark, the distributor
may be at fault. If traces of deposit are
visible, scrape it away to prevent it
shorting the system.

4 Another reason may be pitted points,
which can be filed down. Reset the gap
to manufacturer's specifications.

5 If the ignition switch is at fault, use a
length of wire to bypass the switch.
Connect the + battery terminal to the +
coil connection. Remove it to stop the
engine.

6 If the battery is flat, power can be
made up by using other batteries on
board. Connect the second battery to the
old leads and switch on. If necessary,
turn the engine over by hand.

7 A blockage in the carburettor can be
cleared by blocking the air inlet with a
rag and turning on the engine. If it still
will not run, check the filter; it may be
dirty.

8 Finally, check the fuel lift pump.
Disconnect the downstream connection
and hand-turn the engine. If no fuel
escapes, check the pump diaphragm for
dirt or a leak.

Diesel engine
Diesel engines are more prone to fuel
problems than ignition defects. Ignition
is effected by compression and if the
batteries are not turning the engine over
fast enough to make it start:

1 Use the hand start with the starter
motor or decompress the engine to make
it turn, then push the compression lever
down. It is kind to the battery to make a
habit of doing this, particularly in cold
weather.

2 To boost the speed of engine rotation,
attach two parallel batteries. Always
isolate the alternator from the circuit
and remove the driving belt.

3 If the fuel becomes contaminated, it
must be drawn off and filtered.

4 If the fuel is contaminated with water,
a few drops of methylated spirit will
absorb the water and filter it through the
system.

5 The majority of diesel engines will run
on only one or two cylinders, if a little
reluctantly. If, however, a fracture
develops in one of the high-pressure fuel
pipes, do not bend it back to seal it.

6 If the fuel lift pump fails it is possible
to erect a jury-tank. Use a large jerry
can and filter the fuel through a fine-
mesh cloth or stocking over a funnel.
The tank needs to be topped up
regularly, but if it runs dry, bleed the
engine before re-starting to eliminate air
in the pipes.

7 The injectors are often at fault. If
there is excessive leakage, the nozzle nut
may be loose or the nozzle face may be
distorted or worn. If the nozzle is
dripping the needle may be worn or
jammed or it may not be correctly
positioned. The nozzle spray holes may
become blocked and distort the spray
and the pressure. Symptoms of a faulty
injector include engine knocks, black
smoke, and an engine that stops and
starts instead of running smoothly.

Electrics

Each year electrical systems are used for an increasing number of functions and in any boat the system load is enlarged by the addition of extra lamps or pieces of navigation gear. Unfortunately, consideration is seldom given to battery capacity or to recharging requirements.

Battery Systems

It is easy to calculate the battery capacity required, but usually the first sign of overload is an ineffective radio or RDF, dim lamps or an engine that will not start. All these potentially dangerous factors are avoidable. First, there should be at least two separate battery supplies in the boat, one exclusively for the engine (a 60 amp battery would be adequate), and another for domestic use. The greater its capacity, the less often you will have to run the engine or use another form of charging system; 120 amps would be a realistic minimum. A 180 amp should be satisfactory, unless there is an electric refrigerator, for example, when the load for that should be calculated and separate provision made for it. To check the state of the battery, a voltmeter is required or, better still, a hydrometer, since it also provides a most accurate check on the electrolyte levels. An ammeter is also needed to monitor the charging rate. While 25–30 amps can be accepted for perhaps 10 mins, longer periods should be at lower current. The charging output control on the alternator should take care of this, but the ammeter will allow the adjustment of engine revs to achieve the most efficient charging rate.

Charging

Although engine and domestic supplies need to be separate, they must also be jointly charged through a system which takes into account the needs of each. This can be done by automatic charging controls or by manual switching of the generator output. As long as the wiring is correct, the normal main battery supply on/off switches can be used to determine which battery system is used.

Alternators are almost exclusively used for charging today because they produce higher output at lower revs than dynamos, but they must not be run without an electrical load on the output or damage will result. While most alternators now have protection against this, it is still best never to turn the battery selector switch to 'off' when the engine is running.

Independent chargers

To keep batteries topped up while you are away from the boat, solar panels or wind generators are a considerable help, their choice depending on climatic conditions. Some wind generators can be adapted for use with a towed rotator, so that the boat speed can be used to generate electricity, usually at a much better rate than a wind charger. As a general rule, wind chargers vibrate when rotating, and those which start charging at low wind speeds have a limited output.

Cable connection, plugs and sockets

Proper plastic connector boards are the only real solution, apart from soldering, and the plug board must be kept dry and corrosion free. The best way to ensure this is to coat it in Dow Corning Silicone Sealant.

If soldering is preferred, wrap the two bare ends of wire together and lay a piece of solder alongside the bared wire. Then wrap the whole thing in metallic foil (even cigarette packet material will do) twisting the ends to ensure that liquid solder cannot escape. Light two matches simultaneously and hold the burning ends under the foil. When it has cooled, peel away the foil and wrap the joint in insulating tape.

Electrical do's and don'ts

1 Stow the battery in an accessible place, away from any hot spot in the engine space and in a free air flow. If there is a fuel leak, check that it has not reached the battery, since it may cause corrosion, leakage and dangerous toxic chlorine gas.

2 Keep the surface of the battery clean and dry; condensation on the top may lead to a flat battery.

3 Always identify a lead to its correct terminal when connecting and disconnecting.

4 Always stop the engine and turn off all switches before disconnecting any lead.

5 Always check that the voltage and polarity are correct before connecting a battery into the system.

6 Never run an alternator with the battery disconnected.

7 All wiring should be firmly secured at regular intervals or carried in a cable tray.

8 Fuses or circuit breakers should be used to protect the circuit at source. Fuses should be sealed glass or ceramic.

Cable size

To determine the correct size of cable for a circuit, first divide the total number of watts by the voltage to give the total current. Consult the table, *below*, and select the current which is the same or slightly larger than the circuit current. Follow the column down until you reach a figure equal to or above the length of the circuit in metres. The corresponding cable size is given at the left hand side.

Maximum circuit lengths for PVC insulated cables for 0.25 volt-drop (metres)

Cable Size	Current (amps)			
	1	3	5	10
14/.25	9.2	3.0	1.8	*
14/.3	13.3	4.4	2.6	*
21/.3	20.0	6.6	4.0	2.0
28/.3	26.0	8.8	5.4	2.7
35/.3	33.0	11.0	6.6	3.3
44/.3	41.0	13.9	8.3	4.2
65/.3	62.0	21.0	12.5	6.3
84/.3	80.0	26.0	16.0	8.0
97/.3	92.0	31.0	18.4	9.2
120/.3	110.0	38.0	23.0	11.4
80/.4	135.0	45.0	27.0	13.7
37/.75	225.0	75.0	45.0	22.7
266/.3	250.0	85.0	50.0	25.0

* Do not use this size cable for this or higher current values

Power requirements of electrical fittings

No.	Equipment	Watts
1	Masthead tricolour light	25
1	Bicolour pulpit light	25
1	Stern light	10
1	Masthead/steaming light	25
1	Floodlight at spreaders	20
4	20-W cabin lights	80
4	10-W cabin lights	80
1	Compass light	2
1	Vent fan	24
1	Radio	7.2
1	Log	0.2
1	Echo sounder (LED type)	1.2

Power consumption over 24 hrs

Equipment	Watts	Hours	Total
Ventilator fan	24	$\frac{1}{2}$	12
Radio	7.2	3	21.6
Navigation units, compass, instrument lights	3	7	21
Navigation lights (tricolour masthead)	25	7	175
Cabin lights	2×20	4	160
Cabin lights	3×10	1	30

Total power consumption for one day: 419.6 Watt hours or 35 ampere hours for a 12V system.

Tools

A good set of tools increases the incentive to attempt do-it-yourself repairs and maintenance, and so avoid high boatyard repair bills. The quantity of tools you can carry is inevitably limited by the size and storage capacity of your boat, the rigours you expect to impose upon it, and your bank balance.

Tools must be kept rust free for efficiency. One of the best ways of keeping them is in a plastic tool box, with trays, which is light and easy to move around the boat. It will ensure that the tools stay rust free to a large extent, and also that the box itself does not make rust marks and scratches on the boat. It is a good policy to coat tools with petroleum jelly to keep the damp out, and also to spray them from time to time with WD40. Oil-impregnated tool-kit lining papers will also help to keep corrosion at bay.

Most of the tools needed on a boat are obvious: spanners, screwdrivers and so on; but there are some special items which are particularly useful. For example, epoxy 2-part glue, drills, wheel brace, a mole or any other sort of self-gripping wrench, Allen keys and spanners that will fit every nut or bolt on the engine. A socket set is invaluable because it enables you to reach around corners and get at inaccessible bolts.

An 'American' screwdriver is also very useful. It is a screwdriver on the end of a cranked arm, with a conventional blade at one end, and a Philips type at the other. Again, for getting screws into difficult places, it is a good idea to have a retaining screwdriver with a little spring-clip on the end, which holds the screw in place while you are tightening it up. The same gadget can be used for bolts.

Drill a small hole in the handle of each of your hand tools and attach lanyards to them to help you hold on to them when working up the mast or over the side.

Finally, a mirror on a stalk, the angle of which can be adjusted, is excellent for working on things which are out of sight, usually on the engine. Failing this, any type of mirror is useful, if it can be supported in the position where you require it.

For more difficult repairs, power tools are helpful and will save a great deal of time. While it is possible to run them from a marina berth, it is preferable to obtain a small engine-driven generator which will give an output of 12V or 24V to charge batteries, as well as 240V to run your shore power tools. It is possible to get 12V power tools, and also battery-powered ones, but these usually need frequent recharging.

Remember to take all power tools home in the winter when the boat is laid up and will be damp. At the end of each sailing season, it is also worth while to clear out the toolbox and lockers containing spare parts. Clean up any rusty tools and discard all broken fittings and corroded bolts, screws and wire.

The older any equipment is, the greater will be the need for spare parts. Parts for older engines are particularly difficult to obtain, so it is worth ordering a stock of ignition parts, starters and generators from the manufacturers when you can get them, both as a hedge against inflation and to ensure that your engine will continue to function.

It is better to be well equipped with the right spares in the case of failure, than to risk wasting precious days of a cruise searching for a part. The engine manufacturer will normally supply a list of recommended spare parts and give the names of stockists.

Remember to keep the instruction manual for each piece of equipment on board, since it is possible to make a number of repairs simply with the aid of some commonsense and good instructions.

General tools
A power drill that can be run from the boat's electrical system or a 240V generator and 110V household drill
Hacksaw with 4 extra blades
Knife with multi-purpose blades
Small wood saw
Small screwdriver set (hard plastic handle) with a range of accessories
Counter-sink and drills for steel ($\frac{1}{2}$ in/12 mm size) and shank to fit hand drill, to be used for wood or soft metal
Socket set 6–19 mm
Chisel ($\frac{1}{2}$ in/12 mm size)
Pliers (single joint, side-cutting type)
Claw hammer
Metre rule (extending tape type which shows millimetres and inches)
Adjustable spanner to open up to $1\frac{1}{2}$ in (4 cm)

Rigging and sail-repair tools
Rigging knife
Marlin spike
Hollow fids for splicing
Splicing vice
Serving wire
Serving mallet
Wire cutters for largest size of rigging
Dacron sail twine, plain and waxed
Sailmaker's palm
Needles in various sizes
Grommet tool

Electrical and plumbing tools
Tube cutter
Pipe wrenches
Wirecutters
Soldering iron
Crimping tool
Test meter and light

Engine and mechanical tools
Oil can
Hand pump for engine oil
Set of engine tools
Tappet, ignition, fuel line, carburettor wrenches
Feeler gauge
Wire brush
Bottle gas torch
Vice grip pliers
Slip joint pliers
Punch
Adjustable open-end wrench
Files (rat-tail and flat)

Spare parts

Hulls
For fibreglass: fibreglass mat, cloth, polyester resin, activator, expanded metal sheet, epoxy resin, epoxy resin putty.

For wood: sheet plywood, sheet lead, fastenings, bedding, caulking compound.
For metal: quick-drying cement, epoxy, under-water epoxy, primer paint.

Rigging
Rope for halyards and sheets
Wire, the length of the longest stay
Blocks, shackles
Cotter and clevis pins
Rigging screws/turnbuckles and toggles
Monel seizing wire, plastic adhesive tape
Winch
Winch repair kit and grease, pawls and springs

Sail repair
Sailcloth in a variety of weights
Chafe protection
Sail twine, serving wire, sail tie tape
Jib hanks and sail slides
Battens

Electrical
Wire and fuses
Electrical tape
Starter motor and brushes
Generator or alternator
Distilled water
Hydrometer
Battery lugs, cable
Sealant
Bulbs

Mechanical
For petrol/gasoline engine:
Gasket set
Points
Condenser
Coil
Distributor cap
Ignition leads
Plugs
Waterpump and belts
Filters
Engine oil
Hydraulic fluid
Grease
For diesel engine:
Filters
Belts
Injectors and injector lines
Waterpump impellers
Engine oil
Hydraulic fuel

Plumbing
Repair kit for heads
Pumps
Hose
Pipe fittings

Paint

Painted boats

Repair scuffs as soon as they occur. Any blemishes left will flake back and water will get underneath the paint, causing it to lift off. If it is necessary to repaint using undercoat before a top coat, the latter must be applied as soon as the makers direct, otherwise damp will get in to the undercoat. This may sound like a chore, but it is probably easier than maintaining small areas of the hull of a GRP boat. Modern paint strippers of various types make the task of removing paint easy, and they are relatively clean to use, so there is no excuse for not having a smart-looking boat.

Varnish work

Bright work on a boat shows up neglect more than anything else. To maintain varnish, wash it off with fresh water as often as possible. Salt is very hard on varnish and if any blisters or damage occur during the season, catch the problem immediately. Keep a thinned-down pot of varnish that is 3 parts varnish to 1 of thinner on board all the time for instant repairs. If black weathering marks appear, the varnish and wood must be rubbed back until the wood looks natural, before the thinned-down varnish can be applied. After each coat of varnish, always rub down lightly to get a smooth, matt surface so that the next coat will adhere to it.

It is advisable to prepare for varnishing in the autumn because if two coats of varnish are applied then there is much less work involved the following year in getting the boat ready for the season. When the spring comes it should only be necessary to rub down lightly and apply two more coats of varnish.

There are new varnish surface preparers on the market which are good at getting a matt surface on varnish even in places which are difficult to reach; they will also wash off, without leaving any dust. Opinion is divided as to whether 1- or 2-pot polyurethane varnishes or the old, traditional varnish is best. The new, sealing types are said to stop the wood breathing, but they protect the surface very well against scratches and bumps and provide a much harder, although perhaps brittle, surface.

Anti-fouling

If you are buying a second-hand boat, check what anti-fouling has already been applied because it is important that what you put on top is compatible. There are barrier-type undercoats but this means more work. Some anti-foulings act better in different areas. At the end of the season, if the boat is taken out of the water, it pays to clean off all the weed and slime immediately. This is easy to do while it is wet, and means that the hull is clean and can dry out thoroughly during the winter. At the beginning of the season the hard work starts with getting the bottom as smooth as possible: equally important for both cruising and racing boats. Normally, two coats of anti-fouling are recommended; apply it with a brush, which gives a better finish than a roller.

Paint services

All the paint companies are helpful in giving advice on how to solve problems connected with paintwork, and International (Interlux) the market leader, offers a particularly comprehensive service.

Polish

It is a good plan to polish a GRP hull and the smooth parts of a GRP deck, at least once a year. An ideal opportunity is at laying-up time, or in the autumn. The effect of polishing the hull is to make it more difficult for marine growths to flourish on the GRP, particularly in the area close to the waterline. Polishing also provides an opportunity to inspect the hull closely for small scrapes which need to be repaired. It should also delay the time when the hull has eventually to be painted.

Painting GRP hulls

Painting a GRP hull becomes necessary when either the gelcoat colour has faded too much to be restored by polishing or when, in the case of a white hull, the dirt from near the surface of the water has changed the colour. These problems can be delayed by careful cleaning with the use of fibreglass cleaner, and waxing with a recommended fibreglass polish. Eventually, though, something more serious will have to be done. The usual solution is to repaint with 2-pot polyurethane paints to match the existing colour of the boat; there are professional organizations which will do the work for you.

To get a good surface the boat usually needs to be sprayed, although some professional painters always use a brush or a Scandinavian-type foam roller. When using a brush, dried paint tends to collect in the heel of the brush and work its way down the bristles to the surface being painted. As soon as this happens, clean or change the brush. To ensure an even coating, hold the brush handle at right angles to the surface with the bristles at 45°. The paint should be well stirred until any sediment is thoroughly mixed in before you start painting.

If you employ a professional organization, the job will be first-class, but you will also be able to see more blemishes in the hull afterwards because the restored gloss will highlight them. However, once the boat is in the water, the reflection of the surface is cast down again, and the movement of the water breaks up any imperfections. Certainly, the painting of a GRP hull can considerably improve its watertightness.

The amount of paint you will need

The following formulae can be used as a general guide to estimate the area to be covered. The covering capacities quoted on tins allow for the amount of paint normally wasted. Take measurements in metres.

BELOW WATERLINE
Medium-draft sailing cruisers with rounded bows: 0.75 × Waterline length × (Beam + Draft) = area in sq m
Full-bodied boats such as long-keeled yachts, shallow draft yachts and motor sailers. Waterline length × (Beam + Draft) = area in sq m.

TOPSIDES
(Length overall + Beam) × twice average freeboard = area in sq m.

DECKS
(Length overall × Beam) × 0.75 = area in sq m.

Mixing colours
1 Only mix shades of the same product.
2 Do not mix more than two colours together or the effect may be muddy.
3 Make a test mix of the desired shade and make a note of the proportions.
4 Many colours are already a mixture of hues and may produce surprising results when mixed.
5 Having established the proportions, mix the entire quantity in one go.
6 When tinting white, use small quantities, since strong shades may 'drown' the white altogether.
7 Mixed shades may not retain their colour as well as single colours; pale shades, for example, may fade.
8 Keep surplus for later touch-up.

Covering ability of paint

	sq m/ltrs	sq yds/gls
Primers		
Metallic primer	11	60
Glass fibre primer	18.5	100
Undercoats and enamels		
Undercoating	10	55
Enamel	10	55
Two-pot polyurethane	11	60
Underwater paint		
Anti-fouling–normal	10	55
Anti-fouling–heavy	7	35
Miscellaneous		
Non-slip deck paint	7.2	38
Ordinary deck paint	8.2	44
Marine varnish	13	70

Below decks

The galley

The first essential with the galley is to keep it clean! As soon as it starts to get dirty, it will smell, which does not help people who are prone to seasickness.

It must be possible to remove the cooker so that the area round it can be cleaned, since it is very easy to spill food at sea. Dirt also tends to collect in corners around the sink and it is worth keeping a tube of rubber sealant to fill up these gaps as soon as they appear. Dish washing is best done in a bowl because back pressure from the sea can force out the plug in the sink and you will lose all your hot water. The sink is very useful as a drainer to keep crockery under control while it is being dried.

Fresh water

Whatever type of tanks the boat is fitted with, fresh water will start to taste stale after a while. A frequent cause of trouble is the inlet pipe, and all plastic tubing in the system must be of good quality. Various liquids and tablets are available for keeping the water clean, and if you have trouble it is worth persevering with them, particularly if there is a convenient water supply which enables you to keep flushing out the tank as directed. At the end of the season it is important to clean the tank through with a domestic-type bleach cleanser, to rinse it out again, and then leave it empty during the winter. In cold weather water may freeze and any left in the pipe runs can cause considerable damage which is only apparent the following spring. Most boat piping is thoroughly inaccessible, so it is worth trying to blow the piping system through to ensure that you have a simple start to the next year.

Gas systems

If you suspect a leak in the pipe one way to check it quickly, without any elaborate equipment, is to coat the area with dish-washing liquid to see if you can raise a bubble, in very much the same way as you would check for a puncture in a tyre.

Heads

As with the galley, it is important to keep this equipment clean, and to make sure that everyone knows how to operate it properly. As soon as it starts to get dirty and smells develop, it becomes another cause of seasickness and gloom throughout the boat. The whole area around it also needs to be cleaned regularly with disinfectant. Cleaners suggested by the toilet manufacturers should be used. Many domestic cleaners are too harsh for the surface of a marine toilet and can damage the valves in the system.

Always carry spares for the pumps and valves so that you are not caught out when at sea. When you leave the boat after a cruise or a weekend, make sure that the heads have been flushed through and that the valves are shut off. Check that they are working well at the end of each season when the boat is out of the water; also check the quality and security of the jubilee clips at each end of the pipe. It is a good policy to turn off the seacocks when the toilet is not in use when sailing because they will sometimes tend to siphon back when the boat is heeled, and can flood it.

Bilges

The important thing with the bilge is to try to keep it clean. Avoid brushing dirt and crumbs into it – collect them with a dustpan instead. Make sure that limber holes through bulkheads are clear and also that water can get down from the highest point of the bilge to the bottom where the pump suction is. Rubbish collects very quickly in the bilge and easily causes a smell. It is possible to clean it out by putting dish-washing liquid into the high areas, washing it down to the lower end and then pumping it out. Ensure that there is a proper trap on the end of the bilge suction so that rubbish cannot be drawn into the pump. When moored alongside a marina, take the opportunity to wash out the bilges thoroughly with fresh water.

Ventilation

This is essential for keeping the boat both clean and mildew- and mould-free for a pleasant life on board. But it is equally important during winter, if you have a cover on the boat, to ensure that air can get through underneath it. When you are away from the boat, leave all the locker doors propped open so that they cannot swing and become damaged or chip the varnish. Prop up all seat cushions and allow the air to circulate thoroughly.

Cushions and upholstery

Ideally, all cushions should have loose covers which can be washed easily. Modern polypropylene fabrics are very good in that they resist dirt and water, but they must still be removable to allow cleaning. One of the best ways to keep upholstery mildew-free during the winter, apart from taking it home, is to use electric heating in the boat.

Lighting

Maintaining lighting is a case of maintaining switches. In the event of failure, it is easy to assume that a lamp has blown until checking reveals that salt and corrosion have eaten away the switch. Some switches are difficult to work on and have to be replaced, while others can be taken to pieces – WD40 is very useful in either instance.

Leaving lights on by mistake will flatten the battery. When going ashore, always remember to check first, that the gas is turned off, second, that the main battery switch is off and, third, that all the seacocks are shut.

Marine housework

1 Always clean up any spillages and retrieve dropped food immediately to prevent smells developing.

2 Leave any wet items to dry in the cockpit rather than in the cabin where dampness may impregnate the bunks. Leave wet towels and cloths to air frequently.

3 To clean glass windows, wash with a vinegar and water solution. Plastic windows should be washed very gently with fresh water and a soft cloth or sponge. Do not rub hard!

4 Wash the ice box regularly with soda, ammonia or bleach. When it is empty, keep it wide open to allow any smells to escape. Always keep food wrapped or in containers, never loose.

5 Treat oil spots with dry asbestos cement. It will absorb the oil and can then be wiped off.

6 Avoid cleaners which produce a lot of suds, since they waste water. Detergents work better than soap in salt water. Keep two large sponges handy; one for work tops and the other for grimier tasks.

7 Keep the bilge clean by scrubbing it with bilge cleanser or solvent and add a few drops of pine essence to improve the odour.

8 To whiten enamel sinks or heads, fill with water and add a little bleaching powder. The stain should soak off in a few hours.

9 To clean the cabin, use a tank-type vacuum cleaner in harbour. If the bilge is dry, vacuum up any loose dirt. Use a broom handle with a stuffed sock on the end to reach the corners, behind the cooker, etc.

10 Check cushions, curtains, carpet for stains once a year. Most fabrics used on modern cruisers respond well to a soap and water wash.

11 Use only metal polish produced for boat work, rather than household or industrial types.

12 Leave drawers, lockers and hatchways open as often as possible to prevent mildew and rot.

Boats and the law

The legal problems which occasionally confront a boat owner are often more easily avoided than cured. The following points cannot cover the extensive subject of Maritime Law comprehensively, but are intended to provide some practical guidance to small-boat sailors.

Buying and selling

Although there are few legal constraints in buying or selling a yacht, the position varies from country to country, so current requirements should be verified before entering into such an agreement.

Be particularly wary when buying a boat since, unlike most forms of property, boats can carry debts with them. Claims against a boat for salvage remuneration, collision damage and other debts may survive the sale and be enforced against the new owner. If a boat is registered there may also be registered encumbrances, such as mortgages, which remain binding until cleared off the register.

When buying or selling a second-hand boat it is advisable to record the deal in a written document. It is preferable to seek independent professional advice although standard forms of agreement, such as that sponsored by the Association of Brokers and Yacht Agents in Britain, are available. While a broker will normally assist a purchaser, he is usually the seller's agent.

Boats are invariably sold 'as-is, where-is' and, since most contracts automatically free the seller of any liability for defects in the vessel, a survey is crucial. Buyers should note, however, that some contracts restrict the purchaser's right to withdraw for defects found on survey. The choice of surveyor is also important. If possible select a member of a recognized professional organization; this indicates that he is qualified and carries insurance against professional negligence.

When buying a new boat, either commissioned or from stock, you may be expected to enter into an agreement on the supplier's standard terms. If so, study the contract carefully before signature, paying particular attention to the provisions relating to payment, delays in delivery and the supplier's liability for defects after delivery, but remember that any guarantee is of limited value if the supplier ceases trading after delivery. In the case of a commissioned boat, avoid paying any part of the purchase price unless it is fully secured. Most reputable suppliers will provide a bank guarantee to secure any deposit and stage payments made prior to delivery.

Berthing and mooring

Most boat owners enter into an agreement with a yard or marina for berthing or mooring facilities. The agreement is likely to be in a standard form, but you should check carefully the extent to which the yard's liability is restricted or excluded by the agreement. Check also restrictions imposed on the owner or outside contractors working on the boat, and whether a commission is levied on boats sold from the marina.

Chartering

A written charter agreement should set out plainly the obligations and the responsibilities of both parties. Before taking out a boat on charter, take note of the extent to which you may become personally liable for damage to the boat or third parties and the penalties imposed for late return. You are liable for the consequences of your own negligence, and generally that of the crew, so insurance is essential.

As an owner wishing to let/rent your boat on charter, consult your insurance brokers and legal advisers. Existing insurance should be extended to cover the boat while on charter and the potential liability of charterers. Ensure that there is an insurance cover against misappropriation by the charterer, and against losses arising from any breach of the charter agreement by him.

Insurance

Adequate insurance is essential both for protection against damage to your own craft and against claims by third parties. Most yacht owners arrange their boat insurance through a broker who should be in a position to advise on the range of policies available and to suggest the most suitable cover.

When completing a proposal form for marine insurance, you are obliged to answer all the questions truthfully and to disclose any factors that may influence an underwriter in fixing the premium, or deciding whether to accept the risk. Any non-disclosure or misrepresentation will jeopardize the policy.

It is worth shopping around for insurance. While most yacht policies are broadly similar, the terms sometimes differ and should be examined before acceptance. Policies vary on details such as the extent to which damage by fire is covered. Damage to engines and electrical equipment caused by flooding is often restricted and many policies do not cover theft of outboard motors, unless secured by an independent locking device, or of dinghies, unless permanently marked with the name of the parent vessel.

Losses caused by wear and tear are not covered and it is the owner's responsibility to keep his boat in seaworthy condition. You will not be covered against any loss when navigating outside the permitted cruising limits, or if using the boat during her laid-up period. All warranties must be strictly observed.

Should a claim arise, give full details to the insurers as promptly as possible. If a decision needs to be made urgently and the insurers are not available, an owner is obliged to act prudently, as if he was protecting his own interests. Any claim will generally be processed through a broker who will usually deal with the insurers for the owner.

Salvage and collision

If you have the misfortune to be involved in a collision, make a detailed note of all the circumstances of the casualty as soon as possible after the event. Details of times, headings, course alterations, speeds, signals passed between the vessels, positions, weather and sea conditions should all be noted and recorded in the ship's log. If possible, details of the vessels, their owners and insurers should be exchanged. No admission of liability should be made.

In some circumstances, the Owner or Master of a vessel which causes damage may limit the amount of his liability to a sum prescribed by statute which is often substantially less than the cost of repairing the damage caused. The amount to which liability may be limited and the precise circumstances in which limitation may apply varies from country to country. The possibility that a yachtsman may not be able to recover, in full, damages caused by the negligence of another, emphasizes the importance of maintaining adequate insurance cover.

Salvage is voluntary aid to property in danger at sea. If successful, the salvor is entitled to remuneration, which is assessed by taking into account many factors including the value of the property saved and the degree of danger to both vessels. Salvage takes many forms and any voluntary act which assists an endangered vessel to safety may give rise to a salvage award. Towage assistance is often treated as salvage and anyone who accepts a tow should establish the basis upon which aid is given.

Distress Signals

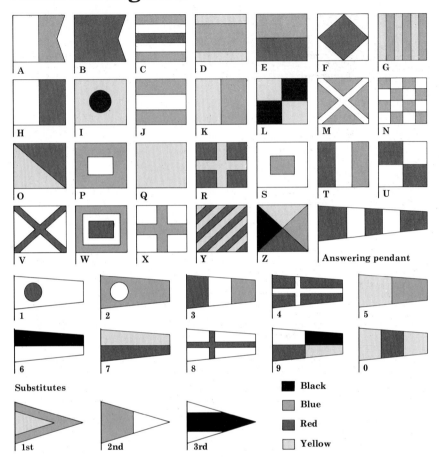

Substitutes

1st   2nd   3rd

■ Black
■ Blue
■ Red
□ Yellow

The phonetic alphabet should be used for radio transmissions in plain language or in code.

A Alpha	H Hotel	O Oscar	V Victor
B Bravo	I India	P Papa	W Whisky
C Charlie	J Juliet	Q Quebec	X X-ray
D Delta	K Kilo	R Romeo	Y Yankee
E Echo	L Lima	S Sierra	Z Zulu
F Foxtrot	M Mike	T Tango	
G Golf	N November	U Uniform	

If you need to spell out a word you should say, 'I spell' after pronouncing the word and then spell it using the phonetic alphabet.

Numerals should be pronounced:

1 wun	3 tree	5 fife	7 seven	9 nin er
2 too	4 fow er	6 six	8 ait	0 zero

Transmit numbers above 9, digit by digit.

International code flags are usually hoisted in groups of four, one below the other, and read from top to bottom. A 6-ft. (2-m) gap is left between groups when more than one is hoisted on a single halyard. Flag signalling is normally used only for code signals. The answering pendant is hoisted half way up the halyard when a signal is acknowledged in the same way. It also indicates a full stop or decimal point. There are three substitute flags, used when a letter or number recurs in a group: the first substitute stands for the first flag and so on.

Morse code is usually transmitted using a bright lamp or torch, but can be conveyed using flags or arm signals. Use sound signals only for single-letter code signals or in an emergency, especially in fog or crowded waters. Plain language or code can be sent.	A ·— B —··· C —·—· D —·· E · F ··—· G ——· H ···· I ·· J ·——— K —·— L ·—·· M —— N —· O ——— P ·——· Q ——·—	R ·—· S ··· T — U ··— V ···— W ·—— X —··— Y —·—— Z ——·· 1 ·———— 2 ··——— 3 ···—— 4 ····— 5 ····· 6 —···· 7 ——···

8 ———··	
9 ————·	
0 —————	
·—·—·	**End of message AR**
·—···	**Waiting signals AS**
·—·—·—	**Full stop or decimal point AAA**
·—·—·	**General call AA**
———————	**Answering Signal TTT TTT**
·····	**Word received signal T**
·········	**Erase signal EEE EEE**

Code signals, sent by any means, are understood internationally.
Each letter of the alphabet except **R** is a complete signal when sent individually:
A I have a diver down; keep well clear at slow speed.
B I am taking in, discharging or carrying dangerous goods.
C Yes.
D Keep clear of me; I am manoeuvring with difficulty.
E I am altering my course to starboard.
F I am disabled; communicate with me.
G I require a pilot.
H I have a pilot on board.
I I am altering my course to port.
J I am on fire and have dangerous cargo on board; keep well clear of me.
K I wish to communicate with you.
L You should stop your vessel instantly.
M My vessel is stopped and making no way through the water.
N No.
O Man overboard.
P *In harbour.* All persons should report aboard as the vessel is about to proceed to sea. *At sea.* My nets have come fast on an obstruction.
Q My vessel is healthy and I request free pratique.
R No meaning in the International Code, but used by vessels at anchor to warn of danger of collision in fog.
S I am operating astern propulsion.
T Keep clear of me; I am engaged in pair trawling.
U You are running into danger.
V I require assistance.
W I require medical assistance.
X Stop carrying out your intentions and wait for my signals.
Y I am dragging my anchor.
Z I require a tug.

Some useful two letter signals are:
AC I am abandoning my vessel.
AN I need a doctor.
BR I require a helicopter urgently.
CB I require immediate assistance.
DV I am drifting.
EF SOS/MAYDAY has been cancelled.
FA Will you give me my position?
GW Man overboard. Please take action to pick him up.
JL You are running the risk of going aground.
LO I am not in my correct position: *used by a light vessel.*
NC I am in distress and require immediate assistance.
PD Your navigation lights are not visible.
PP Keep well clear of me.
QD I am going ahead.
QT I am going astern.
QQ I require health clearance.
QU Anchoring is prohibited.
QX I request permission to anchor.
RU Keep clear of me; I am manoeuvring with difficulty.
SO You should stop your vessel instantly.
UM The harbour is closed to traffic.
UP Permission to enter harbour is urgently requested. I have an emergency.
YU I am going to communicate with your station by means of the International Code of Signals.
ZD1 Please report me to Coastguard, New York.
ZD2 Please report me to Lloyds, London.
ZL Your signal has been received but not understood.

Facts and figures

Feet to Metres

Feet	Metres	Feet	Metres
1	0.30	26	7.92
2	0.61	27	8.23
3	0.91	28	8.84
4	1.22	29	8.84
5	1.52	30	9.14
6	1.83	31	9.45
7	2.13	32	9.75
8	2.44	33	10.06
9	2.74	34	10.36
10	3.05	35	10.67
11	3.35	36	10.97
12	3.66	37	11.28
13	3.96	38	11.58
14	4.27	39	11.89
15	4.57	40	12.19
16	4.88	41	12.50
17	5.18	42	12.80
18	5.49	43	13.11
19	5.79	44	13.41
20	6.10	45	13.72
21	6.40	46	14.02
22	6.71	47	14.33
23	7.01	48	14.63
24	7.31	49	14.94
25	7.62	50	15.24

Metres to Feet

Metres	Feet	Metres	Feet
1	3.28	26	85.30
2	6.56	27	88.58
3	9.84	28	91.86
4	13.12	29	95.14
5	16.40	30	98.43
6	19.69	31	101.71
7	22.97	32	104.99
8	26.25	33	108.27
9	29.53	34	111.55
10	32.81	35	114.83
11	36.09	36	118.11
12	39.37	37	121.39
13	42.65	38	124.67
14	45.93	39	127.95
15	49.21	40	131.23
16	52.49	41	134.51
17	55.77	42	137.80
18	59.06	43	141.08
19	62.34	44	144.36
20	65.62	45	147.64
21	68.90	46	150.92
22	72.18	47	154.20
23	75.46	48	157.48
24	78.74	49	160.76
25	82.02	50	164.04

Fathoms to Metres

Fathoms	Metres	Fathoms	Metres
1	1.83	26	47.55
2	3.66	27	49.38
3	5.49	28	51.21
4	7.32	29	53.04
5	9.14	30	54.86
6	10.97	31	56.69
7	12.80	32	58.52
8	14.63	33	60.35
9	16.48	34	62.18
10	18.29	35	64.00
11	20.12	36	65.84
12	21.95	37	67.67
13	23.77	38	69.49
14	25.60	39	71.32
15	27.43	40	73.15
16	29.26	41	74.98
17	31.09	42	76.81
18	32.92	43	78.64
19	34.75	44	80.47
20	36.58	45	82.30
21	38.40	46	84.12
22	40.23	47	85.95
23	42.06	48	87.78
24	43.89	49	89.61
25	45.72	50	91.44

Metres to Fathoms

Metres	Fathoms	Metres	Fathoms
1	0.547	26	14.217
2	1.094	27	14.764
3	1.640	28	15.311
4	2.187	29	15.857
5	2.734	30	16.404
6	3.281	31	16.951
7	3.828	32	17.498
8	4.374	33	18.045
9	4.921	34	18.591
10	5.468	35	19.138
11	6.015	36	19.685
12	6.562	37	20.232
13	7.108	38	20.779
14	7.655	39	21.325
15	8.202	40	21.872
16	9.749	41	22.419
17	9.296	42	22.966
18	9.842	43	23.513
19	10.389	44	24.059
20	10.936	45	24.606
21	11.483	46	25.153
22	12.030	47	25.700
23	12.577	48	26.247
24	13.123	49	26.793
25	13.670	50	27.340

International nautical miles, kilometres and statute miles

INM	Km	SM	Km	INM	SM	SM	Km	INM
1	1.852	1.15078	1	0.53996	0.62137	1	1.60934	0.86898
2	3.70	2.30	2	1.08	1.24	2	3.22	1.74
3	5.56	3.45	3	1.62	1.86	3	4.83	2.61
4	7.41	4.60	4	2.16	2.49	4	6.44	3.48
5	9.26	5.75	5	2.70	3.11	5	8.05	4.34
6	11.11	6.90	6	3.24	3.73	6	9.66	5.21
7	12.96	8.06	7	3.78	4.35	7	11.27	6.08
8	14.82	9.21	8	4.32	4.97	8	12.87	6.95
9	16.67	10.36	9	4.86	5.59	9	14.48	7.82
10	18.52	11.51	10	5.40	6.21	10	16.09	8.69
11	20.37	12.66	11	5.94	6.84	11	17.70	9.56
12	22.22	13.81	12	6.48	7.46	12	19.31	10.43
13	24.08	14.96	13	7.02	8.08	13	20.92	11.30
14	25.93	16.11	14	7.56	8.70	14	22.53	12.17
15	27.78	17.26	15	8.10	9.32	15	23.14	13.03
16	29.63	18.41	16	8.64	9.94	16	25.75	13.90
17	31.48	19.56	17	9.18	10.56	17	27.36	14.77
18	33.34	20.71	18	9.72	11.18	18	28.97	15.64
19	35.19	21.86	19	10.26	11.81	19	30.58	16.51
20	37.04	23.02	20	10.80	12.43	20	32.19	17.38
21	38.99	24.17	21	11.34	13.05	21	33.80	18.25
22	40.74	25.32	22	11.88	13.67	22	35.41	19.12
23	42.60	26.47	23	12.42	14.29	23	37.01	19.99
24	44.45	27.62	24	12.96	14.91	24	38.62	20.86
25	46.30	28.77	25	13.50	15.53	25	40.23	21.72
26	48.15	29.92	26	14.04	16.16	26	41.84	22.59
27	50.00	31.07	27	14.58	16.78	27	43.45	23.46
28	51.86	32.22	28	15.12	17.40	28	45.06	24.33
29	53.71	33.37	29	15.66	18.02	29	46.67	25.20
30	55.56	34.52	30	16.20	18.64	30	48.28	26.07
31	57.41	35.67	31	16.74	19.26	31	49.89	26.94
32	59.26	36.82	32	17.28	19.88	32	51.50	27.81
33	61.12	37.98	33	17.82	20.51	33	53.11	28.68
34	62.97	39.13	34	18.36	21.13	34	54.72	29.55
35	64.82	40.28	35	18.90	21.75	35	56.33	30.41
36	66.67	41.43	36	19.44	22.37	36	57.94	31.28
37	68.52	42.58	37	19.98	22.99	37	59.55	32.15
38	70.38	43.73	38	20.52	23.61	38	61.15	33.02
39	72.23	44.88	39	21.06	24.23	39	62.76	33.89
40	74.08	46.03	40	21.60	24.85	40	64.37	34.76
45	83.34	51.79	45	24.30	27.96	45	72.42	39.10
50	92.60	57.54	50	27.00	31.07	50	80.47	43.45
55	101.86	63.29	55	29.70	34.18	55	88.51	47.79
60	111.12	69.05	60	32.40	37.28	60	96.56	52.14
65	120.38	74.80	65	35.10	40.39	65	104.61	56.48
70	129.64	80.55	70	37.80	43.50	70	112.65	60.83
75	138.90	86.31	75	40.50	46.60	75	120.70	65.17
80	148.16	92.06	80	43.20	49.71	80	128.75	69.52
85	157.42	97.82	85	45.90	52.82	85	136.79	73.86
90	166.68	103.57	90	48.60	55.92	90	144.84	78.21
95	715.94	109.32	95	51.30	59.03	95	152.89	82.55
100	185.20	115.08	100	54.00	62.14	100	160.93	86.90

Mariner's measure

The old nautical mile (6,080ft) has been replaced by the international nautical mile (6,076ft). The difference, however, is too small to be of any consequence for the yachtsman.

1 fathom = 6ft
1 fathom = 1.8288m
1 cable = 100 fathoms approximately
1 nautical mile = 10 cables
1 nautical mile = 1,852m (6,076.12ft)
1 nautical mile = 1.852km
1 nautical mile = 1.15 miles 1 knot = 1 nautical mile per hour 1 kilometre = 0.539957 nautical miles
1 mile = 0.868976 nautical miles

Electricity

$$Watts = Volts \times Amperes \quad Amperes = \frac{Volts}{Ohms}$$

Estimating speed

A rough idea of a boat's speed can be gained by noting the time it takes to travel its own length by reference to an object in the water.

$$Speed\ in\ knots = \frac{length\ in\ metres}{time\ in\ seconds} \times 1.94$$

$$Speed\ in\ knots = \frac{length\ in\ feet}{time\ in\ seconds} \times 0.59$$

Frequency/wavelength

Frequencies and wavelengths are reciprocal. In other words, 300kHz = 1000m and 1000kHz = 300m. The formulae for converting them are:

$$Metres = \frac{300\,000}{kHz} \quad kHz = \frac{300\,000}{m}$$

1 MHz = 1000 kHz

Barometric pressure

The following conversion factors are calculated at 0°C and standard gravity of 980.665 cm/sec^2

1 millibar = 0.02953in   1 inch = 33.86387mb

Estimating speed

Knots	m/sec	MPH
1.944	1	2.237
3.9	2	4.5
5.8	3	6.7
7.8	4	8.9
9.7	5	11.2
11.7	6	13.4
13.6	7	15.7
15.6	8	17.9
17.5	9	20.1
19.4	10	22.4
21.4	11	24.6
23.3	12	26.8
25.3	13	29.1
27.2	14	31.3
29.2	15	33.6
31.1	16	35.8
33.0	17	38.0
35.0	18	40.3
36.9	19	42.5
38.9	20	44.7
48.6	25	55.9
58.3	30	67.1
68.0	35	78.3

Conversion table (Fahrenheit to Celsius)

°F	°C	°F	°C	°F	°C	°F	°C	°F	°C	°F	°C
00	−18	24	−4	48	9	72	22	96	36	121	49
01	−17	25	−4	49	9	73	23	97	36	122	50
02	−17	26	−3	50	10	74	23	98	37	123	51
03	−16	27	−3	51	11	75	24	100	38	124	51
04	−16	28	−2	52	11	76	24	101	38	125	52
05	−15	29	−2	53	12	77	25	102	39	126	52
06	−14	30	−1	54	12	78	26	103	39	127	53
07	−14	31	−1	55	13	79	26	104	40	128	53
08	−13	32	0	56	13	80	27	105	41	129	54
09	−13	33	1	57	14	81	27	106	41	130	54
10	−12	34	1	58	14	82	28	107	42	131	55
11	−12	35	2	59	15	83	28	108	42	132	56
12	−11	36	2	60	16	84	29	109	43	133	56
13	−11	37	3	61	16	85	29	110	43	134	57
14	−10	38	3	62	17	86	30	111	44	135	57
15	−10	39	4	63	17	87	31	112	44	136	58
16	−9	40	4	64	18	88	31	113	45	137	58
17	−8	41	5	65	18	89	32	114	46	138	59
18	−8	42	6	66	19	90	32	115	46	139	59
19	−7	43	6	67	19	91	33	116	47	140	60
20	−7	44	7	68	20	92	33	117	47	141	61
21	−6	45	7	69	21	93	34	118	48	142	61
22	−6	46	8	70	21	94	34	119	48	143	62
23	−5	47	8	71	22	95	35	120	49	144	62

Freshwater measurements

1 litre weighs 1 kg
1 gallon weighs 10 lb
1 cubic metre weighs 1,000 kg
1 cubic feet weighs 62.4 lb
1 cubic metre is 1,000 litres
1 cubic foot is 6.23 gallons
1 ton occupies 35.96 cubic feet
1 ton is 224 gallons (Imperial)

Conversion Tables

Multiply	By	To obtain
Pints (Imp)	1.201	Pints (US)
Gallons (Imp)	4.546	Litres
Litres	0.22	Gallons (Imp)
Gallons (Imp)	1.201	Gallons (US)
Gallons (US)	0.8327	Gallons (Imp)
Litres/sec	13.20	Gallons/min

Multiply	By	To obtain
Litres/min	3.666×10^3	Gallons/sec
Fluid oz (Imp)	28.41	Cubic cm
Fluid oz (US)	1.041	Fluid oz (Imp)
Minutes (angle)	0.01667	Degrees (angle)
Square yards	0.8361	Square metres
Square metres	1.196	Square yards
Horsepower	1.014	Horsepower (metric)
Miles	1.609	Kilometres
Miles	0.8684	Nautical miles
Miles/hr	1.609	Kilometres/hr
Cubic cm	3.531×10^5	Cubic feet
Cubic metres	1.308	Cubic yards
Cubic metres	220.0	Gallons (Imp)
Cubic yards	0.7646	Cubic metres
Cubic yards	764.5	Litres
Fathoms	1.85	Metres
Feet	0.3048	Metres
Inches	25.40	Millimetres
Kilogrammes	2.205	Pounds
Kilometres	3.281×10^3	Feet
Kilometres	0.6214	Miles
Kilometres/hr	0.5396	Knots
Kilometres/hr	0.6214	Miles/hr
Knots	1.853	Kilometres/hr
Knots	1.152	Miles/hr
Pounds/sq ft	0.03591	Cm of mercury

Distance of horizon for various heights of eye

Height of eye		Horizon distance	Height of eye		Horizon distance
metres	feet	n miles	metres	feet	n miles
1	3.3	2.1	16	52.5	8.3
2	6.6	2.9	17	55.8	8.6
3	9.8	3.6	18	59.1	8.8
4	13.1	4.1	19	62.3	9.1
5	16.4	4.7	20	65.6	9.3
6	19.7	5.1	21	68.9	9.5
7	23.0	5.5	22	72.2	9.8
8	26.2	5.9	23	75.5	10.0
9	29.6	6.2	24	78.7	10.2
10	32.8	6.6	25	82.0	10.4
11	36.1	6.9	26	85.3	10.6
12	39.4	7.2	27	88.6	10.8
13	42.7	7.5	28	91.9	11.0
14	45.9	7.8	29	95.1	11.2
15	49.2	8.1	30	98.4	11.4

Lights – distance off when rising or dipping (n miles)

Height of light		Height of eye							
		metres	1	2	3	4	5	6	7	8
metres	feet	feet	3	7	10	13	16	20	23	26
10	33		8.7	9.5	10.2	10.8	11.3	11.7	12.1	12.5
14	46		9.9	10.7	11.4	12.0	12.5	12.9	13.3	13.7
18	59		10.9	11.7	12.4	13.0	13.5	13.9	14.3	14.7
20	66		11.4	12.2	12.9	13.5	14.0	14.4	14.8	15.2
24	79		12.3	13.1	13.8	14.4	14.9	15.3	15.7	16.1
28	92		13.1	13.9	14.6	15.2	15.7	16.1	16.5	16.9
30	98		13.5	14.3	15.0	15.6	16.1	16.5	16.9	17.3
34	112		14.2	15.0	15.7	16.3	16.8	17.2	17.6	18.0
38	125		14.9	15.7	16.4	17.0	17.5	17.9	18.3	18.7
40	131		15.3	16.1	16.8	17.4	17.9	18.3	18.7	19.1
44	144		15.9	16.7	17.4	18.0	18.5	18.9	19.3	19.7
48	157		16.5	17.3	18.0	18.6	19.1	19.5	19.9	20.3
50	164		16.8	17.6	18.3	18.9	19.4	19.8	20.2	20.6
55	180		17.5	18.3	19.0	19.6	20.1	20.5	20.9	21.3
60	197		18.2	19.0	19.7	20.3	20.8	21.2	21.6	22.0
65	213		18.9	19.7	20.4	21.0	21.5	21.9	22.3	22.7
70	230		19.5	20.3	21.0	21.6	22.1	22.5	22.9	23.2
75	246		20.1	20.9	21.6	22.2	22.7	23.1	23.5	23.9
80	262		20.7	21.5	22.2	22.8	23.3	23.7	24.1	24.5
85	279		21.3	22.1	22.8	23.4	23.9	24.3	24.7	25.1
90	295		21.8	22.6	23.3	23.9	24.4	24.8	25.2	25.6
95	312		22.4	23.2	23.9	24.5	25.0	25.4	25.8	26.2
100	328		23.0	23.8	24.5	25.1	25.6	26.0	26.4	26.8

Vertical sextant angles – for finding distance off

Miles	15m 49ft	20m 66ft	25m 82ft	30m 98ft	35m 115ft	40m 131ft	45m 148ft	50m 164ft	55m 180ft	60m 197ft
0.1	4°38′	6°10′	7°41′	9°13′	10°42′	12°11′	13°39′	15°07′	16°32′	17°57′
0.2	2 19	3 05	3 52	4 38	5 24	6 10	6 56	7 41	8 27	9 12
0.3	1 33	2 04	2 35	3 05	3 36	4 07	4 38	5 09	5 39	6 10
0.4	1 10	1 33	1 56	2 19	2 42	3 05	3 29	3 52	4 15	4 38
0.5	0 56	1 14	1 33	1 51	2 10	2 28	2 47	3 05	3 24	3 42
0.6	0 46	1 02	1 17	1 33	1 48	2 04	2 19	2 35	2 50	3 05
0.7	0 40	0 53	1 06	1 20	1 33	1 46	1 59	2 13	2 26	2 39
0.8	0 35	0 46	0 58	1 10	1 21	1 33	1 44	1 56	2 08	2 19
0.9	0 31	0 41	0 52	1 02	1 12	1 22	1 33	1 43	1 53	2 04
1.0	0 28	0 37	0 46	0 56	1 05	1 14	1 24	1 33	1 42	1 51
1.1	0 25	0 34	0 42	0 51	0 59	1 07	1 16	1 24	1 33	1 41
1.2	0 23	0 31	0 39	0 46	0 49	1 02	1 10	1 17	1 25	1 33
1.3	0 21	0 29	0 36	0 43	0 50	0 57	1 04	1 11	1 19	1 26
1.4	0 20	0 27	0 33	0 40	0 46	0 53	1 00	1 06	1 13	1 20
1.5	0 19	0 25	0 31	0 37	0 43	0 49	0 56	1 02	1 08	1 14
1.6	0 17	0 23	0 29	0 35	0 41	0 46	0 52	0 58	1 04	1 10
1.7	0 16	0 22	0 27	0 33	0 38	0 44	0 49	0 55	1 00	1 06
1.8	0 15	0 21	0 26	0 31	0 36	0 41	0 46	0 52	0 57	1 02
1.9	0 15	0 20	0 24	0 29	0 34	0 39	0 44	0 49	0 54	0 59
2.0	0 14	0 19	0 23	0 28	0 32	0 37	0 42	0 46	0 51	0 56
2.1	0 13	0 18	0 22	0 27	0 31	0 35	0 40	0 44	0 49	0 53
2.2	0 13	0 17	0 21	0 25	0 30	0 34	0 38	0 42	0 46	0 51
2.3	0 12	0 16	0 20	0 24	0 28	0 32	0 36	0 40	0 44	0 48
2.4	0 12	0 15	0 19	0 23	0 27	0 31	0 35	0 39	0 43	0 46
2.5	0 11	0 15	0 19	0 22	0 26	0 29	0 33	0 37	0 41	0 44
2.6	0 11	0 14	0 18	0 21	0 25	0 29	0 32	0 36	0 39	0 43
2.7	0 10	0 14	0 17	0 21	0 24	0 27	0 31	0 34	0 38	0 41
2.8	0 10	0 13	0 17	0 20	0 23	0 27	0 30	0 33	0 36	0 40
2.9	0 10	0 13	0 16	0 19	0 22	0 26	0 29	0 32	0 35	0 38
3.0	0 09	0 12	0 15	0 19	0 22	0 25	0 28	0 31	0 34	0 37
3.1	0 09	0 12	0 15	0 18	0 21	0 24	0 27	0 30	0 33	0 36
3.2	0 09	0 12	0 15	0 17	0 20	0 23	0 26	0 29	0 32	0 35
3.3	0 08	0 11	0 14	0 17	0 20	0 22	0 25	0 28	0 31	0 34
3.4	0 08	0 11	0 14	0 16	0 19	0 22	0 25	0 27	0 30	0 33
3.5	0 08	0 11	0 13	0 16	0 19	0 21	0 24	0 27	0 29	0 32

Anchor comparisons

Length of boat	m	6.5	8.0	9.0	11.0	13.0	15.5	17.5	22.2
	ft	21.0	26.0	30.0	36.0	43.0	51.0	57.5	72.0
CQR (plough)	kg	6.8	9.1	11.3	15.9	20.4	27.2	34.0	47.6
	lb	15.0	20.0	25.0	35.0	45.0	60.0	75.0	105.0
Fisherman	kg	13.5	18	22.5	31.5	40.5	54	67.5	90
	lb	30.0	40	50.0	70.0	90.0	120	150.0	200
Bruce anchor	kg	5	10	10	20	20	30	30	50
	lb	11	22	22	44	44	66	66	110

Beaufort wind scale

Force	Knots	Sign	Description	Open sea – probable wave height in metres
0	Less than 1	◎	Glassy sea; smoke rises vertically	
1	1–3		Small ripples	
2	4–6		Light breeze; wavelets	0.15
3	7–10		Gentle breeze, crests of large wavelets break occasionally	0.60
4	11–16		Moderate breeze; small waves, with breaking crests	1
5	17–21		Fresh breeze; long waves, spray from breaking crests	1.80
6	22–27		Strong breeze; large waves with extensive foamy crests	3
7	28–33		Near gale; sea heaps up, white foam from crests blows in streaks downwind	4
8	34–40		Gale; longer, higher waves, spindrift off crests, streaky foam	5.50
9	41–47		Strong gale; high waves, crests topple	7
10	48–55		Storm; very high waves, long curved crests, sea white from large foam patches	9
11	56–63		Violent storm; huge waves, poor visibility	11.30
12	64 +		Hurricane; air full of foam and spray	13.70

Watch system

A D   D   D   D   D
B   D   D   D   D
MN   4   8   12   16 18 20   MN   4   8

Sk D D D D   D D D D D D
Al   D D   D D   D   D D   D
Ac   D D   D D   D   D D
Bl D   D D   D   D D   D D
Bc D D   D D   D   D D   D D
MN   4   8   12   16   20   MN   4   8

Sk   D   D   D   D   D   D
          D   D   D   D   D   D
       D   D   D   D   D
MN 3 6 9 12 15 18 21 MN 3 6 9 12 15 18 21 MN

The watch system, *above*, divides duties, D, into four-hourly stints. Sk = Skipper Al = Group A watch leader. Ac = Group A watch crew. Bl = Group B watch leader. Bc = Group B watch crew

Port entry signals (international)

Light	Type	Main Message
● R ● R ● R	Flashing	Serious emergency – all vessels stop or divert according to instructions
● R ● R ● R		Vessels shall not proceed
● G ● G ● G	Fixed or slow occulting	Vessels may proceed – one-way traffic
● G ● G ○ W		Vessels may proceed – two-way traffic
● G ○ W ● G		Vessels may proceed only when they have received specific orders to do so

Exemption signals and messages

	Type	
○ Y ● R 　　● R 　　● R	Fixed or slow occulting	Vessels shall not proceed, except that vessels which navigate outside the main channel need not comply with the main message
○ Y ● G 　　○ W 　　● G		A vessel may proceed only when it has received specific orders to do so, except that vessels which navigate outside the main channel need not comply with the main message

Abbreviations for harbour facilities

AB	Alongside berth	**LB**	Lifeboat
Air	Commercial airport	**M**	Mooring
Bar	Licensed bar	**ME**	Marine Engineering repairs
BY	Boatyard	**MRCC**	Marine Rescue
C (x Ton)	Crane (x Ton)		Coordination Centre
CG	Coastguard	**MRSC**	Marine Rescue Sub-Centre
CH	Chandlery	**P**	Petrol/gasoline
D	Diesel	**PO**	Post Office
Dr	Doctor	**R**	Restaurant
EC	Early closing	**Rly**	Railway station
El	Electrical repairs	**SC**	Sailing Club
FW	Fresh water	**Sh**	Shipwright, hull repairs
HMC	Her Majesty's Customs	**Slip**	Slipway
Hosp	Hospital	**V**	Victuals, food stores
Hr Mr	Harbourmaster	**YC**	Yacht Club
L	Landing place		

Glossary

Terms which are referred to in the text without a full explanation are included in the glossary. Some other terms which are clearly defined in the book are not included.

A

Aback: describes a sail when the wind strikes it on its lee side.

Abaft: towards the boat's stern.

Abeam: at right angles to the *centre-line* of the boat.

Aft: at or near the stern.

A-hull: to ride out a storm with no sails set and the helm lashed to *leeward*.

Amidships: the centre of the boat, *athwartships* and fore-and-aft.

Anti-fouling: a poisonous paint compound used to protect the underwater part of a hull from marine growths.

Apparent wind: the direction and speed of the wind felt by the crew. It is a combination of *true wind* and that created by the movement of the boat.

Astern: behind the boat; to go astern is to drive the boat in reverse.

Athwartships: at right angles to the fore-and-aft line of the boat.

Azimuth: angular distance measured on a horizon circle in a clockwise direction, usually between an observer and a heavenly body.

B

Back: when a wind backs, it shifts anticlockwise.

Back a sail: to sheet it to *windward* so that the wind fills it on the side that is normally to *leeward*.

Backstay: a stay that supports the mast from aft and prevents its forward movement.

Baggywrinkle: rope, teased out, plaited together and wound around *stays, shrouds* etc., to prevent chafing.

Ballast: extra weight, usually lead or iron, placed low in the boat or externally on the *keel* to provide stability.

Ballast keel: a mass of ballast bolted to the *keel* to increase stability and prevent a keel boat from capsizing.

Batten: a light, flexible strip, fed into a batten pocket at the *leech* of the sail to support the *roach*.

Beam: 1, the maximum breadth of a boat; **2,** a transverse *member* which supports the deck; **3,** on the beam means that an object is at right angles to the *centre-line*.

Beam ends: a boat on its beam ends is *heeled* over so far that the deck *beams* are almost vertical.

Bear away: to steer the boat away from the wind.

Bearing: the direction of an object from an observer, measured in degrees true or magnetic.

Beat: to sail a zigzag *course* towards the wind, *close-hauled* on alternate *tacks.*

Belay: to make fast a rope around a *cleat,* usually with a figure-of-eight knot.

Bend: 1 to secure a sail to a *spar* before hoisting; **2** to connect two ropes with a knot.

Berth: 1, a place occupied by a boat in harbour; **2,** to moor a boat; **3,** a sleeping place on board.

Bight: a *bend* or loop in a rope.

Bilge: the lower, round part inside the hull where water collects.

Block: a pulley in a wooden or plastic case, consisting of a *sheave* around which a rope runs. It is used to change the direction of pull.

Boot-topping: a narrow coloured stripe painted between the bottom paint and the *topside* enamel.

Bottlescrew see **Rigging screw.**

Broach: when a boat *running* downwind slews broadside to the wind and *heels* dangerously. It is caused by heavy following seas or helmsman's error.

Broad reach: the point of sailing between a beam *reach* and a *run,* when the wind blows over the *quarter.*

Bulkhead: partition wall in a boat normally fitted *athwartships.*

C

Carvel: edge-to-edge wooden planking which gives a smooth hull surface.

Catamaran: a sailing boat with twin hulls, connected by crossbeams, developed from Polynesian craft.

Catboat: a boat with a single sail.

Caulk: to make the seams between wooden planks watertight by filling with cotton, oakum or a compound.

Cavitation: the formation of a vacuum around a propeller, causing loss in efficiency.

Centre-board: a board lowered through a slot in the *keel* to reduce *leeway.*

Centre-line: centre of the boat in a fore-and-aft line.

Centre of effort (COE): the point at which all the

forces acting on the sails are concentrated.

Centre of lateral resistance (CLR): the underwater centre of pressure about which a boat pivots when changing *course*.

Chain pawl: a short lug which drops into a toothed rack to prevent the anchor chain running back.

Chain plate: a metal plate bolted to the boat's side to which the *shrouds* or *backstays* are attached.

Chart datum: reference level on a chart below which the tide is unlikely to fall. Soundings are given below chart datum. The datum level varies according to country and area.

Chine: the line where the bottom of the hull meets the side at an angle.

Claw ring: a fitting, which slips over the boom like a claw, to which the main *sheet* is attached after *reefing* the mainsail.

Cleat: a wooden, metal or plastic fitting around which a rope is secured.

Clevis pin: a locking pin through which a split ring is passed to prevent accidental withdrawal.

Clew: the after, lower corner of a sail where the foot and *leech* meet.

Clinker-built: a construction method in which adjacent wooden planks overlap each other.

Close-hauled: *the point of sailing* closest to the wind; see also *Beat*

Close reach: *the point of sailing* between *close-hauled* and a beam *reach*, when the wind blows forward of the *beam*.

Close-winded: describes a boat able to sail very close to the wind.

Coamings: the raised structure surrounding a *hatch*, cockpit etc., which prevents water entering.

Contrail: a trail of condensation left behind a jet aircraft, giving weather clues.

Cotter pin: soft, metal pin folded back on itself to form an eye.

Course: the direction in which a vessel is steered, usually given in degrees: true, magnetic or compass.

Cringle: 1, a rope loop, found at either end of a line of *reef* points; **2,** an eye in a sail.

D

Dead run: running with the wind blowing exactly *aft*, in line with the *centreline*.

Deviation: the difference between the direction indicated by the compass needle and the magnetic *meridian*; caused by metal objects aboard.

Displacement: 1, the weight of water displaced by a boat is equal to the weight of the boat; **2,** a displacement hull is one that displaces its own weight in water and is only supported by buoyancy, as opposed to a planing hull which can exceed its hull, or displacement, speed.

Downhaul: a rope fitted to pull down a sail or *spar*.

Draft: the vertical distance from the *waterline* to the lowest point of the *keel*.

Drag: 1, an anchor drags when it fails to hold; **2,** the force of wind on the sails, or water on the hull, which impedes the boat's progress.

Drift: 1, to float with the current or wind; **2,** US: the

speed of a current (rate UK); **3,** UK: the distance a boat is carried by a current in a given time.

Drogue: a sea anchor put over the stern of a boat or liferaft to retard *drift*.

Drop keel: a retractable *keel* which can be drawn into the hull, when entering shallow waters and recovering on to a trailer.

E

Eye of the wind: direction from which the *true wind* blows.

F

Fair: a well-faired line or surface is smooth with no bumps, hollows or abrupt changes in direction.

Fairlead: a fitting through which a line is run to alter the direction of the lead of the line.

Fathom: the measurement used for depths of water and lengths of rope. 1 fathom = 6 ft = 1.83 m.

Fid: a tapered tool used for *splicing* heavy rope and for sail-making, often hollow.

Fiddle: a raised border for a cabin table, chart table etc, to prevent objects falling off when the boat *heels*.

Fix: the position of the vessel as plotted from two or more *position lines*.

Forestay: the foremost *stay*, running from the masthead to the stemhead, to which the headsail is hanked.

Freeboard: vertical distance between the *waterline* and the top of the deck.

G

Genoa: a large headsail, in various sizes, which

overlaps the mainsail and is hoisted in light to fresh winds on all *points of sailing*.

Gimbals: two concentric rings, pivoted at right angles which keep objects horizontal despite the boat's motion, e.g. compass and cooker.

Go about: to turn the boat through the *eye of the wind* to change *tack*.

Gooseneck: the fitting attaching the boom to the mast, allowing it to move in all directions.

Goosewing: to boom-out the headsail to *windward* on a *run* by using a *whisker pole* to hold the sail on the opposite side to the mainsail.

Ground tackle: general term used for anchoring gear.

Guard rail: a metal rail fitted around the boat to prevent the crew falling overboard.

Gudgeon: a rudder fitting. It is the eye into which the *pintle* fits.

Guy: a steadying rope for a *spar*; a spinnaker guy controls the fore-and-aft position of the spinnaker pole; the foreguy holds the spinnaker pole forward and down.

Gybe: to change from one *tack* to another by turning the stern through the wind.

H

Halyard: rope used to hoist and lower sails.

Hank: fitting used to attach the *luff* of a sail to a *stay*.

Hatch: an opening in the deck giving access to the interior.

Hawse pipe: see Navel pipe.

Head-to-wind: when the bows are pointing right into the wind.

Headfoil: a streamlined surround to a *forestay*, with a groove into which a headsail *luff* slides.

Heads: the toilet.

Headway: the forward movement of a boat through the water.

Heave-to: to *back* the jib and lash the tiller to *leeward*; used in heavy weather to encourage the boat to lie quietly and to reduce *headway*.

Heaving line: a light line suitable for throwing ashore.

Heel: to lean over to one side.

I

Isobars: lines on a weather map joining places of equal atmospheric pressure.

J

Jackstay: a line running fore-and-aft, on both sides of the boat, to which safety harnesses are clipped.

Jibe: see **Gybe**.

Jury: a temporary device to replace lost or damaged gear.

K

Kedge: a small, light second anchor.

Keel: the main backbone of the boat to which a *ballast keel* is bolted or through which the *centreboard* passes.

Ketch: a two-masted sailing vessel with a *mizzen* mast slightly smaller than the main and stepped forward of the rudder stock/post.

Kicking strap: a line used to pull the boom down, to

keep it horizontal, particularly on a *reach* or *run*.

L

Lanyard: a short line attached to one object, such as a knife, with which it is secured to another.

Lapstrake see **Clinker-built.**

Leech: 1, the after edge of a triangular sail; **2,** both side edges of a square sail.

Lee helm: the tendency of a boat to *bear away* from the wind.

Lee shore: a shore on to which the wind is blowing.

Leeward: away from the wind; the direction to which the wind blows.

Leeway: the sideways movement of a boat off its *course* as a result of the wind blowing on one side of the sails.

Let fly: to let a *sheet* go instantly, spilling the wind from the sails.

Lifeline: a wire or rope rigged around the deck to prevent the crew falling overboard.

Limber holes: gaps left at the lower end of frames above the *keel* to allow water to drain to the lowest point of the *bilges*.

List: a boat's more or less permanent lean to one side, owing to the improper distribution of weight, e.g., *ballast* or water.

Log: 1, an instrument for measuring a boat's speed and distance travelled through the water; **2,** to record in a book the details of a voyage, usually distances covered and weather.

Luff: the forward edge of a sail. To luff up is to turn

the boat's head right into the wind.

Luff groove: a groove in a wooden or metal *spar* into which the *luff* of the headsail is fed.

Lurch: the sudden rolling of a boat.

M

Marinized engine: an auto engine which has been specially adapted for use in boats.

Marlin spike: a pointed steel or wooden spike used to open up the strands of rope or wire when *splicing*.

Mast step: the socket in the *keel* in which the base of the mast is located.

Measured mile: a distance of one nautical mile measured between buoys or *transits/ranges* ashore, and marked on the chart.

Member: a part of the skeleton of the hull, such as a wooden frame or *stringer* laminated into a fibreglass hull to strengthen it.

Meridian: an imaginary line encircling the Earth which passes through the poles and cuts at right angles through the Equator. All lines of longitude are meridians.

Mizzen: 1, the shorter, after-mast on a *ketch* or *yawl*; **2,** the fore-and-aft sail set on this mast.

Mouse: to bind thin line around a hook to prevent it jerking loose.

Moulded plywood: a form of construction whereby a hull is built up by bonding a number of thin skins of wood together over a framework.

N

Navel pipe: a metal pipe in the foredeck through which the anchor chain passes to the locker below.

No go area: the area into which a boat cannot sail without *tacking*.

Noon sight: a vessel's latitude can be found, using a sextant, when a heavenly body on the observer's *meridian* is at its greatest altitude. The sight of the sun at noon is the one most frequently taken.

O

Off the wind: with the *sheets* slacked off, not *close-hauled*.

On the wind: *close-hauled*.

Outhaul: a rope used to pull out the foot of a sail.

Overall length (LOA): the boat's extreme length, measured from the foremost part of the bow to the aftermost part of the stern, excluding bowsprit, self-steering gear etc.

P

Painter: the bow line by which a dinghy, or *tender*, is towed or made fast.

Pay out: to let a rope out gradually.

Pintle: a rudder fitting with a long pin which slips into the *gudgeon* to form a hinged pivot for the rudder.

Pitch: 1, the up and down motion of the bows of a boat plunging over the waves; **2,** the angle of the propeller blades.

Point of sailing: the different angles from the wind on which a boat may sail; the boat's *course* relative to the direction of the wind.

Port: the left-hand side of a boat, looking forward (opp. of *starboard*).

Port tack: a boat is on a port tack when the wind strikes the port side first and the mainsail is out to *starboard*. A boat on the port tack gives way to a boat on a *starboard tack*.

Position line/line of position: a line drawn on a chart, as a result of taking a *bearing*, along which the boat's position must lie. Two position lines give a *fix*.

Pulpit: a metal *guard rail* fitted at the bows of a boat to provide safety for the crew.

Pushpit: a metal *guard rail* fitted at the stern.

Q

Quarter: the portion of the boat mid-way between the stern and the *beam*; on the quarter means about 45° *abaft* the beam.

R

Rake: the fore-and-aft deviation from the perpendicular of a mast or other feature of a boat.

Range: 1, see **Transit; 2,** of tides, the difference between the high- and low-water levels of a *tide*; **3,** the distance at which a light can be seen.

Rating: a method of measuring certain dimensions of a yacht to enable it to take part in handicap races.

Reach: to sail with the wind approximately on the *beam*; all sailing points between *running* and *close-hauled*.

Reef: to reduce the sail area by folding or rolling surplus material on the boom or *forestay*.

Reefing pennant: strong line with which the *luff* or

leech cringle is pulled down to the boom when *reefing*.

Rhumb line: a line cutting all *meridians* at the same angle; the *course* followed by a boat sailing in a fixed direction.

Riding light or **anchor light:** an all-round white light, usually hoisted on the *forestay*, to show that a boat under 50 ft (15 m) is at anchor. It must be visible for 2 mls (3 km).

Riding sail: a small sail hoisted to enable a boat to maintain *steerage way* during a storm.

Rigging screw: a deck fitting with which the tension of *standing rigging*, e.g. *stays, shrouds*, is adjusted.

Righting moment: the point beyond which the boat will no longer right itself when *heeling*, but capsizes.

Roach: the curved part of the *leech* of a sail which extends beyond the direct line from head to *clew*.

Run: to sail with the wind *aft* and with the *sheets* eased well out.

Running rigging: all the moving lines, such as *sheets* and *halyards*, used in the *setting* and *trimming* of sails.

S

Sailmaker's palm: a strong leather protective loop which fits across the palm of the hand. It has a hole for the thumb and metal reinforced plate on the palm to accept the eye of a needle, and is worn when mending sails or *splicing* ropes.

Schooner: a boat with two or more masts, with the mainmast aftermost.

Scope: the length of rope or cable paid out when mooring or anchoring.

Scuppers: holes in the *toe rail* which allow water to drain off the deck.

Seacock: a valve which shuts off an underwater inlet or outlet passing through the hull.

Sea room: room in which a boat can manoeuvre, clear of land or dangers.

Seize: to bind two ropes together, or a rope to a *spar*, with a light line.

Serve: to cover and protect a *splice* or part of a rope with twine bound tightly against the lay.

Serving mallet: tool with a grooved head, used when serving a rope to keep the twine at a constant and high tension.

Set: 1, to hoist a sail; **2,** the way in which the sails fit; **3,** the direction of a tidal current or stream.

Shackle: a metal link with a removable bolt across the open end; of various shapes: D, U.

Sheave: a grooved wheel in a *block* or *spar* for a rope to run on.

Sheet: the rope attached to the *clew* of a sail or to the boom, enabling it to be controlled or *trimmed*.

Shrouds: ropes or wires, usually in pairs, led from the mast to *chain plates* at deck level to prevent the mast falling sideways; part of the *standing rigging*.

Skin fitting: a through-hull fitting where there is a hole in the skin, through which air or water passes. A *seacock* is fitted to close the hole when not in use.

Sloop: a single-masted sailing boat with a mainsail and one headsail.

Spar: a general term for any wood or metal pole,

e.g., mast or boom, used to carry or give shape to sails.

Spindrift: spray blown along the surface of the sea.

Spinnaker: a large, light, balloon-shaped sail *set* when *reaching* or *running*.

Splice: to join ropes or wires by unlaying the strands and interweaving them.

Split pin: see **Cotter pin**.

Spreaders: horizontal struts attached to the mast, which extend to the *shrouds* and help to support the mast.

Stall: a sail stalls when the airflow over it breaks up, causing the boat to lose way.

Stanchion: upright metal post bolted to the deck to support *guard rails* or *lifelines*.

Standing part: the part of a line not used when making a knot; the part of a rope which is made fast, or around which the knot is tied.

Standing rigging: the *shrouds* and *stays* which are permanently set up and support the masts.

Starboard: right-hand side of a boat looking forward (opp. of *port*).

Starboard tack: a boat is on the starboard tack when the wind strikes the starboard side first and the boom is out to *port*.

Stay: wire or rope which supports the mast in a fore-and-aft direction; part of the *standing rigging*.

Steerage way: a boat has steerage way when it has sufficient speed to allow it to be steered, or to answer the helm.

Stem: the timber at the bow, from the *keel* upwards, to which the planking is attached.

Sternway: the backward, stern-first movement of a boat.

Stringer: a fore-and-aft *member*, fitted to strengthen the frames.

Strop: a loop of wire or rope used to attach a *block* to a *spar* or to make a sling.

Strum box: a filter fitted round the suction end of a *bilge-pump* hose to prevent the pump becoming blocked by debris.

T

Tack: 1, the lower forward corner of a sail; 2, to turn the boat through the wind so that it blows on the opposite side of the sails.

Tacking: working to windward by sailing *close-hauled* on alternate *courses* so that the wind is first on one side of the boat, then on the other.

Tack pennant: a length of wire with an eye in each end, used to raise the *tack* of a headsail some distance off the deck.

Tackle: a purchase system comprising rope and *blocks* which is used to gain mechanical advantage.

Tang: a strong metal fitting by which *standing rigging* is attached to the mast or other *spar*.

Tender or **dinghy:** a small boat used to ferry stores and people to a yacht.

Terminal fitting: fitting at the end of a wire rope by which a *shroud* or *stay* can be attached to the mast, a *tang* or a *rigging screw/turnbuckle*.

Tide: the vertical rise and fall of the oceans, caused principally by the gravitational attraction of the moon.

Toe rail: a low strip of wood or moulding running around the edge of the deck.

Topping lift: a line from the masthead to a *spar*, normally the boom, which is used to raise it.

Topsides: the part of a boat's hull which is above the *waterline*.

Track: 1, the *course* a boat has made good; 2, a fitting on the mast or boom into which the slides on a sail fit; 3, a fitting along which a *traveller* runs; used to alter the tension of the *sheets*.

Transit: two fixed objects are in transit when seen in line; two transits give a position *fix*.

Traveller: 1, a ring or hoop which can be hauled along a *spar*; 2, a fitting which slides in a *track* and is used to alter the angle of the *sheets*.

Triatic stay: a *backstay* led from the head of one mast to that of another.

Trim: 1, to adjust the angle of the sails, by means of *sheets*, so that they work most efficiently; 2, to adjust the boat's load, and thus the fore-and-aft angle at which it floats.

True wind: the direction and speed of the wind felt when stationary, at anchor or on land.

Turnbuckle see **Rigging screw**.

U

Under way: a boat is under way when it is not made fast to the shore, at anchor or aground.

Uphaul: a line used to raise something vertically, e.g., the spinnaker pole.

V

Veer: 1, the wind veers

when it shifts in a clockwise direction; 2, to pay out anchor cable or rope in a gradual, controlled way.

W

Wake: the disturbed water left *astern* of a boat.

Waterline: the line along the hull at which a boat floats.

Waterline length (WL): the length of a boat from *stem* to stern at the *waterline*. It governs the maximum speed of a *displacement hull* and affects a boat's *rating*.

Weather helm: (opp. of *lee helm*).

Weather side: the side of a boat on which the wind is blowing.

Wetted surface: the area of the hull under water.

Whisker pole: a light pole used to hold out the *clew* of a headsail when *running*.

Winch: a mechanical device, consisting usually of a metal drum turned by a handle, around which a line is wound to give the crew more purchasing power when hauling taut a line, e.g., a jib *sheet*.

Windage: those parts of a boat which increase *drag*, e.g., rigging, *spars*, crew, etc.

Windlass: a *winch* with a horizontal shaft and a vertical handle, used to haul up the anchor chain.

Windward: the direction from which the wind blows; towards the wind (opp. of *leeward*).

Y

Yawl: a two-masted boat with the *mizzen* stepped *aft* of the rudder stock/post.

Index

Page numbers in bold
indicate a main entry.
Those in italic refer to
illustrations and captions.

A

Abandoning ship 152–3,
 153
Adhesives 179
A-hull *42*
Aluminium boat
 construction 18–19, *19*
 maintenance 179
America 11, 162, *163*
Anchor 80, 107, 140
 Breaking 85
 Bruce *43*, 80, *81*, 82, 211
 chain **80**, *81*, 82, 83, 84, 85,
  86, 87, 88, 89
 CQR 80, *81*, 82, .83, 211
 Danforth *80*
 daymark *89*
 deck fitting 82–3
 Dragging *88*
 Fisherman's *80*, 211
 Fouled *88*
 Kedge 80, 84, 86, 87
 light *89*
 scope *84*, 85, 86, 87
 stowage 82–3, *82*, *83*
 swivel 80, 86, 87
 weight *81*, 89, 211
Anchorage 58, 60, 62, 63,
 64, 66, 68, 72, 74
 Choice of 85, 87
Anchoring 57, 76, 80,
 84–9, *84*, *85*, 107
 under power 87
 with two anchors 86, 87,
  88, 89
Anemometer 33, *134*
Antenna 12, 122, 125, *142*
Anti-fouling **198**, 199
Archer, Colin 8, 11
Auxiliary power **100–7**
 Handling under 106–7,
  107

B

Backstay 12, 20, 21, *149*
Balance 33, 34
Barometer 134, 136
Barometric pressure 118,
 134–7, *136*, 208
Batten 24, 25
Battery 193, **194**, 195
 installation 105, *141*

Bearing
 away *32*
 Beam 110
 Compass 110, *111*
 Magnetic 108, 109
 Relative *110*
 True 108, 109
Beating 26–7, **30–1**
Bermudan rig 11, *12–13*, 24
Bilge 45, **200–1**
 keel 77
 pump 43, 140, 180, 181
Block 189
 and tackle **99**
Bolera 164
Boom preventer 35, 39
Booster sail 38, *39*
Bosun's, bag *91*, 98
 chair **92**, 189
Bow fitting 12, *82*, *83*
Brassey, Lord Thomas 8, *9*
British Oxygen 173
Broach *34*, 106
Buoyage systems 59, 68, 73,
 114, **126–7**, *126*, *127*
Buoyancy aid 52, *55*, 144
Burgee 33, *163*

C

Cabin trunk roof 12, 52
Catamaran *27*, 30, 31, 46,
 47, *172*
Cat ketch *22*, *24*
Cavitation *100*
Centre-board *33*, 35
Centre of effort (COE) *26*,
 33
Centre of lateral
 resistance (CLR) *26*, *33*,
 35
Certificate of Competence
 56
Chafe 45, 47, 79, 87, 190
Chart 48, 59, 61, 63, 67, 68,
 71, 73, 75, 88, 112, *114*
 datum *116*, 117, *118*, 119
 Mercator 109, 114
 plotting **112–13**, *112*, *113*
 symbols 113, *114–5*, 213
Chartering 56, 59, 61, 65,
 66, 67, 71, 75, 202
Chichester, Sir Francis
 161, *171*, 174
Childers, Erskine 8, *9*
Cleat 36, *95*, 184
Close-hauled 27, **30–1**
Clothing **54–5**, 140

 boots 41, 54, *55*
 oilskins *41*, 52, 53, 54, *55*
Cloud **134–5**, *134–5*, 138
Club Mediterranée 170
Coachroof *12*, 52
Cockpit *12*, *16*, 42, 43, 52
Collision regulations *130*,
 131, *203*
Colt Cars GB 173
Compass 44, 108, *108*, 109
 Bulkhead 109
 error 109
 Masthead 109
 north 108
 Steering *108*, 109
Contrail *139*
Conversion tables 206–211
Courageous 163
Course 108–113
Cruiser *12–13*, *12–13*, 27,
 46–7
 buying and selling 202
 choosing **46–7**
 design 8, 10–11
 internal layout **48–9**
Cruising 46–75
 chute *25*, 27, 34, 38
 Club 10
 Coastal 38
 courtesies 57
 documentation 56
 grounds **58–75**
 Long-distance **44–5**
 publications 56–7, 59, 61,
  63, 64, 67, 68, 71, 73, 114

D

Dan buoy 140, *145*
Dead reckoning (DR) 108,
 112, 116
Decca Yacht Navigator
 132, 133
Deck
 construction **15**
 fittings 22, 82–3, 184–5
 Non-slip *53*, 141, 199
 seamanship **90–9**
Deviation 109, 112
 card *109*
Dinghy/tender *89*, 203
Direction
 finding equipment 52,
  124–5
 Measuring 108
Dismasting 93, **148–9**
Distance 56, 108
 Estimating 111

Sea horizon *111*, 210
-off *128*, 21C, 211
Distress signals **142–3**, 158,
　204–5
　code flags 142, *204*, 205
　flares 43, 52, 140, **142–3**,
　　143, 152
　Morse code 142, *205*
　phonetic alphabet 204
Downwind **34–5**
Drift (UK) 77, 107, 113
　(US) *see* Tidal stream
Drive
　Sail *100*, 192
　Straight *100*
　Inboard/outboard *100*
Drogue *see* Sea anchor
Drop keel **35**

E

Echo sounder 85, *116*, 117,
　117, 121
Electrical systems 141, 194,
　195, 208
Electrolysis *103*, 181
Engine
　Choice of **100–1**
　cooling 105
　Diesel 100, *104–5*, 193
　failure 107, **192–3**
　installation **104–5**, *141*
　maintenance 104, **192–3**
　Marinized *102*
　mountings 105
　Outboard 47, 100
　output *102*
　Petrol/gasoline 100, *104–5*
　power curves *103*
　power required 102, 103
　safety 141, *150*
Estimated position (EP)
　112, *113*
Exhaust systems 100, 105
Eye,
　plate 52
　Talurit *93*
　Tucked *96*
　Seized *98*

F

Fender 57, 72, 77, 78, 79, 94
　board 78, *79*
Ferroconcrete boat 19
　maintenance 176, **179**
Fibreglass boat **14–15**
　construction *14*, 15, 19
　maintenance 176–8

painting 198–9
Finger pontoon *78*
Fire **150–1**, *153*
　blanket 140, 150, 151
　extinguisher 140, 141, *150*,
　　151
First aid 156–9
Flags
　Code 142, *202*, 203
　Courtesy 57
　Flare 43, 52, 140, **142–3**,
　　143, 152
Fleming Day, Thomas 8, *9*
Flyer 175
Fog *138*
　Sound signals in 130, 204
Food
　Children's 51
　consumption 45
　stores 50, 51
Forestay *12*, 20, 21, *149*

G

Gaff rig *22, 24*
Galley 48, 49, **50–1**
　maintenance 200–1
Gas (bottled) *50–1*, 141, 200
　warning devices *151*
Genoa 24, 25, 34, 38, 44,
　189
Guard rail 52, 79, 184
Gulf Stream 67, 164, 165
Gybe *34, 35, 37, 160*

H

Halo *139*
Halyard 22, *23*, 28, 29, 45,
　90, 188, 189
Hasler, 'Blondie' 170, 171
Hatch 23, 52, *141*, 143, **182**
Heads 48, *50*
　maintenance 200
Headsails 24, *25, 28*, 29, 34,
　36, 37, 38, 43, 44, 76
　Furling 24
　Reefing 40, *41*
　Stowing *28, 29*
Heave-to 42, *42*
Heavy weather **40–3**
　clothing **41**, *41*, 54
Heel, angle of 26, *27*, 31
Howells, Val *171*
Hull
　Displacement 10, 11, 102,
　103
　Planing 27, 103
　resistance 102

Semi-planing 102, 103
　speed 27, 102, 103
Hypothermia *154*, **155**, 158

I

Imp 164
Inland waterways 57, 58,
　60, 62, 68, 72
Insurance 56, 203
Isobars *136*, 137

J

Jackstay 41, 43, 52, 53, 144
Jib, 28, 32, 34, 189
　Storm 24, *25*, 42, 43
　to set 28, *28*
Jibe *34, 35, 37, 160*
Jolie Brise 11, *165*, 168
Junk rig *22*, 24
Jury
　rigging **148–9**, *148*
　steering **146–7**, *147*

K

Keel *12*, 26, *27*
　Fin *46*, 76, 106
　Lifting *46*
　Long *46*
　maintenance **180**
　Twin *46*
Ketch 13, 42, 44, 147
Kicking strap *34*, 40, 99,
　189
Knight, Edward 8, *9*
Knots 82, **92–5**, 98, 99
　bowline 82, 92, *93*
　clove hitch *94*
　double bowline *93*
　double overhand *92*
　double sheetbend *95*
　figure-of-eight *92*
　figure-of-eight overhand
　　hitch *95*
　fisherman's bend *94*
　half hitch *94*
　hangman's *99*
　marlin-spike hitch *98*
　reef *95*
　rolling hitch *95*
　running figure-of-eight *99*
　sheet bend *95*
Knox-Johnston, Robin 172,
　174, *175*

L

Land breeze 38, 138
Latchway Safety System
　53, *53*, 55

Latitude *108*
Lee helm *33*
Lee shore *86–7*, 139
Leeway *27*, *31*, 112, 113
Let fly *33*
Lewis, David *171*
Life-belt 140, *141*
Life-buoy *145*
Life-jacket 43, 52, 140,
   144, 152, 153
Lifeline 12, 79, *141*, 184
Liferaft 40, 140, *141*, **152–3**,
   153, 154, 155
Lighting 48, 50, 201
Lights, navigation 89, *126,
   127, 131*
   sectored *110*
Log 56, 108, 110, **120–1**,
   120, *121*, 144
   Chip 121
   Dutchman's 121
   Electromagnetic 120
   Electronic 120
   Pitot-static 120
   position 121
   Taffrail 120
   'Walker' *120*
Longitude *108*
Loran C *133*
Luffing *32*, 33

M

McMullen, Richard 8, *9*
Mainsail 24, *25*, 28, *29*, 189
   to set **28–9**, *29*
   tensioning 28
Maintenance of
   below decks **200–1**
   deck **182–5**
   electrics **194–5**
   engine **192–3**
   ferroconcrete 176, **179**
   fibreglass **176–8**, **198–9**
   paintwork **198–9**
   running rigging **188–9**
   sails 91, **190–1**
   skin fittings **180–1**
   standing rigging **186–7**
   steel 176, **179**
   Tools for **196–7**
   wood 176, **178–9**
Man overboard **144–5**, *145*
Marinas 58, 62, 63, 64, 66,
   68, 70, 72, 75, 76, 77, 78,
   80
Marlin spike 52, *91*
Mary 10

Mast *12*, 20, *21*, 43, 148, 149
   head *21*
   Mizzen 43
   sheave 189
Meridian 108
Messenger *88*, 90
Monohull 47, *172*
Mooring **76–9**, 86, 87, 202
   buoy 76, *79*
   piles 78, *79*
   ropes 78, *79*
   Swinging *78*
   swivel 86, 87
   to quay/dock wall 78, *79*
   under power 78, 106, *107*
   under sail *76*, 78
Motor sailer *13*, **39**
Multihulls 10, 35, 46, *47*,
   172

N

Nautical mile 108, 208
Navigation **108–133**
   Astronomical **128–9**
   Coastal 108, 110
   Electronic **132–3**
   instruments *112*, 113, 140
   lights 89, *126, 127, 131*
   port entry signals 213
   Satellite *133*
Navigator's notebook *113*
Noon sight *129*

O

Omega *132*, 133

P

Painting **198–9**
Points of sailing 26, *26*, 27
Position fixing 108, 110,
   111, 116, 122, 128, 132
Position, line of 110
Propeller *12*, 100, *101*, 102,
   106, *107*
   shaft *104*, 192
Pulpit *12*, 52
   turtle 36

R

Races
   Admiral's Cup Series 161,
      166, 167, **168–9**, *168*
   America's Cup 25, 161,
      162–3
   Bermuda 161, **164–5**, *165*
   Early 10–11
   Fastnet 40, 152, 166,
      168–9, *169*

Onion Patch **164–5**
Round Britain 161, **172–3**
Round the World 161,
   174–5
Sidney-Hobart *166*
Single-handed
   Transatlantic 161, **170–1**
SORC 161, 164–5, *164*
Southern Cross Series
   166–7
Racing **160–75**
   boat 10–11, *27*, *48*
   ratings 10, 11, 160
   rules 160–1, *160*, *161*
Radar **122–3**
   beacons 114–115, 122
   equipment *114*
   reflectors *115*, 140
Radio
   EPIRB 140, 142, 152
   in emergency 142, 169
   VHF 133, 140, 142, 152
   wavelengths 208
Radio direction-finding
   124–5
   beacons 124, *125*
   Cost of 125
   equipment *124*, 125
   Errors in 124, 125
   Taking bearing from *124*
Range (US) *see* Transit
Reach **32–3**, *32*, *33*
   Beam 27, *32*
   Broad 27, *32*, 34
   Close 27
Reefing **40–1**, 44
   headsail 40, *41*
   Jiffy/slab *40*
   Points 40, *41*
   Roller 40, *41*, 44
Reliance 163
Rescue services 142, *154*
Riding sail 43, *147*
Rigging
   Jury **148–9**, *148*
   repairs 148, *149*
   Running **22–3**, *23*, 188–9
   screw *21*, 52, 186
   Setting up 187
   Standing 20–1, 186–7
   Steel 92
   Tuning 21
Rigs **20–1**, 22
   Bermudan *12–13*, 24
   Cat ketch *22*, *24*
   Comparison of *13*
   Double spreader *20*

Dutch *22*
Fractional *20*
Gaff *24*
Gunter *148*
Junk *22*, 24
Schooner 22, *24*
Single spreader *21*
Sprit *148*
Rope **90–9**, 187, 189
  Anchor 189
  Care of 90
  Cleating 95
  Coiling *94*
  Colour-coded *90*
  Mooring 189
  repairing 91
  sizes 189
  Wire 187
Rudder 12
  Improvised *146*
  maintenance 180–1
  movement 106
  Skeg 46, *76*, 146
  Spade 46, 76, 146
  Transom-hung 146
Running 27, **34–5**, 42 (*see also* Downwind)

S

Safety **140–159**
  below decks *140, 141*
  Children's 53, **55**
  equipment *140, 141*
  harness 43, *52, 53*, 55, 140, 144
  on deck 53, *140, 141*
Sails, Care of 29, 190–1
  Choice of 24–5
  Cloth for 25, 36, 191
  Cut of *25*
  repair 91, **190–1**
  Soft/wraparound 22, *24*
  Stowing *29*, 190
  Trimming 26, *32*
Salvage 203
Satellite navigation *133*
  Navstar GPS 133
  weather pictures *137*
Schooner 13, *24*, 44
Sea anchor 42, *43, 145*, 152, 155
Sea breeze *38*, 138, *139*
Seacock 43, *141*, 180, 181
Seasickness 43, 56, 154, 155, 159
Secondary Port 118, 119
Seizing 98–9

Self-steering systems **44–5**
  Autohelm 44
  Improvised *45*, **146–7**, *147*
  Sailormat *44*
Sextant **128–9**, *129*, 211
Shackle 28, 52, 81, 86, 87, *87*, 91, 92
Sheets 22, 23, 31, 37, 90, 91, 92, 93, 188, 189
Sheet track *13*, 183
Shroud *12, 21*, 45, *149*
Sight reduction tables *129*
Slip *78*
Slocum, Joshua 8, *9*, 174
Soundings **116–117**
  lead *85*, 117
  line of 116, *117*
Spare parts **197**
Speed, logging **120–1**
  potential 103
Spinnaker *23*, 24, 25, 32, 34, **36–7**, 39, 167, 189
Splicing **96–7**
Spreaders 12, *21*, 45
Standard Port 118, 119
Steel boat
  construction **18–19**
  maintenance 176, **179**
Steering, ahead 106
  astern *76*, 106
  bridle *147*
  failure **146–7**
  system 106
  wheel *146*
  with sails *147*
Stowage *29*, **48–9**, 50, 82–3, 190
Sunburn 39, 155, 159
Survival *144*, 152, **154–5**

T

Tabarly, Eric 170, *171*
Tacking 30, 31, *160*
Tell-tales **31**, *31*, 32, 33
Tidal stream 34, 76, 112, 118
  atlas 56, 112, 118, 119
Tide 57, 77, **118–119**
Tiller 12, 30, 31
  Improvised 146
Tools 91, **196–7**
Topping lift 12, 35, 40, 188, 189
Trade winds 34, 44, 57, 60, 67, 174
Trailer sailer 13, 46, *47*
Transit *88*, 109, *110*

Traveller *23, 33*, 38, 89
Trimaran 47, *172, 173*
Try-sail *43*, 140, 169
Turnbuckle *21*, 52, 186
Turning circles *76, 77, 107*

V

Variation 109, 113
Ventilation 43, **182, 183**, 201
Voss, John 8, *9*

W

Warp 42, 43, 87
Watch systems 43, 45, 56, 88, 212
Water, depth 116–18
  tanks 50, 51, *51*, 200
Wave formations *139*
Weather 56–7, 59, 60, 63, 64, 67, 68, 69, 70, 73, 75, **134–9**
  forecast **136–7**, 138
  Heavy **40–3**
  helm 26, 32, *33*
  Local 138–9
  map plotting *136*
  symbols 137
Whipping **98–9**
Winch 12, *23*, 30, **185**
Wind
  Apparent *27*, 30, 33, 34
  Backing 38, 136
  Beaufort scale 212
  Coastal 138, *139*
  direction *33*, **134**, 136–7
  Katabatic *138*
  pressure 26, **134–5**
  Prevailing *135*
  Seasonal *63, 65, 135*
  speed *134*
  strength 26, **134**
  True *27*, 33, 34
  Veering 38, 136
Windlass *82*, 83, 84
Wire rope *92*, 93, 149, 187
Wooden boat
  construction **16–17**, 19
  maintenance 176, **178–9**
Worth, Claude 8, *9*

Y

Yacht, clubs 10, *11*, 160, *163*, 166, 170, 172
  registration 56
Yawl 13, 42, 44, 147

Acknowledgements

The Publishers received invaluable help from the following people and organizations:
Jazz Wilson, who researched *Cruising Grounds*; Alison Tomlinson; Sonya Larkin; Candy Lee; Jan Storr; Wally Buchanan, Master rigger; David Johnston of Ingledew, Brown, Bennison and Garrett; Roy Flooks; Ted Spears; Brookes and Gatehouse Ltd; Conyer Marine Ltd; Force Four Chandlery; International Association of Lighthouse Authorities; International Paint; Keen International Marine Electronics; Kemp Masts Ltd; Lewmar Marine Ltd; Lucas Marine; Marlow Ropes Ltd; Royal Cork Yacht Club; Royal Ocean Racing Club; Royal Thames Yacht Club; Royal Yachting Association; Schermaly Ltd; Simpson Lawrence Ltd; Sowester; Stowe Equipment Ltd; Thomas Foulkes; Volvo Penta; Westerley Marine Construction Ltd.

PICTURE CREDITS

1	H. Gritscher/Rapho
2/3	Jim Leggett/Daily Telegraph Colour Library
4/5	Yachting World
6/7	Peter Keen/Susan Griggs Agency
9	Mary Evans Picture Library
10/11t	Mary Evans Picture Library
10/11b	Museum of the City of New York/Robert Harding Picture Library
15	Columbus Yachts Ltd. (Sweden Yachts)
17	Geoff Hales
19	META
23	John Watney
24t	Yachting World
24c	Colin Jarman
24b	Alastair Black
30	Alastair Black
34	David R. Kitz/International Yacht Sales
39	Alastair Black
42	P.W. Purser
45	Alastair Black
50	Yachting World
51	John Watney
52	Musto & Hyde
53	Sowester
55	Dick Johnson/Yachting World
58/9	Jim Leggett/Daily Telegraph Colour Library
60/1	Alastair Black
62	Alastair Black
65	Alastair Black
66	Larry Dale Gordon/The Image Bank
69	Alastair Black
70/1	J. Bryson/The Image Bank
72	Paolo Koch/Rapho
74/5	James Davis
80/1	Sowester
82	Yachting World
82/3	John Watney
33	Yachting World
84	George Hall/Susan Griggs Agency
86	Tom Muldoon
90	Peter Smith Studios
91	John Watney
100	Yamaha
116/7	Seafarer Navigation International Ltd.
120	Walker Knotmasters
122/3	Racal-Decca Ltd.
124/5	Brookes & Gatehouse Ltd.
128	Telesonic Marine Ltd.
134	Brian Seed/Art Directors Photo Library
135l	Art Directors Photo Library
135r	Ann Welch
137	Meteorological Office
138	Robert Harding Picture Library
139t	Walter Rawlings/Robert Harding Picture Library
139b	R.K. Pilsbury
143	Peter Smith Studios
145	John Watney
154	Yachting World
163/3	Alastair Black
163	Beken of Cowes Ltd.
164/5	Alastair Black
165	Beken of Cowes Ltd.
166	Ambrose Greenway
167	Alastair Black
168/9	Alastair Black
169	John Frost Historical Newspaper Service
169	Ambrose Greenway/Camera Press
170/1	S. Smith/*Observer*/Camera Press
171t	Western Morning News Co Ltd.
171b	Alastair Black
173	Beken of Cowes Ltd.
175t	Alastair Black
175b	John Frost Historical Newspaper Service